Just Another Car Factory?

compliance
vs
committment
of
workers

Just Another Car Factory?

Lean Production and
Its Discontents

James Rinehart,
Christopher Huxley,
and
David Robertson

ILR Press
An imprint of
Cornell University Press
Ithaca and London

First published 1997 by Cornell University Press
First printing, Cornell Paperbacks, 1997

Printed in the United States of America

Library of Congress Cataloging-in-Publication Data

Rinehart, James W., 1933–
    Just another car factory? : lean production and its discontents /
James Rinehart, Christopher Huxley, and David Robertson.
        p.   cm.
    Includes bibliographical references and index.
    ISBN 0-8014-3373-8 (cloth : alk. paper).—ISBN 0-8014-8407-3
(paper : alk. paper)
    1. Automobile industry and trade—North America—Manage-
ment.   2. Corporations, Japanese—North America.   3. Downsizing of organizations—North America.   4. Automobile
industry workers—North America—Attitudes.   I. Huxley,
Christopher Victor, 1944–   .   II. Robertson, David, 1951–   .
III. Title.
    HD9710.N572R56   1997
    629.2'068—dc21   97-4958

Cornell University Press strives to use environmentally responsible
suppliers and materials to the fullest extent possible in the publishing
of its books. Such materials include vegetable-based, low-VOC inks
and acid-free papers that are recycled, totally chlorine-free, or partly
composed of nonwood fibers.

Cloth printing   10 9 8 7 6 5 4 3 2 1

Paperback printing   10 9 8 7 6 5 4 3 2

Contents

Author Recognition

AS IN THE CASE OF PREVIOUS WORK BY THE AUTHORS, THIS BOOK reflects the collaborative contribution of all members of the CAW (Canadian Auto Workers) Research Group on CAMI. From its inception in late 1989, the Research Group was coordinated by David Robertson from the CAW national office. In addition to the authors of this book, members of the research group were Steve Benedict (CAW Local 112), Alan McGough (CAW Local 27), Herman Rosenfeld (CAW Local 303), and Jeff Wareham (CAW national office). The questionnaire items were formulated by the group, and all members conducted interviews at CAMI. We spent untold hours debating key research issues, and everyone contributed, either verbally or in writing, to virtually every chapter of this book.

Acknowledgments

MANY PERSONS MADE THIS BOOK POSSIBLE. THANKS ARE DUE TO CAW officers Bob White and Buzz Hargrove and to staffers Sam Gindin and Ron Pellerin, who negotiated our access to CAMI and supported us throughout the course of the project. We also thank CAMI management for granting us access to the plant and its employees on company time and premises and for cooperating with us during our site visits. Special thanks go to the members of CAMI's Employee Relations Department for coordinating employee interviews.

We are grateful to the CAW Local 88 in-plant committee and leadership for all the time they spent scheduling interviews, being interviewed, and generally putting up with us. Local 88's first plant chairperson, Tom Grygorcewicz, his successor, Mike Reuter, and President Brian Daley deserve special mention. They were always willing to take time from their hectic schedules to talk to us and facilitate our research. Thanks as well to Local 88 vice-president Dave Binns for helping to keep us apprised of developments at CAMI.

A special thank-you goes to the rank and file workers who took the time to respond thoughtfully to our lengthy list of interview questions. We are indebted as well to the managers who patiently endured long, tape-recorded interview sessions and provided candid answers to our questions.

Acknowledgment is due to Kaiyu Wang and Cynthia Johnston for research assistance and to Lyn Cummings and Sue Paterson for tape transcription. We benefited from the editorial work of Rosemarie Bahr on an earlier report by the Research Group. Bob Andersen did a lot of computer work for us, and our discussion of the correlates of worker commitment at CAMI relied heavily on statistical relationships he had established in his M.A. thesis.

We are indebted to Jane Slaughter for her meticulous editing, questions, constructive criticism, and suggested revisions of our manuscript. Throughout the lengthy process of transforming a rough manuscript into a book Frances Benson of Cornell University Press was a much appreciated source of encouragement, reassurance, and support.

A number of people commented on and offered constructive criticisms of our published and unpublished materials: Paul Adler, Hugh Armstrong, Steve Babson, Jim Conley, Seymour Faber, Jim Geschwender, Sergio Sandoval Godoy, John Holmes, Harry Katz, Tom Kochan, Pradeep Kumar, Kevin McQuillan, Gregor Murray, Ester Reiter, Dick Roman, Paul Stewart, and Donald Swartz. We also thank the two anonymous referees from Cornell University Press, one of whom provided an extraordinarily detailed critique and set of recommendations.

Jim Rinehart and Chris Huxley express thanks to their universities, departments, and secretaries for research support. Chris Huxley gratefully acknowledges the support of a visiting fellowship with the Humanities Research Group at the University of Windsor in 1993–94 and in 1996. David Robertson extends thanks to members of the CAW secretarial staff.

This project could not have been completed without the moral and intellectual support of our wives and comrades Carol Rinehart, Charlene Gannagé, and Moya Beall.

Finally, we would like to acknowledge Labour Canada, which contributed financially to this project. The opinions expressed in this book are those of the authors, not Labour Canada.

This book contains entirely new material and represents a major expansion, synthesis, and update of some previous work. Certain formulations have appeared in earlier versions as J. Rinehart, C. Huxley, and D. Robertson, "Team Concept at CAMI," in Steve Babson, ed., *Lean Work: Empowerment and Exploitation in the Global Auto Industry* (Detroit: Wayne State University Press, 1995); J. Rinehart, C. Huxley, and D. Robertson, "Worker Commitment and Labour Management Relations under Lean Production at CAMI," *Relations industrielles/*

Industrial Relations 49 (1994); and J. Rinehart, D. Robertson, C. Hux-ley, and J. Wareham, "Reunifying Conception and Execution of Work under Japanese Production Management? A Canadian Case Study," in Tony Elger and Chris Smith, eds., *Global Japanization? The Transnational Transformation of the Labour Process* (London: Routledge, 1994).

J. R.
C. H.
D. R.

Just Another Car Factory?

Introduction

WE EMBARKED ON OUR RESEARCH AT A TIME WHEN MASS PRODUCTION
had been diagnosed as terminally ill. In the media and in business circles, its impending death was an occasion not for mourning but for cel-
ebration. Mass production's successor (but certainly not its heir, we were
told) was born in Japan, named lean production, and promised a bright
future as the standard manufacturing mode of the twenty-first century.
The emergent system, which carried few, if any, traces of Fordism,
offered not only optimum efficiency but a humanized work environment. It featured simultaneous precision and flexibility, the capacity to
reduce costs, tight inventories, quick die changes, and low per-unit
assembly hours. It was also characterized by multiskilled workers, challenging jobs, plentiful training opportunities, a participatory environment, a high-trust milieu, and harmonious labor-management relations.

While the lean system was portrayed as mutually beneficial to
employers and workers, the early research concentrated on the system's
efficiencies and was fashioned from reams of corporate statistics, observations of the physical characteristics of workplaces, and interviews
with managers and engineers. In contrast, the impact of lean procedures on workers was the subject of assertion rather than empirical in-
quiry. It wasn't long before the ideas advanced in this early wave of
research were subjected to analytical, methodological, and empirical
criticisms, and by the time we were involved in data collection, con-
troversies were in full swing.

We believe there is an urgency to these debates not because of concerns about national and corporate competitiveness but because more
and more people are spending a good part of their lives in lean workplaces. Lean "transplants"—factories in North America fully or jointly

owned and managed by the Japanese—have become a prominent feature of our industrial landscape. There were no Asian auto assembly transplants on this continent before 1981. Between 1982 and 1990, seven transplants began production in the United States, while the four transplants located in Canada all arrived since 1985. The lean system is no longer the special preserve of Japanese firms, nor is it any longer an emergent development. A rapidly growing number of North American companies, including the Big Three auto makers, have implemented or are striving to emulate the manufacturing methods developed in Japan. If there is one non-debatable proposition in the early literature, it surely must be the claim that lean production will be the standard manufacturing mode of the twenty-first century.

Despite a burgeoning body of literature on the subject, many questions about the lean system require more definitive answers. We entered CAMI—a unionized joint venture of General Motors and Suzuki heralded as a lean production showcase—with a set of research questions that arose from our interest in and involvement in shop floor life and unions. We were interested in the organization of work and the social relations of production. We were interested in how the constellation of practices associated with a lean system affects workers and how they accommodate to, resist, and modify workplace rules, routines, and relationships. And we were interested in how the union is shaped by and shapes not only its rank and file members but also the lean system. These concerns were not exhaustive, but they did provide a central focus that guided and permeated all stages and spheres of our research.

Our use of multiple research methods and a longitudinal research design, and our open access to managers, workers, and the shop floor, afforded an empirically grounded portrayal of the internal operations of a lean plant, the experiences and reactions of workers to the system, and the relationship between the company and the union. (Research methodology is discussed in Appendix I.) As far as we can determine, this is the first study of a Japanese or joint venture plant in North America to draw information, systematically and across time, from a randomly selected sample of workers and to have such unlimited access to the shop floor.

CHAPTER I

The Strike That Was Not Supposed to Happen

O N THE MORNING OF SEPTEMBER 14, 1992, AFTER SEVERAL MONTHS of intense negotiations and a 98.9 percent strike vote, workers at CAMI Automotive in Ingersoll, Ontario, began a strike that was to last five weeks. The media paid close attention to the dispute, and the strike even made international news. The attempt to improve working conditions and wages of relatively well-paid auto workers in the midst of a deep recession, newsworthy in itself, was overshadowed by the historic significance of the action. This was the first time workers had struck a North American transplant.

That the strike was not supposed to happen was a point made repeatedly by the media. A *London Free Press* editorial (Sept. 15, 1992) stated: "The strike this week at the CAMI auto plant in Ingersoll may seem absurd, given the recession and the number of jobs already lost in the auto industry." An *Automotive News* (Chappell 1992) headline read: "CAMI strike wilts transplant rose." Behind this and many media reports lay the question, "What went wrong?" Typical was an account in the *Windsor Star* (Sept. 26): "Young, idealistic, bright—they began at the CAMI Automotive plant believing this was no ordinary factory. It's three and one half years later, and those 2,100 workers are now cynical and embittered, wielding picket signs that ridicule the workplace philosophies they once embraced. What happened?"

The company signaled its determination and ability to withstand a long strike by letting it be known that it had an unusually high inventory. Workers symbolized their resolve by maintaining around-the-clock pickets, burning company T-shirts, and bearing banners on which the company slogans of "open communication, empowerment, kaizen, and team spirit" were crossed out and replaced by the "new values" of "dignity, respect, fairness, and solidarity." Another large banner, displayed at the plant entrance, was inscribed with a symbol similar to a no-smoking sign—a diagonal slash across the word "yosh" set inside a circle. (The term "yosh," akin to the rah-rahs of a cheerleader, is sometimes shouted by workers doing pre-shift calisthenics, and company-oriented workers are derisively called "yoshers.") During the strike, the Canadian Auto Workers union (CAW) put on a series of educational programs for the workers, and strikers were joined by their families and other supporters from the community at a large demonstration at the plant. Throughout the five-week strike the morale and solidarity of the strikers, many of whom had no experience on picket lines, remained high.

As with most strikes, this one had multiple causes. Working conditions—many of which were related to lean procedures—and labor-management relations constituted one major grievance. Workers on the picket lines gave reporters vivid examples of how CAMI had ignored their interests. They poured out a litany of complaints centering around what happened daily on the shop floor, and they condemned the vague language of the contract. One worker, cited in the *London Free Press* (Sept. 25), epitomized this line of criticism: "CAMI was a great place to work until we started making cars. It seems that once we started production, all the values got tossed out." The second major issue was wages and benefits, which were lower than those in Big Three auto plants. Ron Pellerin, the CAW national representative responsible for bargaining with CAMI, put the union's case bluntly: "Benefits, pensions, vacations, wages—in virtually every area Suzuki lags behind the industry standard."

Bargaining Positions

While admitting to in-plant problems, CAMI spokespersons publicly viewed the strike as purely an economic matter. Vice-President of Personnel Rick Jess denied that management style had anything to do with the strike, insisting that it was entirely about wages and benefits (*Toronto Star,* Oct. 18, 1992). The CAW, the company declared, was asking for more than it could pay. Company spokesperson Susan Nicholson told the Toronto *Globe and Mail* (Sept. 15, 1992) that CAMI was opposed to "the rubber stamp approach" of wage parity with Big Three automakers; CAMI was operating in a tough economic environment. The markups on subcompact vehicles are always small, and off-shore competitors enjoyed substantial cost advantages. According to Nicholson, "There is something fundamental at issue here. We are the only car plant in North America making small, economy vehicles. From the outset, the CAW recognized that CAMI would have to have a different kind of structure from the rest of the industry in order to succeed, with a different approach to wages and benefits" (*Automotive News,* Sept. 21, 1992). In a CBC radio interview Nicholson emphasized the company's position: "What we're involved in is a strike which is clearly over economics, and it's an issue on Big Three parity, and we're talking dollars and cents." Nicholson expressed disappointment with the CAW "in that they're trying to abandon their role as a partner in the foundation of CAMI" (*Windsor Star,* Sept. 26, 1992).

CAW president Buzz Hargrove stated the union's position: "Suzuki has to take responsibility for a strike that's about equality, about Suzuki competing on an equal footing. Suzuki's had a four-year labor cost advantage with a workforce and a plant facility that's second to none in North America. As far as we're concerned, Suzuki's not going to compete in the future on the backs of its workers" (CAW *Contact,* Sept. 18, 1992). The CAW viewed wage gains as a matter of equality among members; the union sought economic parity with Big Three plants in Canada so that one auto company would not have a cost advantage that the others could then use to whipsaw workers into making concessions.

The CAW also sought to improve working conditions. In a letter to the president of Suzuki in Japan, Hargrove wrote that the CAW initially agreed to "cooperate with CAMI in meshing our workplace structure with key elements of the Japanese production system (e.g., fewer classifications, work teams, job rotation)." He stressed that "this was done in the spirit of an experiment that would subsequently be evaluated and, where necessary, modified." Hargrove maintained that workers had evaluated the experiment and found it wanting. Workers, he said, wanted "a relationship based on respect for our members and their union, not on paternalism—respect and dignity on the shop floor with real worker input and an end to the autocratic management style of the past three years."

CAMI defined the in-plant issues as key concerns of the local union and economics as the major issue for the national union. Management viewed in-plant problems as a natural result of "growing pains" and as "sub-issues" that could be resolved easily. Susan Nicholson told a CBC radio interviewer that "there is a real difference between what people here, locally, are saying as opposed to the kind of direction they're getting from the national union, which is on the money side of things. And that's the problem."

If left to themselves, CAMI insisted, the local and the company could quickly iron out their differences. This position reflected the negotiation pattern prevailing in Japan. There, collective bargaining is conducted mainly on an enterprise rather than an industry-wide basis, and wages and benefits are tied to the economic performance of each plant. CAMI claimed that it was the national union, not the local, that fomented and prolonged the strike. The company thus tried to drive a wedge between the local and national union by maintaining that each was pursuing different goals. CAMI was joined in this effort by the president of Suzuki Motors in Japan, who stressed in a letter to Hargrove the need to negotiate contracts without disruptions of production and the desire to keep the national office out of the dispute:

> It is a custom in Japan to settle labor negotiations, including demands for wage increases and working condition improvements, through a discussion without work disruption. The Suzuki Workers Union has never elected strike action for settling negotiations for 42 years, after the confused postwar period. All labor issues have been amicably resolved through sincere discussions between labor and management . . . Both parties always demonstrate

patience and spend long hours and many days to gain a mutual understanding and solve issues one by one, while continuing to perform jobs as usual. This practice is common not only for Suzuki, but also for all other Japanese companies . . . Suzuki Auto Workers Union, although it is a member of Japan Auto Workers Federation negotiates with Suzuki management independently without influence of any national level union and federation to settle labor issues. They take into consideration Suzuki's own conditions because issues should be treated as a matter of individual company.

The letter ends with the following request: "Although your [CAW national office] involvement is mandatory in finalizing the negotiation, I believe it should basically be handled between the local union and the management of CAMI. It will be appreciated if you would instruct the chairman of Local 88 and its representatives to carry out the negotiations with their own initiatives."

In a follow-up letter to the union local after the strike, Suzuki's president chided the local for striking and made known his expectation that in the future they would resolve disputes without interrupting production. The letter concludes: "We are very eager for you and the members of Local 88 to positively agree on the approach which I describe above for future negotiation." In reflecting on these words, Hargrove (1992) pointed out that Mr. Suzuki was making the case for a company union, one that would represent the company's but not workers' interests. "This not only ignored Canadian union traditions but, as well, was against the law in Canada so he wrote to me only as a concerned CAMI shareholder rather than the chief executive officer of Suzuki." Hargrove went on to say that neither the local nor the national wanted a strike. "If the company's rhetoric of fairness, worker input and commitment to a non-confrontational relationship with our union had been meaningful, this company would never have forced this strike. Obviously it wasn't."

Workers ratified a new agreement on October 19 and returned to work the following day. They made important gains in wages and benefits and improvements in working conditions, some of which hit directly at the heart of lean production.

The Lean Production Debate

There were good reasons for the media's shocked reaction to the CAMI strike. It cast a new light on a cooperative form of labor-management relations and a new mode of organizing production whose immunity to conflict had been largely taken for granted. Japanese assembly transplants and joint ventures in North America are considered to be at least reasonable facsimiles of their parent companies—Toyota, Subaru-Isuzu, Mitsubishi, Nissan, Honda, Mazda, and Suzuki. Most published accounts credit the Japanese with having exported not only some variant of the efficient Toyota production system, or lean production, but their special brand of harmonious industrial relations as well.

Observers from all points on the political spectrum agree that the remarkable performance of the postwar Japanese economy and particularly that of the Japanese automakers was built on a foundation of labor-management cooperation. Strikes are rare, and Japanese auto workers log substantially more hours of work per year than workers in other industrialized nations.[1] Much less agreement exists, however, on the explanation of these patterns of industrial behavior.

On one side are those who view workers' diligence and cooperativeness as voluntary. "Japanese industry has created a new and more powerful corporate hegemony over everyday life and makes workers align more closely with the company and voluntarily give of themselves in the name of corporate progress" (Kenney and Florida 1993:305). These attitudes are nurtured by the special character of Japanese organizational structures, management practices, and production systems. The corporate environment features low-interest housing loans, job security, multiskilling and challenging jobs, joint consultation and worker participation, and the reunification of mental and manual labor. Corporate concern for workers' welfare and challenging work are buttressed by high-trust relations between labor and capital. "Japanese managers are known for their emphasis on trust and respect, human potential and

1. In the late 1980s, the normal work week at Toyota's Takaoka plant was 60 hours (Williams et al. 1992). In the Japanese auto plants as a whole the average number of hours worked in 1991 was 2,253. Included in this figure is an average of 374 hours of overtime. By comparison, average hours worked in industrialized countries of the West were closer to 1,800 (Watanabe 1993).

dignity, collaboration and mutual help of employees through team work and management-labor cooperation" (Shimada and MacDuffie 1987:30). Cooperation is reinforced by enterprise unions that share a common outlook with management (Shimokawa 1987:242).

These accounts view Japanese management as a win-win system that benefits both workers and the company. So innovative is this constellation of production and management practices that some scholars have depicted it as postFordist, a term that signifies a transcendence of all the negativities of the mass production system of Henry Ford (Florida and Kenney 1988; Womack, Roos, and Jones 1990).

Critics, on the other hand, attribute Japan's peaceful industrial climate to a coercive organizational milieu that creates compliance rather than voluntary cooperation among workers. For Watanabe (1993:8), the three Ks—Kitsui (hard), Kiken (dangerous), and Kitanai (dirty)—describe jobs in Japanese auto plants. Parker and Slaughter (1988) have used the term "management by stress" to characterize a system in which workers are subjected to relentless pressure from the pace of work, the absence of buffers and relief workers, managers, and their own team members. Individualized wage systems enable management to reward cooperative workers and penalize uncooperative ones, including those who refuse overtime, wash up before quitting time, don't hand in suggestions, or are not involved in quality control (QC) circles (Cole 1979; Glaberman 1983; Kamata 1982). Corporate welfare practices and employment guarantees generate dependence on the firm.[2] Collaborative enterprise unions leave workers without an effective collective voice on the shop floor to challenge management demands (Clarke 1990; Glaberman 1983; Junkerman 1982; Kamata 1983; Okayama 1987). Industrial relations in Japan are trouble free, Turnbull (1988:8) maintains, precisely because of the special relationship companies have with unions. The labor process under Japanese production management "is simply the practice of Fordism under conditions in which management prerogatives are largely unlimited" (Dohse, Jürgens, and Malsch 1985:141).

---

2. For example, with housing costs exorbitant in Japan, companies like Toyota offer workers low-interest housing loans. Monthly payments are determined by dividing the value of the loan by the number of years a worker will remain with the company before retiring. Whether this produces worker loyalty is debatable; it clearly breeds dependency (Watanabe 1993:10).

In North America, Japanese auto transplants have indeed been notably strike free. While skeptics might point out that most transplants operate without unions, the aura of high trust that surrounds them has been reinforced by reports on NUMMI, the unionized Toyota–General Motors joint venture in California. NUMMI, whose production and management systems are patterned after Toyota, has been praised for turning a trouble-plagued GM car factory into a model of efficient production and harmonious labor-management relations (Adler 1993a, 1993b, 1995; Brown and Reich 1989; Shimada and MacDuffie 1987). The media, especially influential trade journals like *Automotive News,* have applauded the efficiency and consensual labor relations of Japanese companies and their North American offspring. Dissident views, like Parker and Slaughter's (1988) critical analysis of the team concept or the Fucinis' (1990) description of conflict and resistance at Mazda in Flat Rock, Michigan, are occasionally considered. Such accounts, however, are seen as aberrations. Japanese production management is steadfastly portrayed not only as humane and efficient but also as a necessary model for restoring industrial competitiveness in North America.

The antagonists are worlds apart. One side posits a postFordist workplace where conception and execution are rejoined, where workers' contributions come from what they know as much as from what they do, and where worker empowerment and the spirit of cooperation define production relations. The other side views Japanese production management as an essentially Fordist system where the logic of the assembly line is pervasive, where management dictates go unchallenged, where the driving principle is work intensification, and where workers' rights and well-being are sacrificed on the altar of profitability. Empowerment or subordination, cooperation or concession, working smarter or working harder—our entry to the debate is through the front door at CAMI.

CHAPTER 2

Touring the Plant

C AMI IS A JOINT VENTURE BETWEEN GENERAL MOTORS AND SUZUKI that makes the Geo Metro subcompact car and the GM Tracker and Suzuki Sidekick four-wheel-drive sport utility vehicles. The plant occupies 1.6 million square feet and cost a little over $500 million to construct. It is located in the small town of Ingersoll, Ontario (population 8,500), midway between Toronto and Detroit in what the company refers to as the heart of the Canadian automotive supplier community.[1] CAMI began production in April 1989 and by the end of 1991 was operating two shifts with an hourly workforce of about 2,100. In the model year 1991, it produced 160,000 vehicles.[2] Workers at CAMI are members of Canadian Auto Workers union (CAW) Local 88, making it the

---

1. CAMI received from the province of Ontario $50 million in grants and loans, forgivable if certain investment, production, and employment levels were met. The company received from the Federal Ministry for Industrial and Regional Development an additional $57 million, which the company said it needed to operate its extensive training programs. The city of Ingersoll spent $1.31 million to help with the cost of upgrading services around the plant site, with plans for further spending. While these sums are high, they are less than some Canadian transplants have received and substantially less than what it has cost American states to attract transplant operations (*London Free Press,* November 27, 1991 and August 26, 1992; Perrucci 1994; Yanarella and Green 1990).

2. There were four transplants in Canada—Toyota, Honda, Hyundai and CAMI. Of the three currently operating in Canada (Hyundai has since ceased production), CAMI is

only unionized auto transplant in Canada and one of only four such organized plants in North America.

The Joint Venture

Discussions between GM and Suzuki began in 1984, and the partnership was announced in August 1986. GM entered the venture to take advantage of Suzuki's proven track record in producing small vehicles (Suzuki is the largest producer of small cars in Japan). In addition, the exceptional gas mileage of these small cars would ensure GM's adherence to Corporate Average Fuel Economy (CAFE) standards mandated by the U.S. government. These considerations were underscored in an undated CAMI document: GM "needed a presence in [the subcompact market] to preserve a position until the arrival of its own offerings, and to assist in meeting Corporate Average Fuel Economy Goals." GM was also interested in using CAMI as a showcase plant to demonstrate to its employees the nuts and bolts of lean production, or what GM calls synchronous manufacturing.

Suzuki was interested in joining forces with GM in order to market its vehicles through the GM distribution and dealership network. According to the undated CAMI document, Suzuki "needed capital, North American operating expertise, and the General Motors' dealer network to sell a sufficient volume to make a manufacturing venture viable." At a deeper level, the fear of North American protectionism and the appreciation of the Japanese yen (between 1985 and 1988 the yen doubled in value relative to the U.S. dollar) undoubtedly figured in Suzuki's decision.[3]

---

the only one with Japanese and North American owners. By 1990, the transplants were producing over a quarter of a million vehicles, or roughly 18 per cent of North American transplant output (Holmes 1991; Yanarella and Green 1990).

3. Suzuki began in the 1920s as a manufacturer of textile machines, made armaments during World War II, and returned to textile machines immediately following the war. In the early 1950s the company began to concentrate on mopeds and motorcycles and in 1955 produced its first car. The company was unionized in 1946, and in 1948 the union secured a first contract that included a closed shop, a veto over hiring and firing, and parity on the management council. Subsequently, a counteroffensive against independent unions was launched, and by 1950 the original union had been replaced by a second, enterprise union.

CAMI Culture

CAMI brings together a Canadian union, American and Japanese owners, a Japanese production system, and a North American market. As
CAMI President Masayuki Ikuma told guests at Partners' Appreciation
Day, May 1990: "The best way to create a culture that works for a company like CAMI is to concentrate on the blending process—a process
that respects the strength, weakness, and the values of each other and
combines the best of two cultures."[4]

A visitor to CAMI sees evidence of this cultural blending everywhere. The firm's name is derived from the Japanese word for God or
deity—*kami*—spelled with a C to give it a Canadian flavor. The plant
is a long (nearly one kilometer), narrow, windowless structure linked
to the front office by an overpass corridor. Once inside, the visitor is
struck immediately by signs of CAMI culture. Posted over the recep-
tion desk in the front lobby and throughout the plant are CAMI's four
values: empowerment, *kaizen,* open communications, and team spirit.
Clad in blue pants and white or blue shirts or sweatshirts with first-
name labels above the pocket, employees are easily distinguished from
visitors. What cannot be distinguished at first glance is the rank of the
employee. Male and female, president and production worker—all wear
similar uniforms. Only insiders would notice the thin light blue stripes
on the collars of team leaders or area leaders, or the light blue hats they
sometimes wear. (Team leaders are hourly workers and union members. Area leaders are first-level managers, the equivalent of foremen.)
No one at CAMI punches a time clock.

The visitor might search for an exclusive dining area for managers
but would find only a cafeteria used by all employees. In the parking

---

Suzuki now operates with performance-based wages, QC circles, an extensive supplier
network, and a lean, flexible, levelled system of production. Many of these practices were
borrowed from Toyota (Price 1995). In 1988 Suzuki produced 70.4 vehicles per employee,
compared with Toyota's 61.0 and Honda's 51.2 (data from Chilton Automotive Industries,
April 1989 and April 1990, as reported by the GM Liaison Office, n.d.). In addition to vehicles, Suzuki manufactures motorcycles, boat motors, engines, transmissions, and electrical
power generators. The company has seven assembly plants in Japan and 47 plants around the
world (Price 1995).

4. About 250 CAMI employees, including union members, were sent to the Suzuki
plant in Kosai, Japan to witness the original Suzuki production system in operation.

lot there are no reserved spaces for executives, with the lone exception of the company president. If the visitor were to enter areas where management personnel work, he or she would notice that there are special rooms for meetings, but no one has a private office—only a desk in an open room full of desks. CAMI's seemingly egalitarian philosophy is reflected in the absence of a category of employees called workers. Employees who work on the shop floor and are members of the bargaining unit are known as production associates (PAs), team leaders, or maintenance associates (skilled trades workers).

This egalitarian exterior obscures CAMI's hierarchical structure, which is marked by eight levels—PAs and team leaders; area leaders; assistant managers; managers; director of production; four vice-presidents; the president; and a six-person board of directors. The company incorporates three distinct groups of managers—those from GM, those from Suzuki, and those who have come from other companies. The latter group, the CAMI group, according to one manager, "are developing their own management style." Some management responsibilities are clearly identified as belonging either to Suzuki or to GM. GM handles personnel and Suzuki production engineering, for example. Other functions are mixed. For example, the vice-president for finance and the treasurer are from GM, while the comptroller (a director) is from Suzuki. There are fewer parallel and competing levels than in a traditional plant. CAMI leans toward area management rather than departmental management, which means that managers in charge of production in Stamping, Welding, Paint, and Assembly are also responsible for maintenance and quality within their areas.

That this company is half Japanese-owned is obvious. Japanese words spelled out in English (what someone referred to as "Jenglish") are used and posted throughout the plant. In the training area each room has a Japanese name on the door. A central value of the system is *kaizen,* or continuous incremental improvement. *Andon* cords that enable workers to call for help or stop the line are found at most work stations. *Poka-yokes* (devices to ensure fail-safe operations) are located throughout the plant, and CAMI has begun to institute a *kanban* system to move operations closer to stockless or pull production (work is "pulled" through the system by the needs of the next operation down the line, rather than "pushed" through by the creation of inventory). Employee suggestions go by the name of *teians*. Workers are expected to do pre-shift calisthenics called *taiso,* and on occasion exuberant team members have been heard to chant *"yosh!"* CAMI has adopted the word *Nagare,* referring to a flow motion which is both swift and smooth, to name its production system, and the classroom preparation for working in this system is known as Nagare training. The manual used to train recruits is in both English and Japanese. Occasionally visitors might spot the Japanese president wandering around the plant, as well as trainers from Japan—fewer now than in the early days.[5]

The physical environment of CAMI—its exterior signs of equality and its pervasive Japanese terminology and aura—marks it as distinct from traditional North American auto plants. Indeed, the visitor gets the sense that something different, important, and innovative is happening here. Once on the shop floor, however, the visitor quickly realizes that this is still a factory for assembling automobiles.

Making Vehicles

In technical terms, the plant is low-cost; its planners scrupulously avoided what managers refer to as "overdesign"—no point building a fixture to last forever (a charge often leveled against GM) if it's to be used only for one model. The plant uses proven technology that trails the leading edge. The equipment was installed and debugged by suppliers before it was turned over to CAMI. In any event, the equipment design had already been proven at Kosai, the twin plant in Japan. There are some obvious CAMI modifications, but for CAMI, innovation and change are better in small, low-risk doses.

Material Handling

The plant was constructed for point-of-use receiving: it is ringed with 93 receiving docks around its perimeter, where supplier goods are delivered. The supplier owns the containers, guarantees the scheduled

5. At one time there were 150 Japanese trainers in the plant, but only a handful remained at our last research visit.

why

delivery, and unloads the parts at CAMI. From the outset it was understood that vendors would send designated truck drivers who would unload their own product onto the dock area. Other unloading tasks, such as unpacking sea containers, have been done in-house by the Material Handling department. The approximately 120 PAs in Material Handling are organized in teams. Another 20 or so salaried employees work in the office for Material Control.[6]

Material arrives from all over the globe—engines and transmissions from Japan, mirrors from Australia, seats, bumpers, and J grills from Canada and the United States. All North American vendors operate on a just-in-time (JIT) basis, whether they deliver from 200 miles away— the network stretches from Barrie, Ontario, in the north to the tip of Ohio in the southwest—or from a facility near the plant.

The plant uses some automated processes for delivering components to the assembly line. For example, seats organized in sequence according to the color and type of vehicle for which they are destined arrive at the plant by truck within four hours from the order. They are then mechanically loaded onto a conveyer and transported overhead to an elevator where they are lowered to the appropriate vehicle. Some other parts, such as bumpers, arrive at the loading dock organized in sequence, but they still must be transported to the line by a stock person from Material Handling. The parts are delivered to the line as needed. As one manager explained, "We built the plant so that we physically don't have a lot of space to store parts" (McCammon 1989:112). However, precision delivery is complicated by the shipment of steel and components from Japan.[7]

Despite the commitment to the principle of JIT operations, a kanban card system was not introduced until shortly before the summer 1991 shutdown, and then only as a pilot project on trucks in Assembly.

6. Unless otherwise specified, figures on technology, production rates, job cycles, plant population, etc., refer to November 1991.

7. The company has refused to disclose precise figures on the North American content of its vehicles, but some estimates have run as low as 35 percent. The U.S.-Canada Free Trade Agreement called for a minimum 50 percent North American content in order to avoid paying duty on vehicles shipped to the U.S. The American government claimed CAMI's North American content was below 50 percent. CAMI argued that if interest payments on loans used to purchase machinery were considered in the content calculation, it would meet the required standard (Chappell 1991:44).

[handwritten annotation: NO way! what was decided ↗]

Kanban is a self-scheduling system for restocking the line. The material handler goes to the board, picks up the red card that signals a part needs restocking (green indicates fully stocked and a yellow signal means stock levels are getting low), and brings the required part to the assembly line. Kanban was introduced stage by stage to a new team every week or so until the system was implemented throughout the Assembly department.

Stamping

The plant consists of four consecutive production operations: Stamping, Welding, Paint, and Assembly. At one end of the factory is the stamping shop, a capital-intensive and technologically sophisticated operation. The department is minimally staffed. Fifteen salaried employees (managers and engineers), a maintenance team of six and another seven skilled tradespersons in die repair, 20 PAs, and four team leaders operate the place on one shift. Workers operate presses and cranes; load and unload parts; inspect, sand, and buff parts; and deliver them on forklifts to Assembly and Welding.

Stamping occupies the least space of the four departments and houses three Japanese presses identical to Suzuki's in Japan, plus a blanking line. About one-third of the floor area is occupied by finished storage and rack storage. The rest is occupied by the transfer presses, the blanking line, and, along one wall, the die repair shop. The presses are massive, over two stories high and about the same underground. All are computer controlled. Stamping a different part is as easy as calling up the part number on the PLC (programmable logic controller). Running overhead are the cranes that move the dies from die storage to the presses.

The process begins with the blanking press, which takes coils of steel and stamps out blanks—flat sheets of steel configured in different sizes, shapes, widths, and lengths. The blanks are then loaded into one of the transfer presses, where consecutive sets of dies press out three-dimensional body parts, such as doors, roofs, floor panels, fenders, and sidebodies. Over 70 per cent of the metal weight in the car is stamped in-house. "We don't make the smaller reinforcement pieces, such as hinges or reinforcement crash beams on doors," explained one manager. "They're too small for our presses."

Productivity is measured in strokes per minute (SPM)—the number of times the press goes up and down—and the targets vary depending on the press. At the 1991 rate of 5.5 SPM, a lot of steel is pressed, enough to keep the blanking line consuming around 600 tons of material a week.

Management is pushing to reduce the time required to change dies. The less time a press is idle for die changes, the more time it is running and making money. Moreover, if set-up time is reduced, the size of the production run can also be reduced. The die change is highly automated, and the operation has achieved SMED (single minute exchange of dies—anything under 10 minutes). A manager pointed out that "the old style machine could take 36 hours," but with the new machines "the guys got it down from 20 minutes to about six."

Regardless of the quick die change, the stamping operation still builds to a production forecast. It is the area with the most obvious concentration of stock, and it produces sizable batches. This may change: by our final visit in late 1991, management had adopted the goal of reducing inventory between Stamping and Welding.

Welding

In the body shop, the stampings produced in-house, as well as the smaller outsourced parts, are welded together. The shop is divided into four areas, each supervised by an area leader with about 60 people, most of whom load parts into machines that weld them automatically. There are two separate lines or, more accurately, two series of cells (chassis, main body, front door, white body). On one side of the shop the unitized body of the subcompact car is joined, while on the other side the more complex chassis and frame for the sport utility vehicle are welded together. The body shop is one of the most automated in the industry. The extent of automation is immediately felt. Traveling from Stamping to Welding, one moves from an operation that is relatively sparse and mammoth to a dense jungle of machinery and equipment.

Parts are automatically transferred from one operation to the next; robots tap dance around the parts, welding this spot and the next; gantry-style equipment grabs, welds, and releases the vehicle. In places clusters of Japanese Fanuc robots converge on the vehicle, moving like a group of praying mantises. A total of 367 robots complete about 85 percent of the welds on the truck side and as high as 97 percent on the car side. The robots are concentrated at the front end of the process where rows of them are interspersed with manual stations. The operation was described by a manager: "Our lines are very automatic, basically a lot of robotic welding. People bolt the parts and check for quality. The robots do the welding, and the transfer to the conveyor is done with vertical lifters. The conveyor holds the buffer and it drops down automatically on the next line where people add other small parts." Overhead, a maze of conveyors takes completed parts up and over the next operation. Banks of console lights flash, and computer screens display changing data and shifting graphics.

Forklift drivers from Welding pull body panels from Stamping. Outside suppliers deliver small parts daily, and from Material Receiving they are delivered to the line as required. About half an hour's worth of buffer is held in the conveyors between automation cells.

Productivity in Welding is measured in uptime and throughput. A good day, according to one manager is "seven hours uptime." A big breakdown is defined as four hours down, and this "happens maybe once a week or less." The truck side can produce 270 to 278 bodies per day—both shifts—on a three-minute cycle. A perfect eight-hour day on a three-minute cycle would yield 148. Output is higher on the car side.

Paint

The paint shop is clean and well lit. The separate body lines for cars and trucks come together here. Excluding salary and management, 336 workers over two shifts work in Paint. They are grouped into 22 teams, 11 on each shift. They prepare vehicles for painting by sanding, masking, taping, plugging, and sealing them; paint them; clean, buff, and touch them up. In Paint the geography is less supportive of team processes. In some teams, PAs are physically separated from their co-workers. And unlike the rest of the plant, there are no designated team areas.

On the ground floor, the body is cleaned and dipped in Electrocoat (E coat), an anti-corrosive. It is then moved to the sealer area, to a masking area, and then to underbody coat. After the undercoat is applied, the defects are removed in the dry sanding booth, where PAs hand sand the vehicle. On the second floor the vehicle traverses the full length of the paint shop, up one line and down the next, moving from one operation to another. Along one end of the shop are a series of "black box" radiant zone ovens, and closer to the opposite wall a number of paint booths. For every paint operation there is an oven—the Intermediate Coat booth matched with its corresponding oven and so on through the top coat. Between the various coats are clean-up and touch-up operations.

The paint operation is less automated than other new paint shops. According to some in management, this is where the money ran out. There are only 12 robots, and PAs perform many tasks manually, e.g., paint spraying in Final Repair, that are automated in other plants. The most automated areas are the top coat spray painting and the underbody area.

In production terms, many of the issues in Paint are equipment-related. Painting is a complex process, more like a chemical plant with tanks, pumps, lines, and flow rates than a manufacturing operation. The goal seems simple enough—putting about a gallon of paint and about the same amount of primer onto a vehicle—but the process is complicated. In fact, Paint is one of the only departments that has maintained a core of Japanese advisors in the engineering area. Some in management see Paint as "a potential gold mine of cost savings," but according to one manager, "The tough part is to get the volume. Because of Assembly we're having to go back and take a look at where the bottlenecks are." The paint shop works best with larger batches of vehicles. "It is easier to paint 15 white cars instead of five," explained the manager. "We were averaging three cars per batch and now we're up to six and eight and that's a considerable saving." The problem is balancing those batch sizes in the face of pressure to increase volume (especially when there are already 10 colors and a new two-tone) and to reduce batch size in Assembly.

Scheduling

Once painted, the cars and trucks are waxed and then shunted to Painted Body Storage (PBS), which is located overhead between Paint and Assembly. There are 216 spaces in PBS, roughly half trucks and half cars. The buffer is divided into eight lanes on either side. There is flexibility from side to side and the lanes have random access in and out. PBS runs at about 60 percent of its capacity, which means about 60 vehicles on each side—about two hours' worth of production—in case the paint shop is having problems. If there is any interruption in Assembly, PBS can store about an hour's worth of bodies from Paint. PBS is computer controlled.

Vehicles are selected from the buffer and sent to Assembly on the basis of a pre-programmed set of rules that tries to balance high-labor-content vehicles with low-labor-content vehicles. The various models and option packages of cars and trucks, based on type of transmission, air conditioning, the trim level of the vehicle, whether it is five-door or three-door, are all translated into labor content. "We have standard 'man-minutes' for each body style," explains a manager. "Right now we are using 'A' through 'S,' with 'A' being the easiest type, the lowest labor content." On the truck side, for example, the base model requires about 400 labor minutes, while a high-content vehicle requires about 440. As one manager put it, that "represents a lot of extra manpower you have to find when that vehicle goes down the line." While cycle time (the amount of time workers have to do their assigned tasks before repeating them) accounts for a balanced mixture of high- and low-option models, achieving leveled production has been problematic.

Once a vehicle has been selected, it is automatically pulled from one of the lanes and sent down to either the car or the truck side of the assembly operation. First it passes a scanner that reads the label on the fender of the vehicle and sends all the information for the build mix to printers on the floor. Once the vehicle passes the scanner, there is no way out of the system until the end of the assembly process.

Assembly

The logic and pace of the assembly line pervade the entire plant, which has been engineered so that line speed changes trigger changes in other areas. As a manager observed: "The facilities are set up to where if you slow down the main line or speed it up, everything goes with it. So from an operations standpoint, it's been well put together."

Assembly gets an empty painted body that, after passing by hundreds of different work stations, is driven off the line as a finished vehicle. In between, the thousands of mechanical, plastic, and electrical parts, powertrain components, interior and exterior trim, the glass, the wheels, and so forth are bolted, screwed, or otherwise fastened together. The assembly shop also houses the final inspection, testing, and repair operations. They run the length of the assembly hall in the space between the lines for cars and trucks.

Compared with other modern plants, the CAMI assembly operation is labor-intensive. Assembly uses only 18 robots for operations such as spare wheel load and front and rear glazing. In addition, a few operations are automated: one for unloading and delivering seats to the line; a small Automated Storage and Retrieval System (ASRS) for car engines and transmissions; one for separating the cab from the frame on the truck line; and another for installing the gas tank in the truck and filling it.

Assembly consists of separate lines on either side of the assembly hall for the car and the truck. Each line is composed of three parallel segments that run the length of the assembly shop—snaking up, down, and up again. Off-line subassembly areas no longer exist. Shorter feeder lines for subassemblies, such as the instrument panel and the power train, are tied in to the main line. Small part subassemblies, such as the cluster for the instrument panel, have been dispersed and integrated into the work of various line-based teams. Each segment of the line has a different line speed, as do the feeder lines.[8]

The lines are constantly moving. In places the vehicle travels along a continuous double track on the floor and in other places on an overhead conveyor. On the first line the car is conveyed on an overhead carrier but travels at floor height. At the end of the first line, the conveyor slopes upward, curves around, and carries the car in a raised position for most of the second line, where PAs fasten the underbody parts. Three-quarters of the way down the second line, the car is lowered to the floor. It then passes the tire assembly area on the second curve, and a quarter of the way along the third line, it is automatically removed from the overhead conveyor and transferred to the automated glazing station, after which it continues along a set of tracks at floor level for the rest of the assembly operation.

8. In contrast to CAMI, Suzuki's Kosai plant uses workers from supplier firms to perform some assembly operations. A union rep who had been to Kosai expressed surprise at this practice: "I would say this place [CAMI] is similar [to the Kosai plant]. The difference you have over there is your suppliers. A lot of them work on the line or right beside the line."

Most of the major components and parts are assembled in adjoining subassembly line areas and then conveyed to the main line. A number of examples describe the process.

The car body (without wheels) comes out of PBS and travels high up over the length of the assembly shop on an overhead carrier, which slopes down to floor height at Station #1. The car doors are removed here. The doors are transferred, again overhead, to the door assembly line, where they are built up on a moving line. Once the door team has finished, the doors are again transported overhead in the proper sequence to the middle of the third line, where they are installed just after the seats are put in. Door-off assembly, a departure from the way cars used to be built, makes it easier to install the seats, the instrument panel, and the interior trim. It protects the doors from scratches and bumps and allows parts to be located closer to the line.

The instrument panel is assembled on the IP subassembly line, which is off to one side of the main line. The moving line is fitted with holding fixtures that can be rotated to permit work to be done on both the front and back of the panel. At one end of the subassembly line a bare, molded plastic instrument panel is assigned a bar-code identification (rider sheet). Fifty or 60 feet later it is ready to be installed, in various options packages, on the main assembly line. When the panels come off the feeder line they are automatically marshaled in and out of a buffer storage area, which can take about 10 minutes' worth of production. Whenever the buffer is full, the IP line stops. It can be down for five seconds, a minute, but rarely more than a couple of minutes. When the buffer is drawn down, a bell rings and the line starts again. At IP Install, about halfway up the first line, the panels are manually lifted and installed in the car.

The engine is dressed in an area adjacent to the IP line. Engines and transmissions—shipped from Japan—are stored in the Rackmaster, an Automated Storage Retrieval System. The engines and transmissions are fed into the engine subassembly line, and once assembled, the power train is conveyed overhead past the first and second line to a work station at about the middle of the third line.

PAs walk along with the vehicle, installing whatever parts and components are assigned to their work stations. Hanging above each work station are yellow and red andon cords, and at regular intervals in the aisles hang overhead electronic andon boards. If a worker pulls a yellow cord, the line remains in motion while the andon board lights up the troubled work station and plays annoying tunes until the problem is resolved. The red andon stops the line.

Assembly requires the most workers of all the departments. The car side employs 560 hourly direct and indirect workers over two shifts. Nineteen teams range in size from about eight to 21. On the truck side, just over 400 workers cover two shifts. The PAs in truck produce about 135 units on a shift, and on the car side about 245.

Many of the rules and procedures driving vehicle production at CAMI were developed in Japan by Toyota. Various labels have been attached to these guidelines, but they are most commonly known as lean production. The next chapter lays out the major components of this system and describes how they are applied at CAMI.

Lean Production: The Essentials and CAMI's Version

C AMI IS BUILT AROUND LEAN PRODUCTION PRINCIPLES AND WORK practices that the company calls the Nagare system. The lean model that CAMI strives to emulate (and that General Motors calls synchronous manufacturing) was first developed at Toyota by the company's chief production engineer, Taiichi Ohno. This chapter will first explain the basics of lean production as developed at Toyota, and follow up with some specifics as prescribed at CAMI. Many of the CAMI principles are common to other lean production plants.

Lean production, its proponents argue, is superior to traditional production systems. Traditional mass production is a "robust" just-in-case system that relies on buffers of all kinds—high inventories, large stockpiles between work stations, excessive space, including large repair areas, and a corps of relief workers to cover for absentees. The objectives of lean production are to strip away these buffers, to reduce costs, and to involve workers more systematically in production (Womack, Roos, and Jones 1990). This is accomplished by a series of connected practices.

The just-in-time approach minimizes buffers by making only the amount needed just as it is needed. Subassemblies are made just in time to be attached to the vehicle as it moves through the shop, and parts are produced or delivered just in time to be used in the subassemblies

(Schonberger 1983). This makes for a one-at-a-time, continuous production flow that establishes throughout a plant the equivalent of an invisible, smooth-running conveyor. Monden (1983:68) contrasts this with Fordist practices. Under Fordism, supplier lines and subassemblies produce in lots and are not coordinated with the main line. Large numbers of parts are held as inventory, either in the main factory or at the supplier's plant. At Toyota, in contrast, all subassemblies are done on conveyors that are integrated with the final assembly line. The system includes procedures to ensure that defects are spotted and rectified immediately so that they do not proceed to subsequent work stations (e.g., andon cords that workers can pull to call for help or stop the line) (Monden 1983). This makes it virtually impossible for workers to ignore production problems, to work ahead, or to build up banks. Lean production, then, limits the ability of workers to regulate the pace at which they work.

The smooth operation of JIT is possible only when workers perform their tasks the same way every time, in the same number of minutes or seconds. Lean production requires a rigid standardization of human time and motion that has three aspects: *Cycle time* is the amount of time each operator has to do the assigned tasks. Cycle time provides, as it were, the container to be filled with the tasks, motions, and actions that comprise a worker's job. The *standardized work sequence* is akin to a job description; it specifies the layout of the work area, required tools and equipment, and the steps and sequences of each job. *Standardized-work-in-process* refers to the daily number of units or pieces required for an even and on-time flow through each work station. Standards are grounded in time study and strictly enforced (Monden 1983). Once standards are set, however, the challenge is to change them continuously (kaizen) by eliminating non-value-added labor.

Lean production's proponents define it as a flexible system. It is flexible both in terms of product—the ability to change quantity easily and to produce different versions of the product—and in terms of the "adjustment and rescheduling of human resources" to match fluctuations in production quotas (Monden 1983:100). This ability to adjust human resources assumes the absence of restrictive rules on work assignments (job classifications), the development of multifunctional workers, job rotation, the ability to widen or narrow the range of jobs done by each worker, the ability to alter workforce size, and the right to assign overtime work.

The bare essentials of lean production in the workplace are just-in-time production, standardized work, continuous cost reduction (via the elimination of waste and labor time), and a flexible workforce prepared to adapt to changing demands of production.[1] Our research concentrates on in-plant operations, but another key component of lean production is to have as much work as possible done by lower-paid workers via contractors and suppliers. This involves using employees of an outside company to perform non-value-added jobs, such as cleaning and food service, inside the plant, as well as outsourcing, i.e., purchasing vehicle parts from outside firms.

Lean Production at CAMI

The CAMI training manual defines Nagare as "one-by-one," "mixed type" lot production. This requires production smoothing or "leveled production" *(heijunka)*. Managers are to schedule production so that overall product volume, the order of vehicles (e.g., two-door, two-door, four-door), and variations in vehicle option content are maintained at a constant ratio, and the operation time for all line processes is the same.

---

1. Monden (1983:vi) calls Toyota's manufacturing process a unique, revolutionary system whose goal is to maintain a continuous flow of products in order to adapt flexibly to fluctuations in demand. The basic elements of this system are: 1) JIT production. 2) Kanban—an information system (usually cards indicating how much stock is needed) used to manage JIT. 3) Autonomation—the principle that defective units never pass to a subsequent work station; achieved by visual control systems, andon cords, etc. 4) Production smoothing—a procedure whereby many varieties of a product are made in a single day. 5) Workforce flexibility—multifunctional workers who rotate jobs and whose numbers are varied to meet changing production quotas. 6) Short machine set-up times and quick die changes to facilitate a continuous and variable flow of products. 7) Standardized jobs and operations. 8) Kaizen—improvement activities undertaken by workers via suggestions and QC circles.

Operations at Toyota plants in Japan are among the leanest in the world (Williams et al. 1992). The International Motor Vehicle Program study used Toyota's Takaoka plant as the benchmark for "lean" in their cross-national study of auto assembly plants (Womack, Roos, and Jones 1990).

Because of the small lot sizes and sequential operation, dies must be rapidly changed. Just-in-time production is a key organizing principle. It is a goal, given the long supply lines back to Japan, that is often difficult to achieve, but it does motivate managerial practice. CAMI, as managers readily admit, doesn't have much to teach others when it comes to JIT supplier schedules and relationships, but its organization of work, the discipline of its internal processes, and its efforts to move from a push to a pull production system are consistent with the tenets of lean production. The recent integration of off-line assembly into the main line was motivated by JIT principles and shifts flexibility from the worker to management. As a manager explained, "On a subassembly job, the person doing the subassembly has the ability at times to build ahead or be able to leave that subassembly area at a particular time." Now that they are part of the line team they can no longer do so.

The entire plant operates on the basis of standardized operations and times. The original work standards were brought from Suzuki and re-generated by a computer program. One manager described the formula: "It's a program, and what it says is that the average person, given a proper amount of training, should be able to perform these many elements in this amount of time."

Japanese advisers, along with area and team leaders, set up and refined the jobs, which were then codified in detail on standard operation sheets (SOSs). The SOSs are kept by area leaders and are not available to PAs. Key elements of the SOSs were selected by area and team leaders, placed on sheets called CAMI Operating Standards (COSs), and posted at virtually every work station. The COSs specify the main job elements and sequence of operations to be followed in performing each job. The emphasis on standardized work is illustrated by headlines in the CAMI training manual: "The standardized operation shows the best methods of performing every operation in a process which any associate must strictly observe in doing the job." "Improved efficiency begins with standardized operations." "Everyone performs the same operation the same way." "Thorough enforcement of standardized operations." The manual explains: "If everyone worked in different ways, operation times would vary and quality would suffer. Efficient production of good products would be impossible. As a result, we adopt standardized operations."

Standards are supposed to be constantly revised as more efficient ways are found to perform jobs. "Standardized operations," the CAMI manual states, "are the basis of continuous kaizen in process operations. If everyone performs the operations in the same way, potential problems or waste will be easily identified so that kaizen can be readily made." A manager expressed the relationship between standards and their revision: "The whole secret of it is to do the operation the same way every time, exactly the same way every time. And you'll notice even the COSs on the line are made in pencil so that if you change it, you just erase parts and add to it. And that's from Japan."

Setting standards is not the responsibility of industrial engineers at CAMI, in contrast to normal practice in traditional plants. According to *Automotive News* (Chappell 1991:1), "Industrial engineers are an endangered species at CAMI." In theory, each team serves as its own industrial engineering department. Area and team leaders are trained in industrial engineering techniques such as time study and job task analysis. This work is described in the CAMI manual as one of their most important tasks. Under lean production workers not only are expected to follow the "one best way" but are instructed to ask constantly, "Is there a better way?" Workers are urged to contribute to restandardization through QC circles and by submitting suggestions.

Flexibility is a central goal at CAMI. It entails managerial authority to reassign and transfer workers and to demand overtime. Flexibility means that all production workers, who share a single job classification, are able to perform a variety of tasks. It requires teams whose members are cross-trained, perform direct and indirect work, rotate jobs, and adapt to continuous changes in cycle time and job content.

5Ss, 3Gs, and 3Ms

The 5Ss, 3Gs, and 3Ms are Japanese terms that establish rules of conduct and a philosophy of production. The 5Ss establish a neat, ordered, and clean workplace: keeping necessary items and disregarding the rest *(seiri);* storing everything in its place *(seiton);* keeping work areas clean (seisou); maintaining personal appearance and CAMI uniforms *(seiketsu).* The fifth S is *shitsuke,* which translates into the discipline to accomplish what has been decided. The 5Ss also deal with safety rules and work rules, such as on the job "there is no smoking, eating, drinking, reading material or radios."

The 3G principle refers to *gemba* (work site), *gembutsu* (work piece), and *genjitsu* (reality). The rule is to go to it (work site), see it (work piece), and understand it (reality). From the 3Gs comes the principle of visible management. Management should be able to see and assess what is going on everywhere. There can be no inventory blocking operations, and nothing and no one should be out of sight.[2] Visible management entails posting COSs at the job site; placing workforce information on bulletin boards in team work areas, such as attendance records, cross-training achievements, and teian (suggestion) records; and posting quality ratings or production rates, such as strokes per minute in Stamping.

The 3Ms specify the three sins of production—*muda, muri,* and *mura.* Elimination of the 3Ms leads to an efficient and safe workplace. Muda means waste, identified as overproduction, unnecessary transport, excess inventory, defective parts, unnecessary inspection, unnecessary movement, and idle time. A manager provided an example: "More traditionally we would have a worker waiting on the machine. Here the worker doesn't wait on the machine. If there's any waiting it's the machine, not the worker . . . We essentially utilize the individual's time more effectively than in a traditional [plant]." Muri translates as overburden. It refers to difficult or unnatural actions and movements, as well as to the use of inadequate equipment—using a half-ton truck to transport a one-ton load. Mura, which signifies unevenness, includes idiosyncratic, inconsistent work methods, failure to follow the rules, absence of standardization.

Pokayokes, Andons, TPM, and Kanbans

Pokayokes are devices that either make an operation fail-safe because it can be done only in the right way (presence sensors, limit switches,

---

2. Some think such efforts can be taken too far. A story circulated about a high-level Suzuki executive from Japan who, on his tour of CAMI, ordered staff to take down the peg boards that blocked the view into maintenance work areas, remove the doors from tool cabinets, and move the lockers away from the walls in the tool crib.

photo eyes) or provide the operator with visual aids, such as color coding to reduce uncertainty and the probability of error. On some of the CAMI weld operations, for instance, a particular part can be loaded only in the correct way. If it is stacked incorrectly, the machine will not operate. Similarly, CAMI has color-coded wire harnesses, speedometer cables, lock rods, weatherstripping, and springs.

Kanbans, the physical devices used to move an operation closer to stockless or pull production, can take different forms. The most common techniques involve the use of special kanban cards or squares painted on the floor, the former to trigger stock replacement and the latter to limit its quantity. CAMI, over the course of the study, had begun to undertake some of these kanban initiatives in Assembly.

TPM—Total Productive Maintenance—is CAMI's effort to shift some maintenance responsibilities to production workers. This is one way CAMI keeps skilled trades numbers low (the other is by relying on outside contractors). The ratio of skilled trades to production workers is extremely lean; at last count, 92 maintenance associates were responsible for keeping a plant staffed by 2,100 people up and running. In Welding and Paint, where TPM is most developed, production workers might repair cuts in water hoses, change filters and gun tips, clean the slag off the robots, note and report frayed wires, dress the tips of the robots, and change the shanks. Some of this work is done on weekend overtime. Managers admit there are frictions over TPM, particularly where it stops being minor, as Preventative Maintenance is supposed to be largely a skilled trades responsibility. As one manager put it, "Drawing a line PM/TPM is difficult to do."

Part of the CAMI goal of "building quality in" is to be achieved through PAs responding to missing or damaged pieces or bad fits, rather than letting the job go by without signaling the problem. To this end, workers are authorized to pull yellow and red andons to signal for help or stop the line.

This chapter has outlined the key elements of lean production, drawn from management textbooks and from the CAMI version of lean production—Nagare—as described in corporate manuals. These elements, which represent substantial departures from the ideal typical mass production or traditional plant, prescribe how the system ought to operate.[3] As such, they constitute an idealized model that corresponds more or less well with concrete applications. CAMI has implemented the operations and procedures that define a production system as lean, but, as in other lean plants, efforts to refine and perfect the system are continuous.

3. There is a tendency in the literature to contrast lean production with a static, idealized model of Fordist mass production. This ignores both the uneven development of mass production and its variations across companies and nations. On this point see Elger and Smith (1994:10–13) and Williams et al. (1993).

in a lean system, the top exec's and mangers at the largest companies control all the rest — suppliers, employees, society, musical sets.

CHAPTER 4

Recruitment and Training

AUTO TRANSPLANTS USE HIGHLY SELECTIVE RECRUITMENT procedures, some taking as long as three months to complete. This rigor is particularly North American, as companies in Japan do little screening of recruits (MacDuffie 1988). Both critics and proponents of lean production maintain that rigorous recruitment is a precondition for the system to operate smoothly, although there is some disagreement on what traits and capacities are required. MacDuffie (1988) argues that the system needs skilled workers, while Berggren (1992:43–44) says the transplants look for workers not with skill but with a propensity toward company loyalty. Transplants generally favor greenfield sites in rural or exurban areas where there are plenty of young people with no industrial or union experience, where wages are low (sometimes half as much as paid by the transplant), and unemployment levels are high (Berggren 1992:40; Kenney and Florida 1993:101).[1] Honda managers, for example, acknowledged that they deliberately avoided locating in regions where

1. Transplants ordinarily receive 30 to 100 applications for each job opening (Berggren, Bjorkman and Hollander 1991). Mazda's roughly 3,000 production workers were chosen from 96,500 applicants (Fucini and Fucini 1990). At Toyota in Kentucky over 100,000 applicants vied for 3,100 jobs (Yanarella 1995).

workers had "picked up bad habits" (Kenney and Florida 1993:101). NUMMI (New United Motors Manufacturing Inc. in Fremont, California) is an exception in that former employees of the GM Fremont plant were rehired, and the average age of the workforce at start-up was 41 years (Adler 1993b).

Recruitment at CAMI

In CAMI's case, the decision to locate in Ingersoll was apparently based more on operational criteria (e.g., access to supplier firms) than on the characteristics of the surrounding population. While Ingersoll is a small town, it is located in the industrial heartland of Canada, next to a major highway and an easy commute from several mid-sized cities. Unemployment in southwestern Ontario generally exceeds the average in the United States, but in the late 1980s, when the plant was built, the region was not depressed, the level of unionization was relatively high, and wages were not generally low.

To be hired at CAMI was in itself an accomplishment. The company reported that it processed 43,000 applications to hire roughly 1,200 employees. A screening system based on detailed assessment procedures is part of the CAMI way. Personnel selection tests and interviews were designed by a U.S.-based consulting firm. Apart from its insistence that applicants with previous union membership not be screened out, the CAW had no input into the selection criteria and no involvement in any phase of recruitment. The selection process, according to the company, was designed to "produce a competitive and motivated workforce that shares CAMI's values."

Prospective employees fill out an application form that outlines the company's values and expectations (area leader aspirants must also submit a resumé, and maintenance applicants must file proof of their skilled trades qualifications). The forms are checked by the assessment staff "to verify information regarding applicants' employment, work performance and work habits." The material explains that "successful team members are self-disciplined professionals," who "with training and management support" are expected to:

- take full responsibility for their own work
- be able and willing to do a variety of tasks while maintaining a quick workpace
- be willing and able to assist and train other team members
- be punctual and have perfect attendance
- ensure that the work area is clean and safe
- work a rotating shift schedule (such as two weeks of day shift work followed by two weeks of evening shift work)
- be physically and mentally ready to work at their full potential
- restrict smoking to designated areas in the plant
- maintain a drug- and alcohol-free workplace to ensure the safety of all team members.

The recruitment process consists of six phases. The total time commitment is about 15 hours for production applicants and almost 23 hours for the trades, not including the time involved in making at least five trips to the plant. Applicants are told that the hiring process "requires time and dedication and it is time well spent, because it is designed to help you and CAMI."

Prospective employees complete two written tests, take part in hypothetical problem-solving and team activities, and undergo two interviews. The importance of formal education is downplayed, although applicants are asked if they have completed Grade 12. The first step in the process, "general abilities assessment," is based on a written multiple-choice test that evaluates mechanical aptitude, abstract reasoning, and verbal and numerical skills. Another step looks at teamwork; applicants are put through a series of simulation exercises to test their performance in group problem solving. Finally, provided all has gone well, the applicant takes a physical examination.

In some ways CAMI's hiring decisions were similar to those of most other transplants. The workforce, about 20 percent of whom are women, is young (the average age of our sample of workers was 30.6 years and three-quarters of them were under 36). However, prospective employees with prior auto industry or union experience were not rejected. This was the first job for only eight percent of the original

worker sample, and over half (54 percent) had belonged to a union before they were hired at CAMI.[2]

Training for Lean

If workers under lean production are indeed multiskilled and their jobs
challenging, one would expect to find extensive and continuous training programs in transplants. Womack, Roos, and Jones (1990) reported
that Big Three plants gave new workers 46 hours of training, compared
with about 375 hours in transplants. A study conducted by the U.S.
Office of Technology Assessment (OTA) found that transplants gave
new-hires more initial training than their U.S.-owned counterparts,
and annual hours of training in the former were 50 percent higher (45
vs. 30 hours) (OTA 1990).

These surveys were done in the 1980s when many transplants undoubtedly were still in the process of implementing and refining procedures to reach full production. At this early stage there is not only a
need for training but, importantly, more time for it. Mazda (now called
Auto Alliance International), in Flat Rock, Michigan, for example, initially promised to provide training over the entire course of workers'
careers, and during the first several years of operation the company did
give workers 10 to 12 weeks of orientation and training before they got
to the shop floor (Fucini and Fucini 1990). As production pressures
escalated, Mazda shelved these programs. Now new-hires receive at
most two or three days of instruction (Babson 1993).

In 1993, the International Motor Vehicle Program (IMVP) surveyed
eight transplants and 19 Big Three assembly plants in the United States
on their training. For new employees, on a scale of 0 (less than 40 hours
a year) to 3 (160 hours or more), the Big Three plants scored 1.8 and
the transplants 2.8. For experienced employees, on a scale of 0 (less than

2. At the end of 1993 CAMI began to recruit people who had at least a year's manufacturing experience. A manager explained that CAMI had begun to look for people with
realistic expectations of "what they were getting into." Some union reps believe the recruitment change was an attempt to reduce work-related injuries, to which women allegedly were
particularly vulnerable. The full rationale for the new policy is unclear, but one result has
been a decline in the hiring of women.

20 hours a year) to 5 (80 or more hours a year), the respective scores
were 1.8 and 4.1. Although the training edge favors transplants, these
differences are not nearly as great as those reported by Womack and
his associates.[3] Assuming that transplants generally do place a greater
emphasis on training than traditional plants, what are they teaching,
and do they produce a skilled workforce?

Transplants concentrate on teaching soft skills, such as problem solving and group dynamics, rather than on technical skills, like the mental
and manual capacity to operate equipment and perform jobs (Graham
1995; Hodson, Hooks, and Rieble 1992; Jacobs 1995; Yanarella 1995).
Workers value technical skills more highly than soft skills because they
are more likely to increase workers' confidence and improve their mobility opportunities both within the plant and in the labor market generally.[4] MacDuffie maintains that a major aspect of lean production
training is to impart to workers how their jobs fit into the broad production process. "What's different about lean production is its goal of
developing a broader contextual knowledge in the workforce about the
production system, so that a worker's deep, often tacit knowledge of one
specific task becomes linked to an understanding of how the overall system works, and how one's piece of it relates to other upstream and downstream tasks" (MacDuffie 1995:55–56).

Adler and Cole's (1993) designation of NUMMI as a "learning bureaucracy" refers to organizational rather than individual learning. They
admit that NUMMI may not be sufficiently attentive to broadening
workers' technical skills, but, like MacDuffie, they imply that this neglect
is at least balanced by teaching workers about the overall production process and how to continuously restructure (and restandardize) their own
jobs. "At NUMMI the skill development strategies for individual workers are managed as a component of this process [continuous improvement and organizational learning], rather than as a way of maximizing
personal opportunities. As a result, training focuses on developing *deeper*

3. These data were reported in an unpublished report by John Paul MacDuffie and
Fritz Pil (1994). It is unclear whether the apparent convergence of Big Three and transplant
training agendas reflects a declining training emphasis in transplants, an increasing emphasis in Big Three plants, or a bit of both.

4. See Chapter 5 for a general discussion of skill and the distinction between soft and
technical skills.

knowledge, not only of the relatively narrow jobs but also of the logic of the production system, statistical process control, and problem solving processes" (our emphasis) (Adler and Cole 1993:92).

It is easy to devalue this kind of knowledge and consider only technical skill as real skill. Effective interaction with team members and the ability to detect, analyze, and resolve job-related problems are valuable qualities. To the extent that this kind of knowledge is a central ingredient of transplant training, it is a departure from what workers learn in traditional plants. However, this kind of understanding, as the above authors recognize, cannot be equated with skill accumulation. Much of the soft-skills instruction has a clear ideological bent, geared to breeding worker commitment to the firm and its objectives (Graham 1995; Yanarella 1995). Further, development of technical skills is impeded in some transplants by the absence of transfer rights and clear lines of job progression.

One of the six key elements of lean production delineated by Mac-Duffie (1988:13) is on-the-job training done by experienced workers and team leaders. While he regards this process as "extensive," the length and type of hard-skills training depends, of course, on what job a worker is being taught to perform. Job rotation among production workers and their assumption of indirect duties require more training and more systematic training than what is typically provided in traditional plants. It is misleading, however, to regard this on-the-job instruction as extensive, since it entails nothing more than teaching the fundamentals of these routine tasks. This conclusion is reinforced by descriptions of training at Mazda and NUMMI. A survey of Mazda workers revealed that the great majority felt the company had not lived up to its training promises and regarded their training as either poor or fair (Babson 1993). In none of Adler's (1993a, 1993b, 1995) articles on NUMMI does he devote much attention to training, and he acknowledges (as do Adler and Cole 1993) that the plant offers no opportunity for comprehensive hard skills development.

If transplants do have an edge over traditional plants in time spent on technical training, it is not very great. Moreover, the question of content remains. On the one hand is training in a skill such as metal-finishing, which necessarily takes time to perfect and can be used in a variety of industrial settings. On the other is training to do six specific jobs within one's own team, each of which is minutely choreographed and requires mainly the "skill" of being able to work rapidly and continuously.

It is fair to conclude that technical training in lean production transplants is neither extensive nor continuous. The parameters of instruction are set by lean production's standardized and short-cycled jobs. Technical training is defined by the employer, has little conceptual content, takes place mainly on the job, deals with the firm's processes and equipment, and is job-specific. These restrictions place distinct limits on the extent, accumulation, and portability of workers' technical skills.

CAMI Training

CAMI earmarked for training about $40 million—roughly one-third of the grants and loans it received from various levels of government. This was an average expenditure for a North American transplant (Yanarella 1995:131). CAMI has all the hallmarks of a training organization. This is a lingering first impression reinforced by the physical layout of the plant. The overpass from the Administration building to the plant proper ends in the corridor outside the Training Center. Inside are a number of classrooms and special workrooms where it seems something is always going on. The schedule board shows a busy calendar. In the Yaruke room workers are learning how to kaizen, in the Pokayoke room a visiting delegation from GM's Opel plant in Germany is being briefed, and in the 5S room the flagship of the program, Nagare training, is taking place.

Four days of new recruits' first week are taken up with Nagare training, which is a blend of production basics (it is questionable how much knowledge of the production system can be imparted in this brief time) and cultural hype, packaged as an orientation program. For example, CAMI's "cost-down" emphasis is transmitted to trainees in one session on kaizen and one titled "Let's Think About Cost." According to a manager, the program was developed around several objectives: "First of all to let individuals know what the values of the organization are, how we operate. We want to let individuals know what the objectives of the organization are in respect to cost, quality, and safety. We want to get them familiar with the basic operation of the CAMI production system.

We want to train them in the areas of safety." The link between the company's competitiveness and job security is also stressed: "One of the things that it's really important that we do over time, and we start in our first week of orientation with our employees, is explain the competitive reality. Canada is really losing its competitiveness as a jurisdiction and jobs just aren't guaranteed forever. This company is competing with Japan and Korea and Mexico and different companies for a slice of the mini-car and small sport utility market. We need to be able to compete. That's the bottom line."

Program content has changed over the two-year research period. One manager described the revised format as more "toned down" and less likely to lead to "false expectations." And there is a renewed effort to focus on the soft, interpersonal skills: "We've added one segment dealing with team-building. We have a synergy or a consensus seeking exercise that we've instituted in there. It's to show the benefit of individuals working together in a group, and it is your typical consensus-seeking exercise like Lost at Sea, Lost in Space . . . that sort of thing."

During the early days, training was a central activity. In a ramp-up situation, spending hours on training is not only possible but necessary. Producing 25 cars per day as opposed to every hour leaves a good deal of time for instruction. As production increased, training was cut way down. Management's rationale was a familiar one: "The hard part is freeing up the people on the floor." At times understaffing reached the point where new hires were assigned to their teams as early as their first day, with catch-up arrangements made for training later.[5]

For PAs, training is very soon truncated and job-specific. No career paths are mapped out, with training the vehicle for traveling along them. After that intensive first week, workers tend to see the Training Center merely as a place to trade in their teian coupons rather than as a place where PAs are trained. The Training Department does not keep track of hours. There are no data documenting that every PA averages four,

---

5. During periods of acute staff shortages, cross-training and job rotation were suspended, and production quotas and vehicle quality suffered from the substandard performance of new-hires. Productivity and quality dropped not because lean production requires extensive training but because of CAMI's skeletal staffing and the absence of trained relief workers.

eight, or 30 hours of training per year. Indeed, it is surprising how little instruction PAs actually get. As one manager admits, "As for classroom training for the average associate on the floor, there's been nothing more [than Nagare] at this point."

Outside of some special instruction for jobs such as driving forklifts, operating the crane, paint spraying, and repair work, and for what management refers to as CAMI skills—QC circles, kaizen and TPM—training for PAs is "catch as catch can." "For the associates on the floor," explains one manager, "the only other training would be job-specific training just on rotation." The emphasis is on cross-training and the focus on "performing at line speed." When time permits and when absences and injuries do not disrupt the process, on-the-job training is conscientiously and systematically pursued, and workers are thoroughly trained to perform all jobs in a team. On bulletin boards in team areas, training charts display PAs' level of mastery of each job—trained in a job, experienced, achieved line speed, and can teach others how to do the job. This information is recorded in a circle divided into four quadrants, each shaded as the level of attainment is reached. The emphasis on cross-training arises not only from company policy but also from the demands of workers, most of whom are keen on rotating jobs.

Workers' Evaluation of Training

In round 1 of our set of four interviews, we asked workers in our sample to evaluate their orientation session, offering them two pairs of response alternatives. (For a description of our interview format and research methods, see Appendix I.) Respondents were about evenly split on whether the training was "useful" (47.9 percent) or "a waste of time" (52.1 percent). However, only one-quarter of the sample described the orientation as "effective training," while three-quarters viewed it as "indoctrination."

In round 4, nearly three-quarters of the workers felt they were adequately trained for their jobs. However, more and more of them expressed dissatisfaction with CAMI's overall training effort and their resulting lack of skills development. In round 2, 50.6 percent said that there was too much training on QC circles and not enough on the development of

TABLE I.   Attitudes toward training

		Round 2	Round 3	Round 4
There is too much training on QC circles and	Agree	50.6% (40)	59.1% (42)	61.8% (42)
not enough training that develops my skills.	Disagree	49.4% (39)	40.9% (29)	38.2% (26)
There is too much training on teams and problem	Agree	62.3% (38)	67.2% (41)	75.6% (59)
solving and not enough technical training.	Disagree	37.7% (23)	32.8% (20)	24.4% (19)
There is too much classroom training and not	Agree	42.3% (30)	55.2% (37)	60.5% (46)
enough on-the-job training.	Disagree	57.7% (41)	44.8% (30)	39.5% (21)
I've been provided with the opportunity to up-	Agree	35.0% (28)	29.0% (22)	26.6% (21)
grade myself and learn new skills.	Disagree	65.0% (52)	71.0% (54)	73.4% (58)
The opportunity for training at CAMI makes it	Agree	29.6% (21)	13.5% (10)	10.1% (8)
easy to get the skills you need to get a better job.	Disagree	70.4% (50)	86.5% (64)	89.9% (71)

Note: Percentages in all tables, graphs, and the text are based only on those who responded to the question.

skill (see Table 1).[6] By round 4 the majority of respondents (61.8 percent) answered this way. When asked if there was too much training on teams and problem solving and not enough technical training, 62.3 percent in round 2 and 75.6 percent in the final round agreed. A growing percentage of respondents also agreed (42.3 percent in round 2 and 60.5 percent in round 4) that there was too much classroom and not enough on-the-job training. Clearly, workers increasingly felt that they were not getting enough technical, hands-on training.

This sense of marking time on the shop floor was reflected by the fact that only 26.6 percent of respondents in round 4 agreed they had

6. In hindsight, we should have contrasted QC circle training not with "skill" but with "technical skill," to avoid invidious distinctions between the two.

been given the opportunity to upgrade continually and acquire new skills (down from 35 percent in round 2). In the second round, only 29.6 percent considered that the opportunity for training at CAMI made it easy to get a better job. This was a low level of agreement to begin with, but by the last round only 10.1 percent agreed. Finally, when asked if training increased skills or if all the jobs were about the same, 52.9 percent in round 1 and 72.7 percent in round 4 opted for the latter.

Recruitment at CAMI was a painstaking process aimed at selecting loyal, diligent employees who could function well in a team environment. However, technical training for most production workers was a pragmatically brief experience that differed from that of traditional plants only with respect to systematic cross-training for job rotation and preparing to take on some indirect duties, such as self-inspection and minor maintenance. What distinguished CAMI training from past practice was the emphasis on ideological indoctrination, problem-solving instruction, and interpersonal skills to facilitate working in teams. The brief period of technical training and the absence of programs for continuous skills development were reflected by the preponderance of workers' negative assessments of CAMI's training regimen and opportunities.

✳ CHAPTER 5

Working at CAMI:
Multiskilling or Multitasking?

ADVOCATES OF LEAN PRODUCTION HAVE LITTLE OF SUBSTANCE TO say about the content of work and less to say about how workers feel about their jobs under this system. According to MacDuffie and Krafcik (1989:4), multiple tasks undertaken by work teams—inspection, routine equipment maintenance, housekeeping—in conjunction with job rotation, yield "vertically integrated jobs that require skill development.[1] Womack, Jones, and Roos (1990) repeatedly describe lean production jobs as challenging and workers as multiskilled, but these claims are neither amplified nor empirically grounded.[2] Much the same could be said about Kenney and Florida, although they do present some of the system's negative impacts on workers. They equate multiskilling or "polyvalence" with the demands on workers of a flexible assembly process. Moreover, job rotation "enhances the process of knowledge acquisition," allows workers to "familiarize themselves with various aspects of the work process," and "generates a storehouse of knowledge that can be applied to a variety of work situations" (Kenney and Florida 1993:39).

1. Not all lean auto assembly transplants practice rotation. Nissan no longer does, and it is quite limited at Mazda, for example.
2. Berggren (1992:19) depicts Womack, Jones, and Roos's discussion of work and working conditions under lean production as "sloppy and speculative."

44

Both of these sets of authors avoid discussing standardization. This glaring omission and the superlatives used to describe the labor process yield a romanticized caricature of work under lean production.[3]

Other proponents of lean production are more forthcoming on the design of jobs. Adler (1993a:102–3), for example, observes that NUMMI is "obsessive" about standardization, which is a "distinctive feature" of the labor process at this plant. Adler (1993b:113) refers to "the intense discipline and detail with which jobs at NUMMI are regimented," pointing out how closely this resembles Taylorist ideals. He also acknowledges that workers possess only modest skills and that the company has few structures in place to develop workers' skills. Instead of simply allowing that NUMMI's design of jobs inhibits skill and discretion, Adler puts a positive spin on this matter and, in effect, turns a sows ear into a silk purse. First, he cites a NUMMI manager who declares: "Standardized work has the major benefit of giving control of the job to the person who knows it best—it empowers workers [presumably through their involvement in the kaizen process]" (Adler 1993b:142). Second, he minimizes the salience to workers of intrinsic job satisfaction, arguing that it is not a necessary condition for meaningful work. Routinized jobs can be meaningful when they are democratically shaped and viewed by workers as a requisite for making a quality product and assuring the company's competitive edge.

Adler displays a certain ambivalence about the content of work that is echoed in others' descriptions of the lean production labor process. While giving some substance to their characterizations of work content (as opposed to merely attaching positive labels) and admitting to certain negativities, they find elements of the system that obscure or outweigh what workers on the shop floor do most of the time. For example, MacDuffie (1988:15) views standardization as a keystone of lean production, but it is overshadowed by job rotation and the multiple responsibilities of production workers. The latter "means the jobs are more complicated to learn and perform well," while rotation provides "a continuing opportunity for skill development, and . . . a 'career path' of sorts." A similar ambivalence is evident in Wickens' (a Sunderland,

3. In an earlier paper, Womack (1987:11) wrote that all jobs in Japanese plants are painstakingly "choreographed" through time and motion studies. One wonders why these standardized procedures were not discussed in *The Machine that Changed the World.*

England, Nissan plant manager) discussion of work. He admits that lean production is suffused with Taylorism and the logic of the assembly line, but other aspects of the system—teamwork, enlarged responsibilities of production workers, and worker involvement in kaizen—more than compensate for these rigidities and "allow us to move away from the alienated worker and create fulfilling, meaningful jobs" (Wickens 1993:27).

These sanguine images of work have not gone unchallenged. In his study of six Japanese manufacturing transplants in Great Britain, Bratton (1992:202–207) found that large-batch producers adopted a *deskilling* approach to organizing the labor process. The Japanese owners put a premium on workers' autonomy and technical skills only in small-batch, high-value-added workplaces, i.e., plants whose technology and production processes traditionally have required a skilled workforce. Accounts of work at Mazda (Babson 1993, Fucini and Fucini 1990), Graham's (1995) study of Subaru-Isuzu (SIA), Parker and Slaughter's (1988) descriptions of team concept plants, and Berggren's (1992) observations of transplants in Canada and the U.S. indicate that the content of work in lean plants is not much different from that in auto assembly plants in the 1950s. Most jobs are fragmented, standardized, short-cycled, and repetitive. Workers perform multiple tasks, but all of them are routine and easily learned. Berggren (1993) contrasts this situation with genuinely skilled work, which entails worker knowledge, discretion, and portability from one workplace to another. These authors, then, find little in the lean environment or the design of jobs that compensates for the routinization of work.

Our research group was well positioned to examine the manner in which work was organized and carried out at CAMI. We had open access to the shop floor, where we observed work being done throughout the plant and systematically recorded our observations and discussions with workers in repeated visits to selected work stations.

Job Content

Mike in Stamping

Mike belongs to a six-person team that rotates through five jobs on a ten-hour shift. He operates the press for two hours. "You watch the panels [sheets of metal] go through and being stamped, and you're supposed to walk around the press and check to make sure that no scrap parts get caught and build up on the press or die. If stackers at the end say there's dirt on a part, then your job is to go in and wipe down the die and start it back up again."

After two hours Mike moves to metal finishing, where the main tasks are inspecting finished parts and cleaning, buffing, and sanding imperfect ones, or trashing those that are beyond repair. When heavy parts come off the press the metal finisher helps the stackers unload and rack them. After lunch, Mike, along with one other person, becomes a stacker. Most parts are manually handled by these two, but large parts like side bodies require three workers (the metal finisher helps out) to unload and stack. Small parts are stacked automatically, so Mike's only responsibility is to make sure 40 pieces go on each pallet.

Following an 18-minute break, Mike operates the crane, which loads and unloads dies that weigh up to 20 tons. Since crane operators have a good deal of idle time, they are expected to climb down occasionally to sweep the floor or clean up scrap. "When you have downtime, you're supposed to be 5Sing, but nobody does that anymore." Mike ends the shift by driving a forklift, which picks up racks of the various stamped components and puts them in their assigned areas. Forklifts from Welding pick up the racks and deliver them to the body shop.

Mike was sent to a nearby plant for an eight-hour course on how to operate the crane. It took him one week of working on the press before he was allowed to run it himself. The forklift required four hours of classroom instruction and four hours' practice. Stacking was quickly learned, but for the metal finishing job it took Mike about a week to properly detect and repair defects.

Stacking and metal finishing are the worst jobs in Stamping. They have to keep up with what comes off the press. "That's about as close as we come to having a time cycle. In Stamping there isn't any time limit on you to do anything. They figure if you can get the parts out that you're supposed to do in a day, which we usually do, there aren't any big problems. That's why everyone wants to come down to Stamping."

John in Welding

Welding is noisy, sparks are flying, and everywhere machines are moving. John works at station #210 on the car side of the body shop. It is part of a multi-station job. The COS posted at the station reads:

1. Press the cycle stop button to release the locking pin for the parts tray
2. Remove empty parts tray and roll over to parts bin
3. Load parts from bin into tray, using 2 hands, lifting approximately 10 parts at a time
4. Make sure 3- and 5-door parts are not mixed and in proper position on the tray
5. When tray is full, roll back into line position ensuring proper fit
6. Press button to lock tray into place, make sure button lights up
7. Steer clear of machine after button is pushed
8. Watch 1 cycle of the loading machine to make sure it's working properly
9. Call if any problems exist.

Once John completes the tasks at station #210, he moves on to the loading of the "back inner set" and the "#4 Cowl side set" whose COS sheet is similar to the one at station #210. John spends most of his time loading parts, and outside of breaks he doesn't see many people. In Welding there are more robots than people, and most of the other PAs in the body shop are similarly engaged in loading parts that are then welded automatically. John and his co-workers are also responsible for minor maintenance, such as dressing the tips on the robots, and for some TPM duties, usually conducted on weekend overtime or when the line is down.

Glenn, Welding Millwright

Glenn, a skilled millwright, works in the body shop. He is a troubleshooter. "Basically, they call it firefighting, which is what it really is." He is responsible for fixing whatever breaks down in his zone—usually conveyors and robots—as well as for "teaching" (programming) robots. If the line goes down, Glenn "goes into" the PLC (computer) to find out the source of the problem. "It's [PLC] the brains of the line." Glenn follows no time cycles or fixed procedures, but when something does go wrong, the "snowstorms" (managers) show up very quickly. "You might have six or eight guys standing there watching you. 'How long's it going to take? What do you need? What's the problem? Is there a better way to do it than the way you're doing it? Do you need more help?'" The pressure of keeping the line going leads Glenn to take repair shortcuts, anything to get production running.

When everything is up and running, Glenn has idle time. CAMI wants him to use this time to change the sequence of the lines and to make them run faster and more smoothly. At first, skilled workers went along with this, "but now the guys are saying, 'to hell with it.' The lines are faster than the people. They're [line workers] not going to retire from here." The company has not pushed on this. "They're happy to see us do nothing." Glenn uses the idle time to read books or do "government work" (personal projects or hobbies attended to during working hours). "As long as production is running in your zone, the time is yours." Despite the slack periods, Glenn puts in long hours of overtime that ordinarily are devoted to making more permanent repairs to equipment that was "taped and band-aided during the week."

Bruno in Paint

Bruno enters the paint shop through "blow-off" air locks on the ground floor. He works in Underbody Coating. His team masks, tapes, seals, papers, and plugs vehicles to be automatically undercoated, after which the team removes these materials, does touch-up spray painting, and cleans off areas erroneously sprayed. The team also keeps work stations stocked, does in-line inspection, and some TPMing. Jobs are rotated every two hours. Overhead work is the toughest, especially the spraying, and trucks are more difficult to prepare than cars. Ideally, the model mix is two cars and one truck. "If you get a bunch of trucks in a row [which happens regularly] you fall behind." Bruno is solidly built and works out at a health club, but he is being treated for an upper-body ailment that has left him with a chronically stiff neck, tingling, weak hands, and a painful elbow.

One of the jobs is wheel wells. As the truck moves down the line Bruno tapes paper on the two front shock towers; masks the vehicle's identification number and two parts of the driver-side wheel; tapes paper over the rear shock towers and transmission mounting plates; and tapes six brake lining brackets, two carpet holes, and a stabilizer bar mount. Then he moves to the right side of the truck and repeats these tasks, plus taping paper to the fuel inlet. He has about one minute to complete these operations.

It took Bruno about a week to reach line speed on the wheel job, but once he mastered it learning time for the other jobs declined. With the exception of touch-up spraying, the easiest (but dirtiest) jobs are those performed after the vehicle has been undercoated. Most of these jobs involve removing with pliers the protective materials earlier put on by the team. In the summer months this area can be unbearably hot, as workers are clad in coveralls, helmets, safety glasses, aprons, and gloves.

Linda in Engine Subassembly

After four days of Nagare training, Linda was assigned to work in car engine subassembly. This is a U-shaped feeder line on the outer edge of the factory adjacent to the main assembly line. The operation is a serial build where the engine is dressed as it moves around a waist-high conveyor. The PAs are positioned at work stations along the inside and outside of the U. Fourteen PAs and one team leader work in the area on each shift. Tasks on the team range from connecting the generator (job position #1) to installing the starter wires (job position #13). In addition to the work stations on the line, there is a floater position and one off-line subassembly operation.

Everyone in Linda's team was cross-trained, and everyone is capable of performing all the jobs at line speed. If all goes well, Linda rotates jobs every two hours. Before a week is out, she will have rotated through all the jobs in her team. The rotation schedule is supposed to help balance work effort—alternating the physically more demanding jobs with easier ones, those requiring one set of wrist motions with those requiring a different set of motions.[4] In some positions, Linda will use hand tools (e.g., wrenches), in others, power tools (e.g., air-powered wrenches). In addition to lots of fasteners, there are hoses and clamps, wire harnesses and tabs, metal brackets and plates. Most of the jobs involve some attaching and fastening. When the engine approaches her station, Linda checks the attached rider sheet to determine whether it is a standard or an automatic. Depending on the class of engine, operations will differ. In Linda's area the average cycle time is 1.6 minutes. Although Linda will move to four different positions in a day, all of the jobs will have the same time limits.

In engine subassembly, and for most of the plant, a good day is occupied with tasks that are simultaneously routine and somewhat varied. On bad days, the variety is discordant tasks and the routine a fast-paced treadmill. According to one worker, "Three or four automatics in a row makes it difficult to keep going." One of Linda's co-workers underscores the point, "It is frenzied—you go like hell." Another cuts to the chase, "It's fucking frantic." At one stage during our second visit, the engine line was down—the red andon had been pulled, the "tronic" tunes were blaring, the team leader was moving to respond, and the area leader was on his way over. The question was put, "How often does this happen?" The reply was immediate, "Not often enough." On our last visit everyone on the team had requested a transfer to a different area.

In the language that has become popular to describe the nature of work under lean production, Linda is multiskilled. She doesn't attach only the generator or only the clutch assembly. She does not "own" a particular job, as is common practice in traditional plants. Linda is also expected to perform incidental or indirect duties. If the line goes down, she can be set to cleaning up the area or restocking the bins for small parts. The goal of such indirect activities is the absorption of idle time,

4. Sometimes a PA prepares the rotation schedule on weekend overtime, but it is usually made out by the team leader, who will check it with the team. Sometimes the schedule is prepared by the ergonomics group to address problems of repetitive strain injuries (RSIs).

and is clearly more a matter of work intensity than of skill development.[5] Self-inspection is not so much a skill as it is an attitude and part of the work routine, rarely more than the required 30-second checks at the start of the shift and after breaks, and the check and mark operations (colored markers applied to bolt heads) on specified jobs. In-line inspection ordinarily is nothing more than a quick glance and a rapid assessment: Is there a bolt missing? Is the generator in right? As for the other indirect duties, one of Linda's co-workers makes the point: "There is no time to empty garbage, pick up pieces. There's no time to turn around."

There is a great deal to the job in engine subassembly. It is demanding work. A number of different models of engines are built—standards and automatics require different operations, some have air conditioning, those destined for Germany are different again, and so on. In addition, the jobs change frequently. The elements that used to be done at one work station get moved somewhere else in efforts to rebalance the line. However, each job is limited to a set of elements, sequences, and operations. The responsibility for indirect functions does not change the skill content of the work. The limit of skill is cycle time. Within 96 seconds Linda is expected to complete all the required elements following standard procedures and sequences and to make a quick visual check to ensure preceding operations are done correctly. There is much to keep straight and a lot to do right, but the performance of such tasks does not require multiskilled workers.

Bill in Instrument Panel Assembly

In some traditional plants, instrument panel was a preferred off-line job. At CAMI this is not the case; it is a line job like most others. Bill works on the instrument panel, located across the aisle from the main assembly line. His team—the Dashounds—"there ain't no panel we can't handle"—works two centiminutes (hundredths of a minute) ahead of the main line.

---

5. Adding tasks to a routine job was a major feature of the Quality of Work Life initiatives of the 1970s and 1980s. This practice had more to do with rationalizing than with humanizing work. In addition to the absorption of idle time, "job enrichment" had the effect of eliminating the jobs of specialized workers and thus reducing labor costs. For examples and an analysis of job redesign, see Rinehart (1986).

Posted above the conveyor where the PAs stand are the COSs, some of which are quite abbreviated. For example, at pad installation the COS merely instructs the PA to "fasten pad to IP by turning 17 clips to the right." Visual aids are required for some of the less simple operations. For instance, an IP can receive one of six different radios depending on the options. The rider sheet with the IP will specify which radio is to be installed, and the posted visual aid—hand drawn on Bristol board— shows the different radios with some clear distinguishing marks such as the number and position of knobs. The situation is the same for the ten or so choices of speedometers and gauge panels. The total package of the IP is divided so that each position has a roughly equal amount of work. As the panel moves past each position, the worker attaches parts, controls, instruments, wiring harnesses and so on.

Early on, some of the jobs were harder to complete in the required time than others. The plan, according to the team leader, was to even out the jobs. The build sequence would remain the same—quite simply, you don't put in the radio before you install the wire harness. What can change is the package of tasks assigned to any worker.

This process of shuffling job packages and balancing the work load, especially with line speed changes, is central to team concept and lean production. There are a number of ways to do this. On the IP line, where travel distance is small, the team leader might draw up the individual assignments and the team will determine whether they work—by demonstrating that everyone can do the job in the required time. For the most part the parameters are fixed. The build sequence, the line speed, and the number of workers are not subject to team control. Where there is some say is in the task package of each team member.

The Dashounds agreed that the toughest job on the team is the installation of the ducting. It is awkward and hard on the wrists and fingers. Although the instrument panel was completely redesigned for the 1992 model, it ended up harder to build than the previous one. As one worker said ruefully, "You go to the Health Center with an injury and the first thing they ask you is 'Have you been on the duct job?'" She is wearing a wrist splint, but then so are about half her teammates. A PA summed up the frustrations of many when she reported: "There's a lot of RSIs [repetitive strain injuries] here. When I had six weeks here, my fingers and wrists started giving me problems. I went to the Health Center. They gave me ice and said [the pain] was because I was just getting used to the job. Now I'm used to the job, and my hands are still sore."

Carol on Instrument Panel Install

Finished instrument panels are transferred by an automatic hoist/conveyor across the aisle to the installation station on the main line where Carol works. She picks up a metal box of screws and attaches it to a pole of the frame transporting the car. Then she turns around to lift the 20-pound panel from its rack. With the panel in hand she bends down to climb into the car and then twists her body in an awkward manner to position the panel in front of the driver's seat. She attaches six wires, including the odometer cable, and puts in three screws (each side and one in the middle) with an automatic drill. Then she inserts in the panel two speaker grilles and a center plate. She has one minute and 36 seconds to complete these operations, and then she starts all over again.

Brahim in Material Handling

As in traditional auto plants, off-line departments at CAMI—Stamping, Quality Control, and Material Handling—are preferred areas in which to work. A major reason, according to one union rep, is obvious: "You're not line-tied, eh? You have some mobility to move around, and it's the flexibility, the movement, you know. You can take off and go to the can without having to ask somebody to go." The widely held view of certain areas as preferred places to work has reinforced workers' commitment to the seniority-based transfer policy.

After early 1990 hardly anyone was assigned directly from Nagare training into Material Handling. Now the only way to move into Material Handling is through a transfer. It took Brahim the required waiting period of 12 months before he could apply for a transfer out of Assembly into Material Handling, and after that he waited more than a year before a position opened up for him. Eventually he was successful and was assigned to a team that supplied the car line. The impression that struck him on the first day of his new posting was the relative calm and the relaxed atmosphere of the team area, tucked away in the northeast corner of the plant.

Brahim already knew some PAs in Material Handling, so he had an idea of what to expect. He knew it would be some time before he got to drive a forklift or operate the computer. His first job, as for most new transfers, was known as KD (for Knock Down)—breaking down and unpacking cartons of shipped materials. Trucks arrive with their cargo at the 40 or so unloading docks used for Assembly. In an average shift at least seven sea containers also must be unpacked. Even though workers on off-loading and unpacking wear gloves, they often suffer cuts from the knives used to break down the cartons, and the work can produce the unpleasant symptoms associated with RSIs. Although CAMI management set a weight guideline for lifting of no more than 35 pounds, some PAs developed painful back injuries, often incurred by having to reach too high or stoop too low when moving stock.

Rotation in Material Handling is less frequent than in other departments. Stockpersons initially spend three to four months on each assignment—whether it be KD, driving a forklift, or operating the computer. Like other workers in his department who had no experience driving a forklift, Brahim was glad to receive the in-house instruction to obtain the necessary driver's license. The course did not take long to complete. However, unlike much of what passes for skill development at CAMI, the training could prove useful for a job outside of CAMI, and it had the added advantage of allowing Brahim to rotate into a new and different work assignment. On the downside, fork truck drivers were not immune from back injuries associated with hours of bumpy rides on vehicles with poor suspension systems.

Some areas, such as material handling for Welding, are favored over the same sort of work for Assembly. One material handler who had worked in both areas of the plant expressed his preference for Welding: "I love my job. At times it's hard work. At times it's easier. I like the change of pace. I like the small team of seven workers. I like the weekly rotation. I was in Assembly material handling but it was too stressful. It has a faster pace than Welding. Even the management in Welding is not that bad."

Job Rotation

CAMI managers sometimes refer to PAs as multiskilled, equating the term with job rotation. Almost all PAs at CAMI rotate jobs. This pattern of regularly scheduled rotation within teams has never been central to lean production as it has operated in Japan and is not practiced at Suzuki. As one manager reported, "In Japan they do not rotate on the line. That's a unique CAMI type of thing."

During our first visit, the most frequently observed pattern was partial rotations every four hours, with workers circulating through a limited number of jobs. By the second visit, there was more extensive rotation, and by the third round, most workers were rotating through all of the jobs in their teams, with a change of work station taking place after each of the three breaks in the shift. In round 1, 32.9 percent of survey respondents reported that they regularly rotated through all the jobs on their teams, and a further 25.3 percent said they rotated through most of the jobs. These percentages climbed in rounds 2 and 3, and by round 4 62.5 percent of the respondents were rotating through all the jobs, with a further 26.6 percent rotating through most of them.[6] Rotation varied by department. It was most frequent and extensive in Assembly, and much less prevalent in Material Handling. In Paint, four-hour periods for some jobs were not uncommon. Some workers in Paint, such as those in tack-off, saw few advantages in changing work stations only to find themselves doing the same job on the opposite side of the vehicle.

Job rotation arrangements at CAMI are the product of several factors. First was management's concern for flexibility and leanness. Lean staffing put a premium on cross-training workers. Initially, there were few relief workers or floaters to fill in for absentees or for PAs whose injuries restricted them to doing the easiest jobs.[7] The relationship between lean staffing and a flexible workforce was noted by a worker cited in Feldman and Betzold (1988:167): "If everybody is interchangeable you need fewer people. If I'm working in this house and I have [two] people with me and I can only vacuum and she can only wash dishes

6. This trend of more frequent rotation contrasts with the pattern at Mazda. There workers complained about not enough rotation, its restriction by some supervisors, and supervisors' allocation of gravy jobs to favored workers (Babson 1993).
7. Lean staffing is discussed in more detail in Chapter 6.

and he can only make beds, I need three people, but if I had one person that could do all that, I would only need one." The team leader is the prototypical flexible worker who can substitute for all team members, and CAMI wanted as many workers as possible to achieve this level of flexibility. Moreover, as the plant moved to two shifts, first in trucks and then in cars, rotation through a range of jobs created a cross-trained pool of workers that facilitated putting together a second team to do the same tasks on another shift.

Second, rotation was a response to the growing incidence of RSIs. Since most of the jobs at CAMI are characterized by short cycles and repetitive motions, the potential for RSIs is considerable. The standard reaction of the company ergonomic group has been to increase the rate and extent of rotation in "high frequency" teams. CAMI ergonomists argue that a change is as good as a rest. A manager advanced a less charitable view: "One thing you can say about rotation is, you know, they're sharing the pain. It's not the elimination of it, it's a sharing of pain, a spreading around of pain."

Third, regularly scheduled rotation is a demand of the workforce. When asked, "Do you like the idea of job rotation or would you prefer to stay on one job," 91.5 percent of respondents in the first round and 90.4 percent in the final round said they preferred rotation. While CAMI views rotation as a way to increase its flexibility, the workforce uses rotation not only to relieve monotony but also to regulate work and to restrict managerial flexibility. Since there is no job ownership, no codified rules that limit and protect individual jobs, rotation has emerged as an informal shop floor work rule. One manager commented: "These people out here have gotten used to not having the same job, which is the opposite of most auto companies. Most people want their job defined, and don't mess with me. Here, they like rotation." Another manager observed, "I think if you tried to take rotation away from these people and assign them to one job, you'd have chaos."

While managers' objective of flexibility and workers' preference for rotation converge to some degree, there are signs of strain. Some in management thought they had gone a bit too far, too fast:

> In some cases, we've been trying to slow the rotation down a
> bit . . . You are asking a person to know a lot of elephants, if you
> think about it. Learning those jobs on the assembly line, you're

talking about a lot of different parts, a lot of different sequences, it's tough. So, when you have a change on the job, because of an engineering change or something, sometimes you lose something there if a team rotates through there, and they don't all get the change, then maybe you get a bunch of repairs before you get it straightened out.[8]

This concern was prescient. After we left the plant, many teams managed to institute one-hour rotations. Viewing this as a source of quality problems, management set the maximum rotation frequency back to two hours. When CAMI began building a new car model in the summer of 1994, it set further limits on rotation. Two-hour rotation continued, but throughout Assembly and part of Stamping and Welding rotation was restricted to two jobs. This was done to reduce quality problems arising from inexperienced workers and from tasks not being finished by the person who rotated into a job after a break.

The rotation issue is not a clear-cut case of labor vs. management. Local union reps agree with management on the relationship between quality and rotation. Beyond this, however, some of these unionists oppose rotation on the grounds that it hides overburdened jobs and health and safety problems. Persons who rotate through jobs conducive to injuries are less likely to protest than those who perform the same jobs all day. The issue is a potentially divisive one for the union. While most workers continue to favor rotation, the goal of some union reps is the abolition of teams and job rotation and the establishment of job ownership.

Not surprisingly, workers who occupy what are defined as good jobs resist rotation, while workers who perform line-paced and routine tasks favor more frequent switching. For example, paint sprayers on top coat pointed to the special skills associated with their work and did not want to rotate.

Another worker in Paint changes conveyor belts, rebuilds the gun tips on robots, and makes computer adjustments to control the amount of paint being used, its thickness, and its temperature. It takes about a year to learn this job thoroughly, but when we were in the plant the company refused to formally recognize the skills required by giving it

8. Dassbach (1995) believes job rotation is inconsistent with the demands of lean production, because the closely coordinated and tightly timed jobs can only be performed at line speed by experienced workers.

a special classification. Subsequently, CAMI created teams composed entirely of workers who performed a single, relatively highly skilled job, for example, operators in Paint and receivers in Material Handling. These workers remain in the general PA classification and receive no extra pay. This retreat from multitasking was instituted to negate the right of workers to rotate into these special jobs.

The situation in an Assembly repair area is more ambiguous and divisive. Engine and transmission repairs are done by workers who are licensed mechanics. They don't want to rotate, CAMI doesn't want them to rotate (or to give them a special classification), but other team members want to move into those positions. The problem was exacerbated because the licensed mechanics happened to have the lowest seniority on the team.

A serious dispute arose when management announced it was going to transfer into Welding repair PAs from the general Welding department to learn and do the repair work. No one wanted to leave the repair area, and there was nothing in the contract that prohibited the transfers. This triggered a month-long work slowdown that was settled with a compromise that allowed Welding PAs to transfer into repair for a six-week period, after which they would return to their original teams. This was a band-aid solution, and the issue promises to resurface.

Workers told us that well-established rotation schedules in most teams were often disrupted by injuries and absences. PAs repeatedly complained about being prevented from rotating through all the positions on their team. Some teams had up to a third of their members on some sort of work restriction, resulting in a reduced schedule of rotation for those workers still able to perform all the jobs. This increased the possibility for more injuries, as the remaining workers carried on with the hardest jobs. Workers pointed to the tensions that developed within teams when fewer team members found themselves forever rotating through the most arduous work stations.

Thinking about Skill

Social scientists ordinarily measure skill level in terms of three criteria. *Substantive complexity* refers to the degree, scope, and integration of mental, interpersonal, and manipulative tasks. *Diversity* refers to the

③

range of tasks and responsibilities required by a job. *Autonomy* involves the extent to which the job permits or demands self-direction and individual discretion over, for example, how, when, and at what pace work is performed. Jobs can be arrayed along a continuum of skill by determining the degree to which they allow for or require each of these three dimensions (Gartman 1986:143; Hodson and Sullivan 1995:187). Where do most CAMI jobs fall along this skill spectrum?

As in traditional plants, the best production jobs are found in Quality Control (including repair work), Material Handling, and Stamping. Some of these off-line jobs require relatively long training periods and provide valuable skills that are transferable to other workplaces. The description of Mike's job in Stamping is an example. The skills of the average worker are much more limited, and the work of Linda in engine subassembly is typical. The design of most jobs conforms to an industrial engineering set of strictures. Jobs must be broken down into small units of discrete tasks. Each job must have a detailed definition so that it can be easily rearranged. Each job must take the same amount of time. The skill level for each job must be limited so that it can be quickly learned.

In response to open-ended survey questions that asked about the training time required to do their jobs, most workers said it was very limited—a couple of hours to learn, a couple of days to get to line speed. "Trained monkeys can do it in about 10 minutes," said one worker. Another PA answered, "It took me five minutes," and then, after a long pause, he added, "I'm a fast learner." Answers of five minutes, 20 minutes, several hours are the norm for assembly jobs. Workers report some differences between the first set of tasks learned and subsequent ones. One worker made the point: "A couple of weeks when I started. A couple of minutes on the job I'm on now." A CAMI training manual entitled *How to Train* did not dispute these estimates: "Many of the jobs will be much longer and more difficult to teach than others. Some take hours and even days to learn."

Standardization, the tight schedules and low buffers associated with JIT procedures, and precise time limits to complete a set of tasks leave little room for workers to exercise discretion over what to do, how to do it, and when to do it. On the autonomy dimension of skill, workers in traditional plants have an advantage. Although their jobs are also standardized (but not so rigidly) and short-cycled, they can and do devise shortcuts, work ahead, build up banks, and double up on the assembly line.[9] These practices constitute a de facto, informal system of at least limited discretion over how and when work is done that is not available under lean production.

Most adherents of lean production acknowledge that jobs are standardized and short-cycled but claim that skill arises from job rotation, workers' responsibility for indirect functions, and the ability to continuously improve their jobs and work stations. It is this constellation of practices that sets lean production jobs apart from those in mass production and is the basis for designating lean production workers as multiskilled.

The capacity to engage in a series of jobs of equivalent task composition provides neither continuing opportunities for skill development nor a kind of "career path." Most CAMI workers agree. When rotation was a novelty, workers were more inclined to equate rotation with skill development. On the survey question about the relationship between performing different jobs and skill accumulation, the response change over time was substantial. Those who answered that all the jobs required the same skill level increased from one-half of the sample to three-quarters. Even managers, when pressed, reluctantly agreed. The following passages come from different interviews:

Q: Would you say the jobs here are more skilled than would be the case at another plant in Canada?

A: I would say no, but I could be attacked on that. But there is going to be more opportunity for a person to learn more different jobs over time.

Q: If you know more jobs it might mean more variation, less boredom, but you're not more skilled, are you?

A: No, that's right. But you're looking at the assembly line . . . but that's not all the jobs we've got here.

---

9. Doubling-up is a form of job rotation practised by assemblers. Workers do their own tasks as well as the job of an adjacent person for a period of time, while their buddy rests. Workers double up to relieve boredom and to periodically relax and take breaks. See, for example, Hamper (1991:35–40). For a general discussion of informal shop floor practices, or what one might call "unofficial kaizen," see Faber (1976) and Rinehart (1996:138–144).

Q: What does multiskilling mean?

A: I think of associates being able to perform jobs of other associates on the same team, and that's the way I look at it. But with respect to the associates, I wouldn't see a lot of multiskilling.

Rotation does render work under lean production more diverse than in traditional plants. However, it does not increase worker discretion or make work more substantively complex. The continuous rebalancing of jobs also adds to the diversity of work. Whether workers welcome this kind of diversity is another matter. Some may find constant change in their job packages challenging, but others may view it as a burden and a barrier to ever settling into a comfortable work routine. If workers are involved in rebalancing, their discretion is enhanced. However, at CAMI most rebalancing is done by team leaders and, increasingly, industrial engineers. The conceptual knowledge required to do all the jobs in a team is limited, and competent performance is defined by physical dexterity and reaching line speed. Consequently, multitasking is a more appropriate label than multiskilling.

Production workers' assumption of indirect duties like TPM, monitoring quality, housekeeping, and stocking parts also makes work under lean production more diverse than in traditional plants, at least ideally. These functions do not require much training and, more importantly, their performance is restricted by the constant pressure to produce and by tightly timed jobs that keep workers busy for 57 seconds of every minute. Consequently, the assignment of indirect functions is more a matter of work intensification—filling in all the pores of the work day, especially when the line is down—than of skill.

Workers under lean production, in contrast to their mass production counterparts, do learn more systematic procedures for detecting, analyzing, and resolving operational problems. This process contains elements of cognition and discretion.[10] But when defenders of lean production contrast the kaizen process with mass production's admonition that workers' must leave their brains at the factory gate, they ignore decades of research in industrial settings showing that workers in traditional

10. The relationship between worker discretion (empowerment) and kaizen is discussed in Chapter 10.

plants regularly apply their tacit production knowledge, their "trade se-crets," to make work more effective and easier.[11] The difference is that these often ingenious procedures are used mainly for workers' purposes—to take a break, to alleviate boredom by creating hills and valleys of work activity, to make the job easier, to alternate work rhythms in accordance with the way one feels at any given moment—rather than sharing their ideas with the company. These kinds of activities may be condemned in the name of efficiency, but there is no denying that they entailed knowl-edge and discretion, made work more tolerable, and created a more liv-able workplace.

Skill can also be considered as an attribute of individuals. The extent to which workers acquire skills over time is contingent not on job rota-tion in teams but in large part on the kind of job ladders and mobil-ity opportunities a plant provides. Workers who throughout the course of their employment with a firm can move through a series of depart-ments and jobs which are characterized by more skill through formal job posting and bidding procedures based on seniority can accumulate skills that are valuable and portable. Contracts negotiated with unions in traditional plants guarantee these opportunities. Lean transplants probably vary greatly on this score. CAMI allows team to team and in-terdepartmental transfers based on seniority, but the absorption of indi-rect duties by production workers compresses the range of available jobs.[12] Another CAMI career path, although generally a truncated one, is promotion to team leader, a job that carries multiple responsibili-ties and a fairly broad scope for using conceptual and manual abilities.[13]

The long-term acquisition of skill depends on production work-ers' opportunities to move over time through a series of jobs with dis-tinctly different and progressively greater skill requirements. At CAMI the opportunities for such mobility are less abundant than in traditional

11. On the importance of production workers' tacit knowledge see Kusterer (1978).

12. At a Ford assembly plant near St. Thomas, Ontario, the position of sweeper is val-ued because it is neither line-paced nor subject to the same supervisory pressures as direct pro-duction jobs. Under lean production, the assumption by line workers of this and other indirect labor done by specialized workers in traditional plants eliminates or substantially reduces these kinds of positions. While sweeping floors obviously does not involve skill, it is well suited for older or injured workers who are unable to do more physically demanding jobs.

13. The duties and responsibilities of team leaders are discussed in Chapter 7.

plants. Jobs at CAMI vary greatly in the extent to which they embody the three dimensions of skill. Located at the upper end of the skill continuum are the skilled trades, followed at some distance by the smattering of production workers throughout the plant whose jobs demand a relatively high degree of conceptual and/or technical competence, such as paint sprayers, the operator who controls the quality of paint, and many of those who work in Material Handling, Quality Control, and Stamping. However, most jobs at CAMI, and nearly all that are line-paced, are situated at the lower end of the skill spectrum.

This work is not characterized by substantive complexity, nor can it be defined as vertically integrated. It requires little conceptual acumen, and the emphasis is on physical dexterity and performing at line speed. Workers' discretion as to how, when, and at what pace work is performed is severely limited by standardized procedures and short, fully packed time cycles. One could reasonably argue that the degree of discretion exercised by such workers in traditional plants is greater. Task diversity—due to job rotation, continuous line rebalancing, and indirect duties—can be considered as moderate. Only in regard to this latter criterion of skill—and whatever soft skills they learn—do CAMI workers have a decided edge over their counterparts in traditional plants.

CHAPTER 6

Working Lean

C RITICS AND PROPONENTS OF LEAN PRODUCTION AGREE THAT under this system the work pace is fast and workloads heavy. Debates center not on lean production's heavy demands but on the necessity for these demands and their human consequences. According to Berggren, Bjorkman, and Hollander (1991:7), Japanese car makers have some of the hardest driven and most fragmented assembly lines in the world. These authors were struck by the heavy overtime demands on transplant workers: "From a biological and medical perspective they [the transplants] are simply understaffed." At NUMMI workers put in 57 seconds of labor every minute, compared with about 45 seconds per minute when the plant was operated by GM (Adler 1993b). "Mazda," Fucini and Fucini (1990:199) observe, "keeps a thinly stretched work force in perpetual motion." A survey of Mazda workers found that three-quarters reported having difficulty keeping up, and 73 percent said they would likely be injured or worn out before retirement (Babson 1993). Graham (1995:71) found that workers at the Subaru-Isuzu (SIA) plant in Indiana "experienced constant pressure from the assembly line [and were] forced to work at a continuous, rapid pace." This, in conjunction with the design of jobs, was the source of a high rate of injuries, especially RSIs. MacDuffie (1988:16) believes that American workers may rebel against the pressures and work pace of lean production. Kochan et al. (1989:25) discuss the rapid pace and stress associated with lean production, but they suggest that, from a worker's point of view, such problems may be outweighed by the system's relaxed supervision, high-trust relations, multiple job tasks, and problem-solving opportunities. Kenney and Florida (1993:25) acknowledge that work in Japanese factories and in transplants can be grueling. They argue, however, that the Japanese system is no worse than GM's Lordstown plant in the late 1960s, when cars rolled off the line every 36 seconds. What Kenney and Florida fail to mention is that Lordstown was an extreme case, not the norm, that workers rebelled against the line speed by striking, and that ultimately the line was slowed down.

Staffing at CAMI: The Lean Formula

CAMI projects production volume in the following way: Each shift includes 444 minutes of work time (eight and a half hours minus a 30-minute lunch and two 18-minute breaks). Allowing time for line stoppages, 93 percent uptime translates into actual run minutes of 413. Divided by a line speed of 1.65 minutes per vehicle, 413 minutes equals a projected volume of about 250 vehicles per shift. Using the actual number of vehicles desired, the model mix, line speed, work standards brought from Japan, and a computer program of standard times needed to perform each fraction of a task, management establishes the theoretical number of workers required to achieve production quotas.

As we discovered, this equation does not adequately allow for individual absences, turnover, maternity leaves, injuries, an especially difficult model mix, or other unexpected developments. Ideally, disparities between the theoretical and actual numbers needed to meet scheduled production are realized by flexible team members covering for their missing or injured co-workers by working harder. Given this formula for lean staffing, and the fact that CAMI makes subcompact vehicles, it is not surprising that in 1991 CAMI required fewer workers to assemble a car (2.40) than any of 40 North American auto assembly plants surveyed.[1]

1. As reported by the GM/CAMI Liaison Office, n.d. The survey was done by Chilton Automotive Industries. Second on the list was the Ford Atlanta plant (2.66 workers to build

Experiencing Lean Production

We asked survey respondents a series of questions about work pace, workloads, and mental and physical stress associated with their jobs. In rounds 1 and 4, 18.7 percent and 18.8 percent respectively said the pace of their jobs was too fast "all the time" or "often" (see Table 2). Small increases in perceptions of a too-rapid pace of work were registered in all areas except Paint. The percentage reporting that the line speed was too fast "all the time" or "often" increased from 23.5 in round 1 to 29 in round 4, for the total sample. Responses varied across the plant, but there was a growing concern about line speed among workers from all areas.

Given the contentiousness of staffing and work intensity at CAMI, we anticipated greater concern among workers over work pace. In talking with workers, we learned that they saw the problem not so much as the pace being too fast but, as one said, "It's more a question of how much work is piled into a job." Workers often use the term "overburdened" to describe this condition. Following this lead, in round 4 we formulated a new question that asked respondents if their teams were doing too much work with too few people. Just over one-half (50.7 percent) said they were, with marked differences across the plant: 85.7 percent in Welding, 45.2 in Assembly, 55.6 in off-line jobs, and 43.8 in Paint. Over three-quarters (77.6 percent) gave an affirmative answer when asked, in round 4, if they thought they worked harder than workers in traditional auto plants.

Table 3 shows that a little under one-third of the sample in round 1 and a little over one-third in round 4 reported that a) their jobs were physically tiring, and b) they felt burned out when they got home from work. These problems were most pronounced in Assembly and Paint.

---

the Taurus and Sable), while the GM Hamtramack plant was last, using 7.85 workers to build E and K cars. Worker-car ratios for other transplants in 1991 were as follows: Honda in Alliston, Ontario (2.88 for the Civic); Nissan in Smyrna, Tennessee (2.98 for the Sentra); Diamond Star in Illinois (3.00 to build the Eclipse and Laser); Toyota in Georgetown, Kentucky (3.54 for the Camry); NUMMI in California (3.73 to build the Prizm and Corolla). These productivity statistics should be treated cautiously, because they do not control for differences in vehicle design, size, assembly complexity, option content, etc. Nor is any account taken of the hours of work, especially overtime hours, required to achieve production levels. This is a critical omission given the dependence of lean production plants on overtime to compensate for downtime and the absence of inventory.

TABLE 2. Perceptions of work pace and line speed

			Total sample	Assembly	Paint	Welding	Off-line jobs
How often do you feel the pace of your job is too fast?	RD1	all the time/ often	18.7% (14)	20.6% (7)	28.6% (6)	10.0% (1)	0.0%
		once in a while/ never	81.3% (61)	79.4% (27)	71.4% (15)	90.0% (9)	100% (10)
	RD4	all the time/ often	18.8% (15)	22.8% (8)	17.6% (3)	11.1% (1)	10.5% (2)
		once in a while/ never	81.2% (65)	77.2% (27)	82.4% (14)	88.9% (8)	89.5% (17)
How often does the line go too fast?	RD1	all the time/ often	23.5% (16)	29.4% (10)	18.8% (3)	20.0% (2)	12.5% (1)
		once in a while/ never	76.5% (52)	70.6% (24)	81.3% (13)	80.0% (8)	87.5% (7)
	RD4	all the time/ often	29.0% (18)	31.0% (9)	30.8% (4)	22.2% (2)	27.3% (3)
		once in a while/ never	71.0% (44)	69.0% (18)	69.2% (9)	77.8% (7)	72.7% (8)

Note: Off-line jobs include those in Maintenance, Quality Control, Quality Control Parts, Material Handling, and Stamping.

Reports of job stress increased from 18.7 percent to 27.5 percent of the sample, with the least stress (in round 4) indicated by workers in Welding and off-line jobs and the most by workers in Paint. In the first and final rounds about one-third of the sample indicated they were frequently exposed to muscle fatigue and strains, with Assembly and Paint reporting (in round 4) the greatest concerns. Frequent exposure to RSIs was reported by 42.3 percent of respondents in round 4, up from 36 percent in the first round. Just over one-half of assemblers and 50 percent of welders in the last round indicated they were frequently at risk.

These results show a rough pattern, although they are also marked by certain inconsistencies. Assemblers were more likely than workers from other areas to report higher levels of work intensity and stress; workers doing off-line jobs generally reported lower levels. The responses of workers in Paint and Welding were more variable, not only in their perceived degree of work intensity but also in their unevenness across the several questions.

Staffing Problems

Problems began to emerge in the fall of 1990, around the time of our second visit, and persisted throughout the course of the study. At this time the car line had been operating at capacity for nearly three months, and the truck side was working steady 48-hour weeks. The company maintained a strict policy of not keeping a relief corps to cover for absences and injuries. When absences occurred, not enough workers were available to staff to full complement. Teams were forced to operate short-handed, and those with floater positions lost them to other teams that needed people just to staff the line.

A car assembly team leader complained about the difficulty of getting replacement PAs on his team, calling it "a hell of a battle." Model mix was a major source of the problem. Five-door models are supposed to be followed by three-door models, but when that doesn't happen workers have difficulty keeping up and are prone to injury. The team leader said that you can tell when there are three five-doors in a row: you can follow their progression down the line on the andon board.

Observing one team on the truck line, we learned that team members were regularly working eight hours' overtime a week, and four of the 13 members had RSIs. The team leader said, "Everybody is getting tired. You come in and it's dark. You leave and it's dark. They're [PAs] turning down a lot of extra overtime because they're so tired."

Another team leader remarked: "The staffing problems were [that] they [only] had on the lines exactly what we needed, so if we had a

TABLE 3. Percentage of Respondents Who Reported Physical and Mental Stress

		Total sample	Assembly	Paint	Welding	Off-line jobs
How often is your job tiring?	RD1 all the time/ often	29.3% (22)	39.5% (17)	29.2% (7)	26.7% (4)	0.0%
	once in a while/ never	70.7% (53)	60.5% (26)	70.8% (17)	73.3% (11)	100.0% (16)
	RD4 all the time/ often	37.5% (30)	45.5% (15)	52.6% (10)	10.0% (1)	22.2% (4)
	once in a while/ never	62.5% (50)	54.5% (18)	47.4% (9)	90.0% (9)	77.8% (14)
How often is your job stressful?	RD1 all the time/ often	18.7% (14)	20.9% (9)	12.5% (3)	26.7% (4)	22.2% (4)
	once in a while/ never	81.3% (61)	79.1% (34)	87.5% (21)	73.3% (11)	77.8% (14)
	RD4 all the time/ often	27.5% (22)	27.3% (9)	36.8% (7)	20.0% (2)	20.0% (4)
	once in a while/ never	72.5% (58)	72.7% (22)	63.2% (12)	80.0% (8)	80.0% (16)
How often do you feel burned out when you get home from work?	RD1 all the time/ often	32.0% (24)	46.5% (20)	25.0% (6)	26.7% (4)	16.7% (3)
	once in a while/ never	68.0% (51)	53.5% (23)	75.0% (18)	73.3% (11)	83.3% (15)
	RD4 all the time/ often	37.5% (30)	46.9% (15)	52.7% (10)	10.0% (1)	21.1% (4)
	once in a while/ never	62.5% (50)	53.1% (17)	47.3% (9)	90.0% (9)	78.9% (15)
How often does your job expose you to muscle fatigue?	RD1 all the time/ often	33.3% (25)	37.2% (16)	37.5% (9)	40.0% (6)	5.6% (1)
	once in a while/ never	66.7% (50)	62.8% (27)	62.5% (15)	60.0% (9)	94.4% (17)
	RD4 all the time/ often	36.2% (29)	48.5% (16)	36.8% (7)	30.0% (3)	21.1% (4)
	once in a while/ never	63.8% (51)	51.5% (17)	63.2% (12)	70.0% (7)	78.9% (15)
How often does your job expose you to repetitive strains?	RD1 all the time/ often	36.0% (27)	44.2% (19)	25.0% (6)	40.0% (6)	22.2% (4)
	once in a while/ never	64.0% (48)	55.8% (24)	75.0% (18)	60.0% (9)	77.8% (14)
	RD4 all the time/ often	42.3% (33)	51.5% (17)	27.8% (5)	50.0% (5)	35.2% (6)
	once in a while/ never	57.7% (45)	48.5% (16)	72.2% (13)	50.0% (13)	64.7% (11)

Note: Off-line jobs include those in Maintenance, Quality Control, Quality Control Parts, Material Handling, and Stamping.

person off or a person hurt or something, we were scraping—we were working twice as hard as we should be. We weren't getting the help we needed to run the line."

When asked to comment on this, a manager stated: "I appreciate that people feel that there's a shortage of manpower, and I guess in areas of the plant there are shortages. In certain teams they're shorter than others. Certain teams, I know, are not short on manpower, and maybe it's a case of line balance as well." This tight staffing policy meant teams could not finish cross-training newer workers, rotation was often suspended or interrupted, and workers were not getting regular relief from more difficult jobs and jobs tied directly to the line. One result was a sharp increase of RSIs. Having recognized this, one manager emphasized the importance of safer job designs: "We're at maximum capacity right now, maximum line speeds, and now what we need to do is work more aggressively in areas of ergonomics. It's probably the highest on my priority list now . . . We had people waiting, teams waiting four weeks, six weeks, two months, and of course you're borrowing and begging from somebody else to help the team out in the meantime. We got caught with turnover we didn't expect."

Staffing had not been adequately addressed by our third research visit in June 1991, after the start-up of a second shift on the car side. A team leader in Welding stated: "Everybody's tired right now. I think that's why we had a big upswing of RSIs. After a couple of months of 10 hours, that's when you really started to notice it." At one point his 16-person team included five people with RSIs. He observed: "It was down to where we were in really bad shape. We were always borrowing people just to keep running, but we couldn't actually train them in every job to keep our rotation going."

Staffing difficulties were not limited to Assembly. A team leader from Quality Control Parts stated: "Yesterday we were short two people. We eventually had to park 52 vehicles outside that we couldn't handle with that amount of people." When asked how often this happens, he replied: "Just about every day. There's a bad manpower shortage here, and I don't think management's opening their eyes to it at this point."

The woman installing instrument panels told us it took her several weeks before she was able to keep up with the line, but even after mastering the operation she had no time between completing one job and beginning the next one. Another worker told us he preferred the IP install because he knew it so well that he had 10 seconds to rest between jobs. This team also installs seat belts on cars sold in Canada; cars destined for the U.S. already have them attached. The worker doing this job was upset because he felt the cars should be better staggered so he would not have a run of cars requiring extra work.

Difficult model mix was a continuing problem, as indicated by the observations of a manager:

> We have had some frustrations out there because of the imbalance of product load . . . We have that up-level truck that has power steering and power windows and stuff, and we'll be short on a component, like a power steering pump. It's in short supply out of Japan. So they'll run all base models, or a high percentage of base models, and the people really got it made. And then, lo and behold, here comes all those orders [with high option content], and then you've got an overloaded situation . . . We've been unlevel not because we're trying to mastermind some plot out there but because we go through all kinds of shenanigans here . . . because of some of the supply problems we've had.

Another manager stated: "It can be very hectic out there at times with manpower problems . . . We end up getting replacements, but it's probably not as rapid as we would like, that's for sure."

A manager reported that in the summer of 1991 an unspecified number of workers from Material Handling signed a petition complaining about staffing and workloads. "Probably the biggest thing it derived from was manpower. Everyone's bitching because they felt they were overworked. And overtime was another issue. A lot of people seemed to get very frustrated from the amount of overtime they were working."

According to a union Health and Safety rep, difficult model mix is a major issue and a source of work refusals. He provided the following example: "That particular day they had 10 deluxes in a row, so that means it's extra work for them—extra air conditioners, power windows on doors, extra trim, extra stickers. You don't get extra time to do this . . . Now, you have guys on restrictions who can't do this extra work, and the other guys have to pick it up. So you can see the snowballing effect, and you've got yourselves another big issue."

The shortage of workers had developed to the extent that some managers and area leaders started siding with the union on demands for extra staffing. One union rep put it this way: "Believe it or not, sometimes the area leaders come to us and say, 'We need more manpower and we've tried everything.' It's like, 'Will you do anything for us?'" Another union rep declared: "We'll talk to the area leaders and we'll talk to the managers and they'll agree with us, but then they have to process the manning requirements through the Japanese management, and that seems to be where the stumbling block is—they put it on hold. Their favorite line is, 'Well, we don't do it this way in Japan.' But our line is, 'This isn't Japan, this is Canada.'"

Managers said they were taking steps to deal with staffing. A stopgap measure involved bringing in temporary workers. A manager noted that students were being hired for the summer, "but in September we have the potential of having the same problem all over again." Another solution was a permanent pool of workers ready to fill in on teams and departments short of people. Management referred to this pool as an "attrition float," an "RSI pool," or

> . . . the preventative head count allocation . . . I'm allocating the head count in such a way that they can do the cross-training to avoid and prevent RSI injuries in the future . . . I'll just keep adding people to cover people that are injured, but my first step is to stop the hemorrhaging and allocate the people to prevent it. Those people are coming in, as a matter of fact, tomorrow. They're in Nagare right now . . . we'll have in excess of 30, 35 people over and above the budget . . . and that'll solve our problem. I think we'll be out of trouble.

By our final visit at the end of November 1991, staffing was still an issue. An excessive number of teams still had workers on medical restrictions. One union rep estimated that 10 of 15 teams on truck assembly and 15 of 17 on car assembly included workers with restrictions. Although the parts problem had been solved, the model mix imbalance had not. A team leader from Paint felt staffing was getting worse: "It's been the general problem from day one. They're [management] bitching at me—'you've gotta get your ass in gear, you've gotta get those people training and rotating.' But I can't rotate if I've got nowhere to rotate.

I've got so many people off I can't rotate. By the time I get somebody trained on a new spot, I've got somebody else that's on ice."

A former team leader said he stepped down and moved to another department because of personnel shortages. "The biggest reason I switched jobs is we could never get enough people to run the line. They were always taking people away from us and giving us new people that weren't experienced, putting more pressure on the team. And I just got fed up and left."

On our final visit to the instrument panel subassembly, seven of the 19 team members were suffering from RSIs—either on restriction or off work. As one worker said, "I only have six weeks here and my fingers and wrists are giving me problems. I went to the Health Center. They gave me ice and said [the pain] was because I was just getting used to my job. Now I'm used to the job and my hands are still sore."

Observing a team on the truck line, we were told that the job could be handled for eight hours, but after that, "it's a bitch." PAs on this team complained that most of the team's jobs allowed them only 10 seconds idle time in a work cycle of 2.97 minutes. The team had a floater, but he was available only once or twice a week due to absences elsewhere in the area.

A manager acknowledged the removal of floaters but argued that this was an aspect of team concept. "If team one has a floater and team three has a couple of people absent one day, yeah, we might take that floater and help out team three. You know, this is part of our teamwork concept that we try to help each other out."

Managers did not deny that staffing remained problematic. One manager attributed the problem to poor model mix but held out some hope for a remedy: "We're still fine-tuning. We've come up with a little computer program that shows us, depending on a certain model mix, we'll need a certain number of people on the line. And this gives us another tool to go to [upper] management and say, 'Hey, this is what's happening. If you send us a bad model mix we're gonna need more people for two hours of the day or four hours of the day.' So we're still pushing along those lines to make sure that we're fully staffed."

Another manager stated: "We've just increased the five-door ratio and the automatic transmission ratio, but it's having a big impact on the people. I'm having a real hard look at that now, so I can make a case to perhaps bring some more people in. Because, in my opinion, right now, we need to adjust for the ratios and the increase in the options . . . Manpower is one of the biggest issues for me since I've been here. That's all I ever talk about is manpower."

According to one manager,

> We're just trying to reconcile the areas where they're putting up their hand and saying, "Hey, we're too tight," and seeing if it makes sense from a theoretical point of view. You know, I want the assembly department to have enough people to do the job. I really do. I don't expect people to be running up and down the assembly line or any sort of that stuff. We need to have a man on every job, and we need to understand that people get sick, and we need to understand that people need to have time off when they're pre-approved, and that we need to man ourselves accordingly. And I plan on doing that . . .

Despite that recognition, relief staff were not being hired in significant numbers. One manager provided a reason for the slow response to staffing crises:

> There's more of a slow down and think through stuff with the Japanese approach, like, whether it's manpower or whatever you're gonna do. Maybe in some cases it's too slow . . . Here they slow the process down and sometimes that's good, but the Japanese people here didn't know how to respond to that many RSIs and stuff when it just kind of exploded overnight. So we agonized with what does that mean? Are we going to be able to rehabilitate them? Are we going to be able to get them back? Because one of the things that they [the Japanese managers] are real high on—they're dead set against getting too many people and then having to have a layoff.

Another manager put it this way:

> I've never worked anywhere where [staffing] hasn't been an issue . . . We're always pulling out our hair to have enough people to run the plant, whether it's in [a traditional plant] or at CAMI. I mean, to hire new people is a big decision, because, especially at CAMI, when your volumes are volatile. The volumes are high now, so we need more people. What do we do in the spring when the volumes level off? What do we do with the people? So it's a

big decision to bring new people in. And I understand that. At the same time, I also gotta have enough people to run the plant.

Managers described weekly meetings that took place to look at the number of workers on maternity leave, worker compensation (WCB), Sickness and Accident (S&A), etc. As a result, "We have people dribbling in," said one manager. Union reps acknowledged seeing workers coming in to cover for absences but not in sufficient numbers to resolve the issue. A union rep observed: "They seem to be nibbling away, like we get six people every week, but that just covers the six people that have gone off on some kind of leave, like WCB or maternity or parental or medical or whatever. Six a week is not enough, we're not catching up. I don't think we're even staying even . . . We need basically a person a team."

According to the union, what hadn't been addressed was the fundamental problem of being too lean to begin with—of not having enough staff to do the job properly without workers getting hurt. A union rep stated: "We're still running, from our perspective, [at a] bare-bones minimum. People are coming up to our office, saying: 'I've been denied my request to take a day off,' and they're asking us, you know, 'What should we do?' . . . It's to the point where people can't plan time off, because if there's one person off in their area, on a Friday, [the] supervisor will deny any other time off because he wants to cover his ass just in case anybody calls in sick."

Challenges to Lean Staffing

In the 1992 contract negotiations the union challenged CAMI's lean staffing policy. With their five-week strike workers won 24 hours (three days) supplemental vacation time. More important, the company agreed to the principle of permanent relief workers. The size of the relief crews—called Production Support Groups (PSGs)—was set at 4.5 percent of each department.

This human buffer eased but did not resolve the staffing shortage. Over one-half of the workforce was regularly putting in a 10-hour day. "Down here in Welding," a union committeeperson observed, "we consider an eight-hour day a rest" (*Off the Line*—the union newsletter—December 1994). Complaints about overtime and the difficulty of booking vacations and personal days off continued, as did the union's call for hiring more workers. Union reps maintained that the PSG ratio was too low, that the PSGs' effectiveness was limited because management placed some injured workers in the groups, and that at times they were depleted by a rash of injuries and absences.

The 1995 contract addressed some of these complaints, and the union managed to further chip away at CAMI's lean staffing policy. Workers won an additional 10 minutes a day of paid relief time, to be phased in over three years. Two more days of vacation time were agreed upon. The contract provided each worker with a special paid week off which is to be taken at a time determined by a process of random selection. This requirement not only gave workers more leisure; it also required (under normal conditions) the hiring of more workers (about 60, according to union sources) to compensate for those on vacation.

These encroachments on the principle of lean staffing did not constitute a final solution for the union, but head count issues were overshadowed when in early 1996 a new and different kind of crisis emerged. In March 1996 CAMI produced its one millionth vehicle. This should have been an occasion to celebrate, but it came at a time when sales of the Suzuki Sidekick and Geo Tracker were in a slump. While plant capacity is 200,000 vehicles annually, and 175,000 vehicles were scheduled to be made in 1996, in early 1996 production was cut back to 150,000. In April sluggish sales and high inventories (240 days' worth) caused the company to further reduce production to 130,000 vehicles. A third cutback to 120,000 was announced at the end of May.

Initially, these volume reductions were handled by notching down line speeds, removing workers from teams, and assigning them to PSGs. Subsequently, however, CAMI announced that in the summer of 1996 it would be cutting its workforce by 10 percent—about 250 employees. The company offered voluntary buy-outs and early retirement packages (as of June 1996 60 persons had taken the buy-out), but the remainder of the downsizing would come from indefinite layoffs.[2]

2. Unlike unionized transplants in the United States, CAMI had made no promises to avoid laying workers off. Union reps attributed falling sales to a conflict between GM and Suzuki over GM's agreement to purchase the powertrain from Suzuki in Japan for a 20-year period. As the story goes, GM wanted to back out of this arrangement in order to buy cheaper powertrains in North America, but Suzuki refused. In response, GM stopped advertising and pushing sales of the sport utility vehicles.

Work Intensification

For CAMI management, maximum workloads and minimum staffing levels are fundamental measures of what it takes to be lean and competitive. Staffing levels, workloads, and work pace are defined by notions of full jobs, minimal idle time, and hard work. One manager, when asked if the goal of the Suzuki production system was the constant reduction of labor costs, explained the intent this way: "I would say it's not reducing but just to keep it really efficient, not let it get sloppy. It certainly is a tight system, there's no question about it, it's very tight. The system is also that jobs should be reviewed almost constantly and changed almost constantly to keep the operators at a very high work content. And I guess that's a little different from [traditional plants]."

When asked if CAMI was a lean plant, a manager responded: "Yeah, it's a lean plant. You don't have a lot of the fat of the existing or traditional plants, and I wouldn't say you'd want to . . . We have the PAs responsible for their own housekeeping, stuff like that. The leanness to some extent, I guess, is the fact that everybody gives you a good day's work out there. There's not a lot of screwing off going on out there."

Most managers who were asked agreed that workers at CAMI worked harder than their counterparts in traditional plants. When asked if for every minute of the work day CAMI gets a minute's worth of work, one manager replied, "Well, it's probably not that, but there's certainly more than in your general plant, yes, no question."

The intensification of work operates through a number of mechanisms. One way of maintaining minimal labor hours per vehicle is to ensure that workloads approach maximum efficiency (60 seconds for every minute of work time available). Area leaders are trained to monitor jobs visually for signs of "muda" or idle time. Through the kaizen process workers are expected to come up with ideas for eliminating non-value-added labor. Kaizen may result in greater efficiency without additional labor input, i.e., working smarter rather than harder. However, it does not translate into lighter workloads, because any idle time created by kaizen can then be filled up with another task. The objective is to pare away continuously the workers needed to handle a set of operations.

Lean production is a dynamic and flexible system. It is designed to respond quickly to fluctuating production quotas, equipment breakdowns, parts shortages, and unbalanced workloads through a combination of frequent line speed changes, oscillating overtime requirements, and almost constant job rebalancing, both within and across teams. Accordingly, another mode of intensifying work is what CAMI managers refer to as "tweaking the system." This entails increasing line speed, at times in the middle of a shift, and the constant rebalancing and kaizening of team workloads and individual jobs to keep the work content high. One manager described how the production system is continually being stressed and how the andon cords are used in this process:

> Where this system is different . . . is that you have the andon at each operation so that an operator can . . . use the yellow andon saying, "Hey, I have a problem," and that problem may be that he's cross-threaded a bolt or something like that. But that problem may also be that "I can't finish my job operation, I've done three in a row and I can't finish the fourth one, somebody come down and give me help." The andon is supposed to show up those spots where you might have jobs overburdened.
>
> So as we bring the line speed up, if an operator is too busy they use the andon to get help, and that would signify to the team leader and area leader that, hey, we should take a look at this job. In Japan, what they would do is often increase the line speed without adding manpower. Just like line speed today is at a minute and a half [per vehicle], for example, and we'll increase it by three seconds tomorrow [i.e., cut workers' cycle time by three seconds, from 90 to 87 seconds per vehicle], and then that will show if there are some spots that we should look at. And that's kind of a concept that we're not too used to here [in North America] . . . but we have done it here in the plant in CAMI.

The drive continually to improve labor productivity becomes clear. Line speeds are increased without adding workers, workers are expected to do their jobs in less time, and the company relies on the andon system to signal if workers are having problems keeping up. As one worker put it: "Basically when the line goes down they realize there's a problem. If the line doesn't go down, then there's no problem."

This continual stressing of the system is not an uncommon practice in auto assembly plants. But over the years, when management has attempted to increase line speeds without increasing the workforce, workers and their unions have resisted this speed-up vigorously. As a result, a compromise was reached in traditional Big Three plants whereby line speed increases and increased staffing became inseparable. But at CAMI things are different. One manager explained: "You may at a point increase the line speed without adding people, and that's sort of foreign, because in GM, like I say, whenever you increase the line they figure you're going to add manpower. The two things go hand in hand." The same manager joked about what would happen at a traditional plant if the line speed were increased without adding workers: "In General Motors you couldn't do it . . . If you did it in GM, everybody would be waiting for you out in the parking lot."[3]

Working Hurt

Given the intensity of work and the repetitive content of many jobs, we were not surprised to find a high incidence of work-related injuries at CAMI. In 1992 the company began systematically to record data on health and safety problems. For that year the plant recorded 2,678 injuries, 314 (11.7 percent) of which were classified as repetitive strain. CAMI's average injury frequency rate—11.81 per 100 workers—exceeded the industry average (11.41) in Canada. CAMI's average climbed to 13.08 in 1993, substantially higher than the industry average of 10.87. During this year workers reported 2,841 injuries, 604 (21.3 percent) of which were repetitive strains. In 1994 the number of injuries rose slightly to 2,945, with 30.1 percent repetitive strains. However, the frequency rate dropped to 9.26. (After 1993 CAMI stopped providing industrial average statistics.) For the first five months of 1995 the plant reported 1,343 injuries, 32.7 percent of which were repetitive strains, with a frequency rate for these months of 9.23.[4]

These data indicate some improvement in the overall injury rate, but the record was sullied by the escalation of RSIs. In the years for

3. This manager's reference is to conditions at GM that have not prevailed for some time. In their drive to get lean, all Big Three auto plants have increased production without adding people. In the U.S. a GM slogan of the 1990s is "no new Social Security numbers."

4. There were 150 work refusals over health and safety problems in 1992, 161 in 1993, 156 in 1994, and 84 during the first five months of 1995.

which the plant kept reliable statistics, RSIs were the single largest injury category and represented a growing proportion of total injuries.

In response to these conditions, the union demanded and won two full-time health and safety reps, union-appointed but company-paid, who receive ergonomics training and certification. These reps sit on the Joint Health and Safety Commmittee (JHSC). This committee's rights and duties were expanded in each round of bargaining. It now has access to all monitoring equipment, conducts a monthly inspection of all departments, and reviews plant-wide ergonomic concerns, trends in accident and injury rates, and the implementation of corrective measures.

According to local unionists, CAMI was beginning to respond to health and safety concerns. As one union rep observed in June 1995, "Over the last three years we've seen more tilt tables, more ergonomically-designed guns, air tools, assist arms. We have seen the company try to do things [to deal with injuries], but they're very minimal things." While CAMI has shown a greater sensitivity to health and safety problems, ergonomic improvements are outweighed by heavily loaded, repetitive jobs and overtime demands.

Contesting Work Intensification

In a Letter of Agreement in the 1992 contract, CAMI agreed in principle to base workloads on "fairness and equity" and the "reasonable working capacity of normal, experienced operators." The company also agreed to review changes to job elements with the worker before they were implemented; not to increase the speed of the lines "beyond the level for which they are adequately staffed or for the purpose of making up lost production"; and to assess methods used in other plants to avoid confrontations over line speed.

However, according to one union rep, the agreement was "toothless" because CAMI still had a free hand in job loading, job timing, and what is known on the floor as "overcycling," i.e., sending down the line batches of successive vehicles requiring heavy trim ("bad mixes"). "There is no restriction on the company on job loading, job movement, job mixes and overcycling," complained a writer in the union newsletter.

"Our lines are improperly balanced and staffed, causing overburden on the worker which means undue pressure on us to complete our cycles in the time allotted" (*Off the Line*, Oct. 1994).

Just after the strike, CAMI adopted a system of generating time studies called MOST (Maynard Operating Standard Time) that has been used in the industry for decades. The national office of the CAW paid for commiteepersons to take a week's course on MOST (CAMI's offer of a two-hour course was regarded as inadequate), but the company's constant work process changes and shuffling of tasks between work stations and teams made it difficult for the union to pinpoint overburdened work stations reliably. As one committeeperson observed, "We need to seriously address the state of constant flux that the company uses as a means to give us the smoke and mirrors routine. Production problems are not solved, they are merely shuffled around." Another committeeperson complained about the inadequacy of time studies to demonstrate inadequate staffing: "The company either hides the information from us or delays it in an effort to keep us from showing that they are overburdening our workers" (*Off the Line*, Oct. 1994).

Time studies and workloads were a major issue in the 1995 negotiations. In the contract CAMI agreed to allow the union to select a PA as a full-time production standards rep and to institute a dispute mechanism for time standards and workloads. The procedure has five steps, and if not resolved at the fifth stage the matter can be submitted as a grievance.[5] This was an important breakthrough, especially considering that no GM plant in Canada has agreed to such measures.

Copies of MOST studies are available to all workers. They list the standard times for each specific task in a job. These times are then added up to yield a Weighted Time Average (WTA) for the job. When divided by cycle time, the result gives what is called a percentage of job load. For example, if WTA is 2.084 minutes and the cycle time is 2.15 minutes, the percentage is .969, or 97 percent job load. As agreed to in the contract, any worker whose job load is over 95 percent can seek redress through

5. The union wanted the procedure to apply as well to poor model mix, but CAMI refused. Accordingly, disputes in this area can be dealt with only by an appeal to management or, ultimately, a work refusal on the grounds the job is unsafe.

the dispute mechanism. These struggles over time studies and job standards are reminiscent of what has taken place in traditional auto plants.

Our surveys indicated that a majority of CAMI workers did not see work pace and line speed as excessive. Rather, the issue for workers was what they called "overburdened" jobs. In other words, the problem was seen as one of understaffing—doing too much work with too few people.

Three factors contributed to perceptions of overburdening. One was management's inability to achieve leveled production. At times workers could routinely handle their jobs, but all too often runs of high-option models required intense effort and resulted in a failure to keep up. A second was heavy overtime demands. Third, workers were unable to get pre-approved days off or to schedule their vacations at desired times.

We anticipated more concern with physical and mental stress, but fear of RSIs was widespread. Company statistics showing a high incidence of this type of injury indicated that this was not an irrational fear.

The character of CAMI workers is relevant to interpreting these results. CAMI selected people who were conscientious, hard-working, and eager to prove themselves. Fast-paced jobs might be seen as problematic only when there were not enough workers to handle the work, when a difficult model mix required Herculean effort, and when overtime demands were excessive. Then, too, some workers tend to internalize their difficulties. To the extent that workload problems were acknowledged by such persons, they may have attributed them to themselves rather than to CAMI's work process. For example, one worker who kept falling behind reported that day after day she would ask herself, "What's wrong with me? Why can't I keep up?" Eventually she concluded it was not her but the process that was at fault. Moreover, some workers may find it ego-threatening to admit that work pace and workloads are too fast or heavy for them to handle.

It is also important to consider the youth of the workforce. Subjective evaluation of work pace, line speed, workloads, and stress is, at least in part, a function of age. Young workers are capable of handling more physically demanding jobs than are their older counterparts. We can only speculate about how these same workers might answer the work intensity and stress questions in 15 or 20 years. That workers were aware that age mattered was revealed by a survey Local 88 conducted in preparation for 1992 bargaining. Half of the more than 1,000 respondents felt that if the present intensity of work were to continue they would likely be injured or worn out before retirement.

Lean production places greater demands on workers' time and effort than does mass production. The lean system strives to fill in all the pores of the work day by designing fully loaded jobs. The system is defined as lean not only because of the relative absence of buffers, but also because it operates with a minimal workforce. CAMI uses a staffing formula that does not adequately incorporate unanticipated but regularly occurring events such as injuries, absences, and particularly difficult model mixes. Staffing problems are exacerbated rather than solved by the constant modifications of line speed, cycle times, and workloads within and between teams. When production quotas cannot be met, overtime is scheduled and relief workers are hired on an ad hoc basis—much like plugging the holes in a dyke that constantly springs leaks. CAMI executives may genuinely prefer not to hire core workers and then have to lay them off when production quotas fall, but this is not their only reason for avoiding hiring: the very logic of lean dictates minimal staffing. Such conditions set the stage for recurring conflict over staffing levels.

The union negotiated both in 1992 and 1995 several significant modifications of the lean staffing formula. Permanent crews of relief workers were established in 1992 and supplemented in 1995. Workers got longer rest breaks and more paid vacation time, necessitating additional hiring. Time studies and workloads can now be challenged and grieved, and there is now a full-time union production standards rep to handle these matters.

CHAPTER 7

Team Concept
and Working in Teams

*A*LL TRANSPLANT AUTOMAKERS IN NORTH AMERICA PROMOTE SOME variant of team concept. It is "perhaps the most important concept in the management of production activities in Japanese corporations" (Shimada and MacDuffie 1987:63). The term applies both to the shop floor work groups themselves and to the overall enterprise, and it entails "'togetherness,' in the sense of working together, helping each other, and sharing information" (Shimada and MacDuffie 1987:63). Womack, Jones, and Roos (1990:99) regard the work team as "the heart of the lean factory."[1]

According to Kenney and Florida (1993:16), the "underlying organizational feature" of lean production is what they repeatedly call "self-managing work teams." They provide a long list of activities undertaken by teams. Teams move the locus of decision making to the shop floor; "tap the collective knowledge of a group"; facilitate the functional integration of tasks and eliminate the extreme specialization of Fordism; socialize and train recruits; are the medium for job rotation, which

---

1. Having imputed to teams such a central role, the authors turn their attention to other matters. Their discussion of the "heart" of lean production occupies about three-quarters of one page of their book.

"allows workers to familiarize themselves with various aspects of the work process, thus creating a powerful learning dynamic"; are "a source of motivation, discipline, and social control for team members, driving them to work harder and more collectively." They claim there is "ample documentation" that team-based production is associated with productivity increases, although their only source is Monden (1983).[2] These authors conclude that work teams "reduce certain aspects of worker alienation which resulted in high rates of sabotage and absenteeism under Fordism" (Kenney and Florida 1993:37).

Self-Managing Teams?

Kenney and Florida stand alone in depicting teams under lean production as self-managing. Shimada and MacDuffie (1987) use the phrase "self-managing," but they qualify the term so thoroughly that it is clearly inappropriate to describe the way teams operate in the transplants. The Japanese approach "de-emphasizes team autonomy"; teams may be involved in problem-solving activities, but managers are responsible for surveillance and administration. In contrast, "a Scandinavian team is likely to have more independence to control its work methods and pace, and more administrative responsibilities than a Japanese team" (MacDuffie and Krafcik 1989:6). While teams may be the heart of lean production for Womack, Jones, and Roos (1990:101–102), they make no claims for teams' autonomy. Wood (1989, 1991:462) found that team autonomy in Japan is compromised by the central role played by foremen and supervisors, who actively control and evaluate workers. At auto plants in Japan, teams are under the direction of several levels of immediate supervisors who allocate work, set operations time, and evaluate workers. For example, in the 1980s at Toyota there was one sub-foreman for every five workers, one foreman for every 14, and one senior foreman for every 43. "This dense management structure plays a critical role both in avoiding disturbances and in mobilizing workers in rationalization activities" (Berggren 1992:32).

2. This is a curious reference in that Monden nowhere mentions work teams and only briefly discusses QC circles.

Adler (1993b:135–6) argues that NUMMI's standardized jobs and the absence of buffers under a JIT system preclude workers not only from regulating the pace of work but also from determining how they will organize themselves to accomplish it. Teams at NUMMI "had little of the emphasis on team autonomy that characterizes many work redesign efforts . . . [they] were tightly coupled with teams upstream and downstream . . . their work methods were tightly coupled with the corresponding team on other shifts . . . " (Adler 1993b:174).[3] In the plant Klein (1989:64) studied, autonomous work groups became disempowered with the introduction of JIT procedures. Under JIT "individual team autonomy is replaced by carefully structured patterns of collaboration," and "tasks are more tightly coupled than ever before."

From Parker and Slaughter's (1988) perspective, the only autonomy enjoyed by transplant teams—the capacity to exert peer pressure in the pursuit of production goals—is driven by the rigorous demands of the lean system. As a consequence, they view work teams as little more than administrative units. They also argue that "team concept tries to break down the solidarity and teamwork of natural work groups that develop on the shop floor by trying—usually unsuccessfully—to channel that sentiment into formal, highly controlled, company-designed team structures" (Parker and Slaughter 1988:45).

Teams Essential to Success?

A report on nine Japanese and nine British auto components plants indicates that teams are not central to the success of manufacturing operations. Plants rated "world class" (those with the highest productivity and

---

3. Adler (1993b:145) cites a team leader who preferred the NUMMI way over what prevailed when GM ran the plant: "The work teams at NUMMI aren't like the autonomous teams you read about in other plants. Here, we're not autonomous because we're all tied together really tightly." At first glance this appears like a complaint, but the team leader goes on to describe how under the old system workers could work ahead and build up a stock cushion to enable them to take a break for a few minutes. "That kind of 'hurry up and wait' game," the team leader declares, "made work really tiring." What the team leader does not explain is why workers would voluntarily engage in an exercise that made work tiring. His commentary appears to be grounded less in a grasp of worker psychology than in the desire to justify the removal of these limited forms of worker autonomy under lean production.

quality) were substantially less likely than their lower-ranked counter-parts to assign broad responsibilities like inspection, rectification, routine maintenance, and quality improvement to team members. These "pivotal" activities were undertaken in the higher-performance plants by team leaders. "These findings suggest that the role of the 'empowered' operator in world class manufacturing may have been overstated and that the crucial differences lie at team leader rather than operator [and team] level" (Andersen Consulting 1993:14). The authors of this report, one of whom (Daniel Jones) co-authored *The Machine That Changed the World,* clearly distance themselves from those who view work teams as the heart of the lean factory, as an empowering force, or as a basic source of productivity increases.

Peer Pressure

Few discussions of teams fail to mention peer pressure. Transplant managers interviewed by Kenney and Florida (1993:265) said that teams "keep most workers in line." These authors (1993:271) argue that the Japanese system uses a form of hegemonic control that establishes among workers an identification with the company and its goals. Workers feel they are at one with the company, and this translates into "implicit and subtle forms of coercion and motivation, spurring workers to work hard, think for the company, and assist in motivating fellow workers." Peer pressure to work hard may arise from identification with corporate goals. It also may arise because the presence of slow or injured workers impels others to compensate. In some transplants team members are expected to counsel absentees, inform on those who deviate from company policy, and sit on committees that formally review and sanction their peers. This "deflects attention from what usually is an important area of labor-management conflict" (Kenney and Florida 1993:279).

NUMMI workers reported intense stress whenever production was interrupted, and this, according to one worker cited by Adler (1993b:136), induced pressure within teams that pitted workers against each other. Workers at SIA often pushed each other to get work done, and team members who fell behind or made mistakes were targets of resentment

(Graham 1993:159). Nevertheless, these forms of control, Kenney and Florida (1993:304) declare, are only one aspect of team concept, "not its essence." MacDuffie and Krafcik (1989:4) admit that peer pressure can be stressful, but they too provide the upbeat assessment that it reinforces a sense of common purpose. These observations suggest, as does Rehder (1990:90), that "the informal work group of traditional organizations has now been largely brought under management's control in the transplants' team system."

Teams provide a lateral control system in which peer pressure is combined with more traditional supervision. Good team members look out for one another, assist those who fall behind in their work, attend to their jobs faithfully, and are careful to do their tasks in such a way that they do not create more work for others. Lateral control may shape behavior more powerfully than hierarchical control. "When we care about those with whom we work and have a common set of expectations, we are 'under control' whenever we are in their presence. If we want to be accepted, we try to live up to their expectations. In this sense, social control systems can operate more effectively than most formal systems" (O'Reilly 1989:12).

Researchers debate whether workers view peer pressure in a negative or positive light. Adler (personal communication, Feb. 12, 1993) maintains workers may well feel that peer pressure is an appropriate way to handle those who don't pull their weight. This is true, but one could argue that some workers' not keeping up arises from a lean system that produces multiple stresses, most notably through minimal staffing and heavy workloads. In short, workers' use of peer pressure may derive not so much from their identification with corporate output goals, which is what Adler implies, but from the self-interested and quite sensible desire to avoid working even harder than normal.

Team Leaders

Team leaders are key personnel in transplants. At four non-union transplants and NUMMI, team leaders "are the first line of supervision and play crucial roles in the organization, design and allocation of work on a daily basis" (Kenney and Florida 1993:104). Parker and Slaughter (1988) agree that NUMMI team leaders have "critical supervisory responsibilities"; however, they have no formal disciplinary power. Transplant team leaders advise, train, keep records, and fill in for absentees, but their supervisory discretion is much more limited than that of a conventional foreman (Shimada and MacDuffie 1987:63).

The parameters of team leaders' authority and their behavior on the shop floor are important issues for workers. "Most [NUMMI] workers we interviewed," Parker and Slaughter (1988:103) report, "felt that the personality and role of the team leader was the single most important factor in determining how bearable work is." It follows that the position is bound to be a contentious one. Team leaders routinely deal with situations where the interests of the team conflict with those of management. In these cases, whose side does the team leader take, and with what consequences?

The union at GM's Van Nuys, California, team concept plant fought to remove from team leaders duties normally undertaken by first-line supervisors (Parker and Slaughter 1988:171). Mazda workers complained that team leaders often acted like junior foremen who sided with management rather than the team. This precipitated a tug-of-war over the weight that should be given to seniority and workers' preferences in the selection of team leaders (Babson 1993). The loyalties of team leaders, the procedures to select them, and the boundaries of their role undoubtedly are most contentious in unionized shops, where the position is held by union members. The ambiguities of the role are least pronounced where the team leader is a foreman, as at Toyota's Kentucky plant (Berggren, 1992:48).

As a company that has gone to great lengths to construct teams and cultivate team spirit, CAMI is a prime research site for evaluating the functions and dynamics of teams under lean production.

Team Concept at CAMI

Team concept on the shop floor is built into the CAMI-CAW collective agreement, which states: "CAMI will utilize team concept, with employees organized into teams determined in accordance with the nature of an operation or process. All members of a team share responsibility for the work performed by the team and for participation in quality and productivity improvement programs." A central CAMI guideline is to "be a good team member," and management has tried to recruit people who can communicate and cooperate with others. According to the CAMI guidelines, "A good team member involves others in the decision making process, considers and utilizes the new ideas and suggestions of others, understands and is committed to team objectives [yet] understands that the integrity of the line of authority must be maintained to keep an effective team."

Team concept permeates CAMI, and the layout of the plant facilitates its implementation. Production workers are organized into teams, as are electricians and millwrights in the skilled trades. Teams in Assembly, Welding, Material Handling, and Paint have assigned work areas, usually consisting of numbered work stations. Near each of these work areas (with the exception of the paint shop) are spaces for the team to meet, take breaks, eat lunch, and hold QC circle meetings. These areas are furnished with tables, chairs, lockers and shelves, blackboards, and bulletin boards on which is posted information relating to attendance, rotation schedules, jobs learned by each worker, teians, and so on.

Workers are encouraged to adopt team names. In Assembly, a few team names were Body Slammers, Airgun Cowboys, Trim Busters, Justin Times, and Triminators. One team had an elaborately hand-painted sign emblazoned above the rest area, on which they described their work: "We'll rip your doors off." Every day teams meet briefly before the start of a shift. This is unpaid time. While attendance is voluntary, everyone is expected to attend.

CAMI's version of team concept has at least three dimensions. At the most general level, team concept refers to a collaborative partnership between management and workers. Everyone employed by CAMI, from the top to the bottom of the organization, is regarded as a member of one big company team that pulls together to attain company goals. This element of team concept is expressed in the CAMI value of team spirit and symbolized by CAMI's egalitarian exterior.

Team concept also refers to small groups of employees who engage in improvement activities. CAMI views teams as a medium for the realization of kaizen. Team members are expected to pass on their improvement ideas to team leaders, and teams, operating as QC circles, are encouraged to issue formal proposals for reducing costs and non-value-added activity. Teams, then, take on some of the functions of industrial engineers.

The third dimension of team concept is a mode of organizing the workforce in teams that work under the direction of a team leader. It is important to note that "teamwork" here does not mean that team members work cooperatively to complete assigned tasks. Just as in a traditional auto plant, CAMI vehicles are still put together in the way pioneered by Henry Ford, in which all major tasks follow the logic and pace of the drag chain, and each individual essentially works alone on his or her set of assignments. In a few cases, the cooperation of pairs of workers is demanded by the nature of the task. For example, a real cooperative team effort is required when two workers help each other install the rag-top on a Tracker/Sidekick convertible. Cooperative work like this arises from the technical nature of a particular task and is not commonly required at CAMI. Such paired jobs also exist in plants that do not organize the workforce in teams.

It would be more accurate, then, to say that CAMI does not for the most part use a team-based *production system,* but rather a system of teams superimposed on a traditional assembly line operation in which each person works as an individual. The team can support and reinforce individual effort, but for most tasks, the individual has not been supplanted by the team as the operative unit of production. Teams are more an expression of social engineering than of a fundamentally new system of production.

What difference, then, does the team concept make? Several key features represent a marked departure from the practice of traditional auto plants. In the latter, a job consists of a single task, or a bundle of tasks performed by an individual worker, who has acquired the right to the job through the exercise of seniority and transfer rights, or who performs a particular job due to low seniority. This traditional concept of job ownership, which was reflected by a multitude of job classifications, has been eliminated at CAMI. The single classification for production workers mirrors Japanese practice. Instead of job ownership, team members are cross-trained and rotate jobs. The team, then, is the unit within which cross-training and rotation take place.

Teams also absorb indirect duties performed in traditional auto plants by special categories of workers: housekeeping, inspection, repair, stockhandling.

The Contested Role of Team Leaders

Team leaders, who occupy a position somewhere in between front-line supervisors and lead hands, are union members who are paid $1 per hour more than production associates. They are expected to prepare rotation schedules, canvass for overtime, and do paperwork, such as filling out safety checksheets, making daily productivity reports, and updating COSs. They help train workers, fill in for absentees, and assist those who fall behind in their work. In the daily information briefings, team leaders relay the day's production quota and announce any last-minute changes in the job rotation schedule. They are also expected to monitor quality, do safety checks, and correct production glitches. As one manager observed, "There's absolutely no question the team leader is the busiest person in the plant."

CAMI provides team leaders with special training. One course helps the company and the prospective team leader decide whether he or she is suitable for the job and whether the team leader job is acceptable to the person. Another develops social and communication skills. A course attended by both team and area leaders was described by one trainee as a "mini-course on industrial engineering." After completing her first team leader training session, one woman said, "It's horseshit. It's all management training." She complained that the session had nothing to do with what she is required to do most of the time. A team leader who had just completed a five-day course on leadership reported that it spent nearly two days on employee relations, including procedures for discipline and counseling workers. He described this as "how to go out and make a clean arrest, you know, get somebody for doing some-thing wrong . . . get all your facts right because we're gonna burn you. Get it right the first time—we don't want to give him a second chance. It's pretty hard to make the guys think you're one of them when you start using authority like that."

In June 1994 CAMI scheduled team leaders for an all-day course titled "Dealing with Change." The course covered how to anticipate and deal with workers' concerns about change, how to handle their resistance to change, and how to handle the change process in a team environment. This company attention to team leaders signals how central they are to the operation of a lean system.

The position of team leader is a focal point of tension and conflict between company and union. The company would like team leaders to identify with corporate goals and act in concert with first-line management. The union makes it clear that it wants team leaders to identify with union goals and act in a manner consistent with their status as union members. Thus the company may want to expand the role of the team leader, while the union does not want the team leader to participate in the exercise of management authority.

Some team leaders are not bothered by the conflicting expectations of management and their teams. When asked if he felt caught between management and his team, a team leader replied: "No, I've got no problem with that. I know what side I'm on—the team's side." On the truck line, a team leader divulged how his team had benefited from a mistake made by the time study engineer, who accidentally counted a work station from an adjoining team as part of his team's workload. The error brought a welcome reduction in the burden of work. It never occurred to this team leader to report the miscalculation to the area leader: he had no doubt where his loyalty lay. A third team leader said: "The way I see it, the team leader can really be nothing more than a kind of lead hand and just kind of help the guys out during the course of the day . . . I don't think I have the right to make judgment on someone else. It's pretty hard to make the guys think you're one of them when you start using authority, kind of trying to throw your weight around, thinking you're somebody you're not."

Others find themselves caught between the conflicting demands of management and workers and sometimes their own divided loyalties. Team leaders complain they are often berated by workers for policies and practices over which they have no control, such as not getting replacements for injured or transferred workers. On the other hand, when a team refuses to do taiso, participate in QC circles, or submit teians, which are supposed to be voluntary activities, it is the team leader who is most likely to be taken to task by management. Consider the following comments by one team leader: "I really don't get the respect from the union, and I don't get the respect from management either. I'm somewhere in between. I have a problem with that because I'm a brother just like the next guy."[4] When asked if she felt closer to management or her team, another team leader said, "Some days I might say the workers, other days I might say management. I don't know." A third team leader observed: "It would be nice to have a line to define where my job ends and where management starts. You know, you feel kind of uncomfortable sometimes to have to deal with somebody who's in the union, when you're in the union yourself . . . You don't feel really like you belong with the hourly guys sometimes and yet you feel really caught. You're getting pressure both ways."

The special responsibilities attached to the role of team leader are not accompanied by formal managerial authority. This is spelled out in the contract: "The team leader shall not have any disciplinary authority." Their authority is supposed to be a moral kind—to set an example, advise, and support the team. Discipline is meted out by area leaders, who are the first line of management. Nevertheless, in the early days at CAMI, no clear line demarcated the duties of team leaders and area leaders. While they had no formal power, some team leaders still tried to exercise it.

Eventually, some of the ambiguities were removed when Local 88 issued a set of union guidelines for team leaders. In early 1990, 400 workers attended Local 88's meeting to discuss the role of team leader, and some months later the local produced a short handbook. The handbook says it is "intended to be used as a guide by all team members" and has been designed "to help team leaders in performing their team leader functions and be good union members." The guidelines stress that the team leader is a unionized worker who is a "technical advisor, not a personnel manager." The guidelines offer the following counsel: "Remember that you are the team members' union brother/sister. Work with your team, *not against them.*" The distinction between team leaders and managers is summed up: the function of the team leader "is

4. This team leader, who originally was interviewed as a PA, early on was enthusiastic about working for CAMI and evinced commitment to the company and its objectives. Later, disillusionment set in, and ultimately he left the company.

to support your team and to keep production running," while that of the area leader "is to manage people." Team leader duties reflecting the union's interpretation were spelled out in the 1992 contract.

According to our survey respondents, most workers did not want to be team leaders. In fact, the percentage interested in being a team leader dropped from 33.8 in the first round to a mere 13.2 by the fourth round. Support for the idea of having team leaders declined from a high of nearly 80 percent in round 1 to 63.6 percent in round 4. Prior to the 1992 strike, team leaders were chosen by management following a process of peer review within the team. Survey respondents expressed dissatisfaction with this selection process; most favored some form of election. In round 4, 78.5 percent thought team leaders should be elected. Other options, such as rotating the position, were not considered particularly attractive in the early rounds of the survey, but by round 4, over half supported a system of team leader rotation.

Reflecting workers' dissatisfaction with the mode of team leader selection, the union persuaded the company to agree to a one-year "experiment" in which team members would vote for team leaders. After a year, management terminated the experiment. A May 13, 1994, bulletin from the vice-president for production explained, "Instead of having clear direction as to the requirements of their assignments many team leaders have been forced to respond to pressures within the team to accommodate their individual desires, personality conflicts and sometimes unrealistic demands for such things as relief. All this with the threat of being recalled by the team hanging over them." One result, the vice-president complained, was an extraordinarily high turnover rate among team leaders. Between April 1993 and May 1994, of the approximately 220 team leaders, 135 new ones were selected; 97 voluntarily stepped down from their positions. "It is entirely unacceptable that . . . this many gave up their assignment." It seems clear that the company felt team leaders were too beholden and responsive to their teams, and therefore unable to adhere to management expectations of what a person in this position ought to be and do.

CAMI also rationalized the decision to end elections by maintaining that elections conflicted with the Ontario Employment Equity Act provisions on women. The company implied that it believed workers would not elect women, thus disadvantaging them. This logic is questionable, since one of CAMI's own important criteria for prospective team leaders also disadvantaged women: that of attending training courses held after the end of shift and thus acting as a barrier to those with household and child care responsibilities.

Team leader selection and demotion are now entirely in the hands of management. The criteria for selection are quantified, with the maximum possible score 90 points: 24 points for having taken eight courses (3 points per course) in "Leadership Training" (these courses cover topics such as problem solving, Suzuki production system, leadership skills, line-balancing, standardization, and kaizen); 36 points for "experience" (attendance record, length of service, length of service on the team, and team preference—a maximum of 6 points for the candidate most favored by the team); 20 points for performance on leadership exercises administered by the Personnel Department; 10 points for an interview conducted by members of the Personnel Department and an area leader. The input of the team is now minimal—a maximum of six out of 90 points.

Most respondents reported a good relationship between their teams and team leaders, and most were favorably disposed toward their own team leader. Over time, certain aspects of the relationship showed some improvement. In the first round, 42 percent reported that their team leader thought more like management than like one of them. By the second visit, the proportion thinking this way had fallen to less than one in three (29 percent), with little change occurring over the next two rounds. The proportion who felt their team leader was pressuring them to submit suggestions "all the time or often" declined sharply, from 25 percent to 6 between rounds 1 and 4. It is likely that team leaders backed off as a result of the local union's clarification of their role and its assurance that individuals could refuse to participate with impunity.

Our work station observations provided additional insights into the team leader's role. Workers complained about the behavior of some team leaders; they were liable to take strong exception if a team leader acted too much like management or displayed favoritism or discrimination toward particular team members. The most common complaint concerned team leaders who "act like supervisors." On some teams, workers maintained a strong feeling of loyalty and solidarity towards other members but disliked their team leader. One worker in Welding was particularly blunt: "Mind you, there isn't anything I wouldn't do for members of my team, but if my team leader tries to tell me to do something I shouldn't have to do, I just tell him to fuck off."

How Workers View Team Concept

The broad definition of team concept—CAMI as one big team—is meaningless to most workers on the shop floor. The company's attempt to instill in workers team spirit—a feeling that working at CAMI is like being on a baseball or hockey team—has not been successful. For workers, team concept means neither equality of all employees nor partnership with management, and the CAMI value of team spirit increasingly is regarded as little more than an empty slogan. For example, when survey respondents were asked if working in teams helped them feel like part of CAMI, 65.8 percent in round 1, but only 15.9 percent in round 4, agreed (see Table 4). A team leader pointed out one difference between workers' and managers' views of team concept: "We consider ourselves a team, and we like to operate as a team, but management seems to have a different idea of what a team is. They're team oriented as long as it's to their benefit. But as soon as it isn't to their benefit, the whole plant becomes the team instead of the team itself."

For most workers, team concept has an immediate, concrete referent: where and with whom they work day after day. When workers think at all of team concept, then, their image is of their own teams.

How do CAMI workers feel about working in teams? The answer is not simple; teams are seen as a mixture of good and bad, and workers disagree about the advantages and disadvantages. A majority of workers did not feel empowered by working in teams. This limited sense of control is discussed more fully in the chapter on kaizen. Here it is sufficient to report that when asked if working in teams "gives me a say over how my job is done," the percentage who agreed dropped from 80.3 in the first round to 45.6 in the last.

However, only 16.9 percent of the respondents in round 1 and 25.3 percent in round 4 felt that working in teams was a waste of time. Throughout the survey, the great majority (90 percent in round 4) said they liked the *idea* of working in teams very much or somewhat. An even greater proportion reported that they liked being members of their

TABLE 4. All things considered, working in a team:

		Round 1	Round 2	Round 3	Round 4
Helps me feel like I'm part of CAMI	Agree	65.8% (48)	44.9% (35)	31.6% (25)	15.9% (11)
	Disagree	34.2% (25)	55.1% (43)	68.4% (54)	84.1% (58)
Gives me a say over how my job is done	Agree	80.3% (57)	75.9% (60)	59.0% (46)	45.6% (36)
	Disagree	19.7% (14)	24.1% (19)	41.0% (32)	54.4% (43)
Is a waste of time	Agree	16.9% (12)	11.5% (10)	17.9% (14)	25.3% (20)
	Disagree	83.1% (59)	88.5% (77)	82.1% (64)	74.7% (59)
Gives me a chance to know people	Agree	71.2% (52)	90.9% (70)	89.7% (70)	86.1% (68)
	Disagree	28.8% (21)	9.1% (7)	10.3% (8)	13.9% (11)
Gives me a chance to raise my concerns	Agree	86.3% (63)	84.0% (63)	75.6% (59)	73.7% (56)
	Disagree	13.7% (10)	16.0% (12)	24.4% (19)	26.3% (20)
Is a way to get us to work harder	Agree	39.7% (29)	46.1% (35)	51.2% (41)	69.2% (54)
	Disagree	60.3% (44)	53.9% (41)	48.8% (39)	30.8% (24)
Gets us all pressuring one another	Agree	19.2% (14)	40.3% (31)	50.0% (39)	59.0% (46)
	Disagree	80.8% (59)	59.7% (46)	50.0% (39)	41.0% (32)
Helps CAMI but not me	Agree	20.8% (15)	24.4% (19)	31.2% (24)	50.6% (40)
	Disagree	79.2% (57)	75.6% (59)	68.8% (53)	49.4% (39)
Allows team members to act together to express complaints	Agree	—	92.0% (69)	91.0% (71)	84.8% (67)
	Disagree	—	8.0% (6)	9.0% (7)	15.2% (12)

Note: The last question was first asked in Round 2.

own teams. When asked, "What do you like about team concept at CAMI?" most of those interviewed mentioned social aspects, such as friendship, helping each other out, and sticking up for each other. In rounds 1 and 4, 71.2 percent and 86.1 percent respectively said working in teams gave them a chance to get to know people. Throughout the study, respondents continued to cite getting to know people, working together, and helping one another as things they liked about team concept.[5] Apparently it is the social solidarity emerging out of the team experience that accounts for workers' generally positive evaluation of working in teams.

These answers suggest a relatively high degree of team cohesion. But whose interests are served by team cohesion? Do workers use cohesion as a resource to challenge management authority and company goals, or to adhere to those goals? Does team cohesion make life on the job more tolerable, or more stressful for some members? Again, the answer is not a simple one. Cohesion takes different forms and has a range of consequences. Team behaviors are shaped by situational demands, the distinct and sometimes inconsistent motives of team members, the relationship between team leaders and workers, and the extent to which the team is worker- or company-centered.

Team solidarity facilitates the achievement of demanding production quotas. This can give team members a sense of pride in their work and in each other. A team leader said he was blessed with a very positive team. "We look out for each other, and what happens is if I happen to finish my quota ahead of time because I had a real good day and I see somebody struggling, we help out. Only because we're pulling together has it worked." Another team leader gave a similar account: "We have a lot of people off and hurt and all that stuff. We have a good team, like everybody sticks together. Like yesterday, when there were only seven of us [out of nine], everybody tries to help out everybody."

5. Some respondents made the point that these social bonds would have developed in the absence of team concept. One worker, who liked the idea of team concept, said he often socialized with team members after work. This, he added, is "just the same everywhere—there's really nothing different here." The adaptation of team structure to social purposes parallels what ordinarily happens in most workplaces, where informal groups emerge naturally and provide similar forms of social support. See Krahn and Lowe (1993) and Rinehart (1996).

As indicated in Table 4, respondents said working in teams gave them the opportunity to raise their concerns (86.3 percent in round 1 and 73.7 percent in round 4) and allowed them to act together to express complaints (92 percent in round 2, when the question was first asked, and 84.8 percent in round 4). Respondents, then, expressed support for the position of one worker who believed "sticking together" was necessary to "deal with management collectively." Another worker said she liked "working together" with her team, but stressed that there was no alternative in a workplace she described as "a battle between management and employees." "In our group," a team leader observed, "everyone sticks together . . . If we decide we're not working overtime, then no one works overtime." A worker cited in the *London Free Press* (Sept. 11, 1992) said teams are "locked in a battle with management which is seen as anything but consultative. The teams are sticking together, bucking the system. There's a clash going on between teams and managers, an us-against-them mentality." Teams have acted in solidarity to obtain relief workers, to resist losing a floater, to regain an off-line subassembly position, and to protest unsafe working conditions or the company's stringent dress code.

In July 1990 a team in Welding Repair decided to stop doing taiso. This upset the manager, and he threatened to transfer the workers to Welding (a less preferred area). As one of the participants said, "We got together and talked about it and said, 'Well, you can transfer us, because we're not doing it. You're not going to threaten us with it.'" As the story circulated throughout the plant, there was an "uproar," and signs began to appear declaring "taiso or transfer." It was only after the signs appeared that the union settled the matter with management— to the satisfaction of the workers.

The union made clear its support for collective team efforts to deal with shop floor problems. The June 1991 issue of *Off the Line* contained a half-page picture of an assembly team in Final 4 that had collectively invoked Section 23 of the provincial Health and Safety Act and refused to work. The team was protesting a lack of relief and rotation and a failure to replace workers placed on restricted work because of RSIs. The title was "Changing the Definition of Teamwork," and the caption read, "What does teamwork mean to you? To the members of Final 4 YOE Assembly it means solidarity." These examples illustrate that team concept, which is implemented to realize management's goals, can be turned upside down by workers to achieve workers' ends.

Nearly all of the survey group mentioned something they disliked about teams. Criticisms were more pronounced in the final interviews, with more complaints that teamwork was a means of making people cover for absent or injured workers, show up for work, and work harder. In round 1, 39.7 percent said working in teams was "a way to get us to work harder," and by the fourth round, 69.2 percent agreed. Similarly, the percentage who said working in teams "gets us all pressuring one another" climbed from 19.2 in round 1 to 59 in round 4 (see Table 4). One worker said team concept "pits worker against worker" and believed CAMI deliberately set it up this way.

Interviewees sometimes expressed dissatisfaction with work performance of particular team members. Although it was not a widespread refrain, some workers blamed "slackers" for undermining the team system. As one worker complained, "Not everyone pulls their weight." A team leader reported, "The only time they would do that [exert peer pressure] is if they see that one of the other team members isn't pulling their weight, especially if they know that person can pull their weight and don't." Some workers went further, to blame injured or absent workers. A worker on the truck line said he resented two co-workers with RSIs; he believed they were faking their injuries so they would be assigned the easy jobs on the team. This attitude was deeply disturbing for persons unfortunate enough to have suffered an injury, who were working under some kind of restriction, or who missed work. "When you're sick or injured," one worker observed, "you feel guilty because they won't replace you." Small group dynamics, then, can deflect criticism of management onto the team itself. In an article in the local union newsletter, a former Local 88 president advised members to hold CAMI's policy of understaffing responsible for the need to work hard when others were injured or absent: "Team concept has proved to be no more than a method of using peer pressure to improve attendance and to keep people from leaving the line to report small injuries or pains . . . I am shocked by the flack received from other team members by a worker who is injured and must go on light duty. This is related strictly to the Japanese concept of not having replacements for those injured" (*Off the Line,* Feb. 1991).

Another set of questions zeroed in on specific areas in which teams had pressured team members. We asked how often team pressure was put on members to engage in 10 specific activities. As Table 5 shows, in seven of the 10 cases—work harder, improve quality, improve attendance, improve attitude, reduce waste, do housekeeping, and agree to work overtime—the percentage reporting that such pressure was applied "all the time" or "often" declined between rounds 2 and 4. Peer pressure eased most noticeably in regard to improving quality and reducing waste. In two of the three instances in which more workers reported pressure in the final round than in the first—that is, pressure to work slower and to file a grievance—the persuasion was exerted *against* the interests of the company. In no case in round 4 did as many as one-quarter of the respondents indicate that their teams pressured members all the time or often.

We also asked respondents how often they themselves felt pressure from their teams. Over three-quarters said they had never been targets of peer pressure (80 percent and 78.5 percent in the first and final rounds respectively).

On the one hand, our respondents indicated that teams made little effort to pressure *individuals* to take specific actions (Table 5). On the other hand, as time passed substantially more respondents perceived teams as a *general* source of peer pressure (Table 4). How are we to understand this discrepancy? It may be that experience in teams and an awareness of the union's criticism of misplaced peer pressure (as expressed in the union newsletter) led workers to conclude a) that the company set up teams precisely to generate peer pressure in the context of minimal staffing, and b) that such pressure was not in workers' interests. The trend toward viewing teams as a source of *general* pressure, then, could arise from workers' heightened awareness of CAMI's agenda for teams, while the decline in reports of specific pressures could reflect their resistance to such an agenda.

This interpretation is bolstered by the responses that indicate a growing sense that working in teams benefited the company more than workers. In round 1, just one in five respondents believed that working in teams "helps CAMI but not me"; by the final interview, half shared this view (see Table 4). And when asked if teams worked more for the good of the company than for the good of the workers, 71.1 percent in round

TABLE 5. In your experience, how often is team pressure put on members to do the following?

		Round 2	Round 3	Round 4
Work harder	all the time/often	26.0% (20)	24.7% (19)	15.2% (12)
	once in a while/never	74.0% (57)	75.3% (58)	84.8% (67)
Improve quality	all the time/often	43.8% (35)	28.9% (22)	22.8% (18)
	once in a while/never	56.2% (45)	71.1% (54)	77.2% (61)
Improve attendance	all the time/often	17.3% (13)	15.9% (11)	16.5% (13)
	once in a while/never	82.7% (62)	84.1% (58)	83.5% (66)
Improve attitude	all the time/often	18.6% (13)	10.1% (8)	6.3% (5)
	once in a while/never	81.4% (57)	89.9% (71)	93.7% (74)
Reduce personal breaks	all the time/often	8.6% (6)	8.7% (6)	8.9% (7)
	once in a while/never	91.4% (64)	92.3% (63)	91.1% (72)
Reduce waste	all the time/often	13.7% (10)	13.0% (10)	5.1% (4)
	once in a while/never	86.3% (63)	87.0% (67)	94.9% (75)
Do housekeeping	all the time/often	26.0% (20)	21.8% (17)	19.0% (15)
	once in a while/never	74.0% (57)	78.2% (61)	81.0% (64)
Work overtime	all the time/often	22.2% (16)	10.1% (8)	7.6% (6)
	once in a while/never	77.8% (56)	89.9% (71)	92.4% (73)
Work slower	all the time/often	0.0%	1.4% (1)	3.8% (3)
	once in a while/never	100% (77)	98.6% (73)	96.2% (76)
File a grievance	all the time/often	2.5% (2)	4.4% (3)	5.1% (4)
	once in a while/never	97.5% (77)	92.6% (65)	94.9% (75)

1, and 82.7 percent in round 4, agreed or agreed somewhat. Those who expressed outright agreement with this statement rose steadily over the four rounds, from 14.5 percent to 42.7 percent.

Workers had strong opinions about what they liked and disliked about teams, and over time these opinions increasingly took on a critical tone that was reflected in behavior. Of the multiple uses management had envisaged for team areas, rest breaks and lunch were the only activities that endured; problem-solving sessions were undertaken only when teams faced a pressing issue. Team names often fell into disuse or their significance was downplayed. By the final round, teams were more likely to use the technical language of the plant to describe themselves, such as "Line 2, Team 5" in the case of the car engine subassembly—or simply "car engine subassembly." Attendance at pre-shift team meetings declined markedly. In round 1, 85 percent of those surveyed said they always attended, compared to 46 percent in the final round.

Teams as Contested Terrain

While work under lean production could be performed without teams, their multiple functions and their development of internal cohesion indicate that teams at CAMI are something more than administrative units. However, the teams cannot legitimately be labeled "self-managing" and in no way resemble the autonomous groups described in the classic study of coal mining by Trist and Bamforth (1951) and accorded such a central role in the theory of the socio-technical systems school of work redesign. The absence of team autonomy at CAMI is underscored when compared to team activities at Volvo's Uddevalla plant. Small, parallel work teams, each of which built a car from start to finish, handled *all* inspection and repairs, determined the allocation of tasks, were able to vary the pace at which they worked, and took on recruitment responsibilities. Team autonomy was insured by an extremely flat control hierarchy consisting of only two layers of management and no first-line supervisors (Berggren 1992). CAMI workers enjoyed none of this discretion. To the extent that CAMI is typical of transplants, and we have seen no evidence to the contrary, to call transplant teams "self-managing" borders on the absurd.

There are no foremen in team concept plants, but this does not make for a milieu that is less authoritarian than traditional factories. We did not ask CAMI workers with previous industrial experience for comparisons, so we can only speculate about the differences. Auto assembly factories of whatever stripe are characterized by pervasive technical control, since "the entire production process or large segments of it are based on a technology that paces and directs the labor process"

(Edwards 1979:113). Using historical data, Edwards demonstrated that the emergence of the assembly line substantially reduced not only the number but the responsibilities of foremen. At CAMI the assembly line, JIT procedures, and electronic monitoring devices (elements of what CAMI calls visual management) constitute a formidable system of technical control that can be more oppressive than having a foreman watching over your shoulder. In addition, CAMI maintains a distinct management hierarchy consisting of eight levels of authority, and supervisory controls remain intact.

A major difference between traditional and team concept auto plants, then, is team leaders' assumption of some functions performed by foremen, and the broader span of control of first-line supervisors (called area leaders at CAMI). The actions and kinds of managerial responsibilities taken on by team leaders are crucial in determining how authority is exercised. This is why the role of the team leader is so pivotal and contentious in some plants. At CAMI, where team leaders have no formal managerial authority, supervision undoubtedly is less direct, constant, and onerous than in traditional factories. However, the roles and responsibilities of team leaders in lean production transplants vary, and in some, for example SIA and Toyota's Kentucky plant, they are essentially indistinguishable from foremen (Berggren 1992; Graham 1995).

Elton Mayo (1933) and his Harvard colleagues, along with much subsequent research in industrial settings, demonstrated years ago at the Hawthorne Works in Chicago that it was within informal work groups that arise spontaneously on the shop floor that resistance to company objectives and directives emerges, sustained by group codes and sanctions for violating them. Mayo's solution was straightforward: replace these informal work groups with management-constructed groups whose goals are aligned with rather than resistant to corporate interests and ends. While the remedy appeared simple enough, its application generally has proved elusive.

Our results indicate that the teams set up by CAMI did produce some behaviors, such as helping each other out, keeping up with the work, sanctioning slackers, and discouraging absenteeism, that were consistent with the company's objectives. These behaviors reflect an amalgam of self-interest, mutual care and concern, and the exercise of peer pressure. It is this melange of motivations within the small group that is perhaps the key to understanding teams' centrality to lean production. Given the problems created by the policy of very lean staffing, which were compounded by injuries and absenteeism, lateral controls are supposed to operate as a kind of fail-safe mechanism to promote behaviors that are consistent with CAMI goals *in the absence of worker commitment to the company and its values.*[6]

However, the fail-safe mechanism was not entirely effective. CAMI teams did not always act as the company would have liked. Teams were not carriers of an enterprise consciousness; the negative consequences of peer pressure increasingly were recognized; and only a minority of workers we talked to reported constant pressures from co-workers. Increasingly, teams became a base to resist some of management's more excessive directives and policies; workers use the team as a lever to advance their own demands.

In the give-and-take on the shop floor, the team leader is a critical figure. Team leaders can identify with the team or with management. Their relations with team members can be cordial and supportive or surly and authoritarian. They can make workers' lives on the job tolerable or miserable. In helping to shape the boundaries of this role, the initiatives of workers and the union local made a difference. As a result of informal pressures and the union's delineation of a clear line between team leaders and management, team leaders increasingly were viewed by workers as one of themselves rather than as representatives of the company. It is not surprising that the great majority of workers favored an alternative—either elections or rotation—to management selection of team leaders.

The frontiers of shop floor control are always shifting, and the extent to which teams and team leaders at CAMI will operate as arms of management or as a medium for defending workers' interests will be repeatedly contested.

6. These lateral controls help to explain why Japanese workers toil assiduously (Besser 1993; Feldman and Betzold 1988; Kamata 1982).

CHAPTER 8

Gender on the Line

AFTER LONG PERIODS OF VIRTUAL EXCLUSION, BOTH IN NORTH America and Japan, women are finally making progress towards becoming part of the auto assembly workforce. To varying degrees, women have been hired in all the auto transplants that have set up shop in Greenfield and exurban sites in Canada and the United States.

Are lean production car factories any more conducive to equitable gender relations at work than traditional mass production plants? In view of the entrenched patriarchal traditions associated with the Japanese factory (Roberts 1994), no one claims that lean production offers greater gender equality there. But several factors could be cited in support of the proposition that the North American transplants are likely to foster equality: hiring practices that do not emphasize previous auto industry experience; less emphasis on the skills traditionally associated with the largely male trades; and the claim of a more egalitarian and more cooperative workplace environment. As a lean production facility that started with a workforce that was one-fifth female, CAMI provides a fair test of the question whether lean production offers greater gender equality.

Women in the North American and Japanese Auto Industries

Research on work and industrial relations has often been criticized for being gender blind (Gannagé 1986; Forrest 1993). This is particularly true for the study of automobile assembly work. Rarely, if ever, do women workers—or even the wives of male auto workers—feature in the pages of the classic post–World War II studies of workers in the North American auto industry (e.g., Chinoy 1955; Walker and Guest 1952). And despite more than two decades of feminist scholarship on women and work, the same holds largely true of more contemporary research on the industry, such as that by Katz (1987), the work on lean production by Womack, Jones, and Roos (1990), and the output by investigators associated with the Massachusetts Institute of Technology-based International Motor Vehicle Research Program IR/HR Project (MacDuffie 1995).

Many investigations into workplace gender issues have focused on employment sectors predominantly staffed by women, such as the garment industry, retail sales, services, and the public sector. Another important set of contributions to the literature has looked at trades traditionally dominated by men, such as printing, with the focus on the gendered conceptions of skill that male workers have consciously or unconsciously propagated (Cockburn 1981). Research on workplaces where men and women seemingly do similar work, or where management may tolerate, or even promote, the idea of a unisex workforce, raises further issues that have not been sufficiently explored (West 1990:258).

For most of the twentieth century, the automobile industry in both North America and Japan has employed relatively few female workers in direct production. When women first entered the industry in Canada and the United States during World War II, single women were hired first, then widows, and married women last. Segregated patterns of work prevailed, with separate job classifications. Women were concentrated in cutting and sewing material for the seats, and in wiring harness assembly. The numbers of women in the industry quickly declined after the war. Where women workers were still to be found in any numbers, such as at the General Motors Oshawa plants in the early 1960s, it was predominantly in cutting, sewing, and wiring harness.

Union support for women's equality was qualified in the early days. Union backing for the hiring of women during World War II was conditional on opening up a new shift—the so-called "victory shift"—with a separate seniority list for women. Sugiman (1992:2) comments on the contradictory role played by the United Auto Workers (UAW) in Canada: "Notwithstanding the union's impressive record, most UAW members in Canada worked in the automotive sector, an industry that was long dominated by white men and based on sex-specific job classifications, wage rates, and seniority lists. In spite of the UAW's forthright stance against sexual discrimination, many union leaders and members both sanctioned these arrangements and engaged in similarly sexist practices in their day-to-day encounters with their union sisters."

In Japan, the pioneering post–World War II Toyota model of lean production was characterized by the hiring of men only. Toyota did not hire women to work on the assembly line. Most other auto companies pursued similar practices. Price (1994:97) cites Suzuki as "rare among Japan's automakers in that it allowed women to work on the line." But despite this more enlightened policy, "wage discrimination was explicit in the lower starting rates and women did not advance up the wage scale as quickly as men."

One reason often cited for Japanese auto makers' reluctance to hire women for assembly jobs was the labor law in that country prohibiting women's employment on the night shift. However, other considerations, such as concerns over a labor shortage in the late 1980s, proved sufficient to persuade more auto companies to employ women in final assembly.[1]

Women Workers at CAMI

During the first four years of CAMI's operation, the local union estimated that women workers accounted for about 20 percent of the hourly workforce. This proportion of women workers, which has been exceeded at some other North American transplants,[2] is higher than in most Big Three

---

1. Research visit to Japan by David Robertson, spring 1994. A recent brochure for a new Toyota plant in Japan proudly notes the presence of women workers.

2. Slightly higher proportions of female workers have been recorded at some transplants. For example, Fucini and Fucini (1990:63) note that "women accounted for less than 28 percent of the work force" when Mazda opened its plant at Flat Rock, Michigan.

auto plants in Canada and the United States with long established, pre-dominantly male workforces.

In response to the research team's questions, CAMI managers reported that they were not aware of any gender-related problems with or criticisms of their assessment and recruitment procedures, and they did not recall having heard any accusation of biases in hiring. Managers were asked whether the company had ever had any preferences, targets, or quotas in recruiting certain categories of workers who might be under-represented in the CAMI workforce, based on such factors as age, sex, visible minority status, or physical disability. Answers invariably focused on the claim that any such strategy would contradict the "objectivity" of the assessment process.

So far as one manager was aware, discussion of affirmative action programs had "never featured in our discussions in terms of hiring." Researchers were told that the question of the sex composition of the workforce was simply not considered relevant to the selection process. The same manager stated: "We look at it [the assessment process] based on the standard . . . [to see] if people meet the standard at each step in the process. We are not looking at their sex at any point."

No difference in this approach was noted in other interviews with staff involved in assessment, except for the case of potential recruits having some sort of disability. A manager explained: "The only group where we've really highlighted at all, or made any kind of exception, if exception is the right word, or given special consideration to, would be the disabled, and that is the only group that was identified a little bit separately from the rest of the population."

Over the course of the four research visits, the proportion of women at CAMI remained about constant as the workforce was augmented to operate two shifts. However, after we left the plant, the proportion of women PAs appeared to decline. In contrast to past practice, in 1993 CAMI began to recruit people with at least one year's manufacturing experience. A manager explained that CAMI had begun to look for people with realistic expectations of "what they were getting into." Some union reps believe the change was a controversial way of attempting to lessen injuries that the company sometimes claimed were gender-related.[3]

3. This issue was discussed with a focus group meeting with members of the local union executive board and in-plant committee attending the CAW Council meeting in Windsor, Ontario, December 3, 1993, and with union reps in June 1995.

The full rationale for the new policy is unclear, but one result has been a decline in the hiring of women. The local union's Women's Committee noted the negative implications for women in a 1993 report.[4] Over the next two years there was no evidence of a greater willingness by management to hire women. In June 1995 a union rep observed, "Out of the last 80 hired I would say we only have about half a dozen women."

CAMI management, with the support of the union, cooperated with the provisions of the Employment Equity legislation introduced by the New Democratic provincial government in Ontario during its term of office from 1990 to 1995. When this legislation was repealed following the 1995 election of a Progressive Conservative government, CAMI confirmed its ongoing willingness to participate with the union in a Joint Employment Equity Committee made up of three representatives from each side, and the 1995 collective agreement includes such a committee. Each party agreed to ensure that one of their members was from one of the four groups designated in the original employment equity legislation (women, visible minorities, aboriginals, and the disabled).

Who Gets Assigned Where?

In round 1 of our interviews, women (19 percent) were more likely than men (3 percent) to report that their job at CAMI was their first.[5] Women (6 percent) were far less likely to have moved to take up their job at CAMI than men (26 percent).

We observed certain gender-specific patterns in where men and women worked. All the skilled trades, all workers in Stamping, and a disproportionate number of PAs in Welding were male. By round 3, only five percent of respondents reported having a woman as a team leader.

---

4. The Women's Committee has functioned as a volunteer non-elected standing committee since the early days of Local 88. It has addressed wider community issues such as support for local women's shelters. In-plant campaigns have been waged for company-provided day care, thus far with no success.

5. As explained in Appendix I on Methodology, women were slightly over-represented in our interview sample. For example, in the third round of interviews, conducted in June 1991, 28 per cent of our sample were women.

Despite this general appearance of job segregation by sex, we found that no matter how the question was posed, over all four rounds of interviews, a majority of both men and women did not think management tended to assign women to certain work areas, departments, or jobs.[6] However, when we probed those interviewees (usually male) who *did* see gender-based patterns in job assignments, responses showed some consistency. Jobs that interviewees thought tended to be done by men included stamping (especially die changing), some work on the chassis line, particularly where high-torque guns were required, door removal, windshields, some underbody jobs requiring much stretching, and the spray booths in Paint. Several women commented that in the first year or so of operations, the Japanese trainers actively discouraged women from working in the spray booths. Those who saw a gender-based pattern in job assignments thought women were more likely to work in Material Handling, Paint, especially on some jobs such as tack-off, and in Assembly on subassemblies such as instrument panel.

Some male workers expressed the view that women were assigned easier jobs. One man claimed that women "get easier jobs for physical reasons." Another complained that women were "assigned the easiest jobs which do not demand experience with tools." In each of rounds 2, 3, and 4, among the minority of men who thought that women were assigned to certain jobs because they were women, most thought that they were assigned to jobs with better working conditions. Although these were minority views, they proved to be persistent.

Local union leaders recognized the existence of some tensions over gender relations at CAMI. One committeeperson reported: "Initially, what you used to hear from some of the males was they're putting a lot of the females into lighter, easier jobs, such as QC, Paint, and some of the subassembly jobs." Notwithstanding these and other specific concerns, in all four rounds women and men responded similarly when asked whether they thought men and women were treated about equally at CAMI. About three-quarters of the respondents, both men and women, answered in the affirmative.

6. In round 1 workers were asked if, in their experience, women were assigned to certain work areas because they were women. In rounds 2 through 4 we asked two separate questions: first, if women were assigned to certain departments because they were women, and second, if women were assigned to certain jobs because they were women.

For their part, some female PAs objected that they were not given enough opportunity to gain experience on jobs that tended to be performed by men, such as in Stamping. One woman reported that her male co-workers did not always know how to act: "Some feel like they should always help a woman; others stand back and let me see if I can do it."

One woman manager expressed an interest in encouraging women to enter nontraditional jobs. She commented on the resistance she sometimes encountered when talking to women about going into areas of the plant such as Welding where women were underrepresented: "Quite a few women I've talked to don't really like the idea of Welding. Because you get dirty. Because there's a lot of equipment, or they are intimidated by the robots, by the sparks. [That's the view of] a lot of people actually, because welding is just dirtier, it's noisy, and it's hard work too."

The same manager was quick to add that she made a habit of pointing out the advantages of skill development in Welding: "I've told a lot of people that in Welding, you're learning a skill that you may use in another job. That's not so much the case in Assembly, where you're not really going to use those skills again. . . . You learn to MIG weld, you learn to braze and solder, and robotics, you learn a lot, sheet metal and so on." The manager also related her perspective on the need to develop equality of opportunity for the sexes in the workplace: "Now I did have a team leader say to me that women would have a hard time on his line. It's a difficult line. I just told him that every person who comes in has to be able to do the work. And a small man would have trouble too— so it's more [a question of] a small person. But you have to give them the opportunity."

Although some women experienced, and may have continued to experience, difficulties in negotiating certain work roles, the local union, with encouragement from the national office, pointed to progress in helping to open up the range of opportunities for women at CAMI. One committeeperson noted that many of her union sisters from the first year of hiring in 1989 were quick to take advantage of their seniority in bidding for new postings. She rejected the suggestion that women had gained anything from training programs at CAMI. Rather, she insisted, "the improvements that I have seen have been attained through seniority."

Gender Differences at Work

Some PAs observed that, since CAMI had included women in the initial hiring, women did not experience the same challenges faced by their sisters in older establishments, where they would have had to enter a domain traditionally dominated by men. The fact that CAMI had hired a relatively young workforce was also noted, and some women felt this circumstance worked in their favor, with younger males being more open to working side by side with women. A woman member of the in-plant committee said she liked the unisex uniforms issued by the company, because it saved workers money and because it made for an improved working atmosphere for women in a predominantly male workplace.

In our survey, women and men responded differently to some non-gender-related questions, and these can be grouped in two categories. In the first category, we can note a few significantly different responses to questions, especially in the first round, which could be taken to imply a greater skepticism on the part of women toward certain features of team concept. For example, in round 1 (the only time we asked the question), women were more likely than men to reflect back on the orientation session as a waste of time (65 percent of women, compared to 46 percent of men). Women interviewed in the first round were also more likely to say that team meetings were dominated by one person, and that kaizen activities were more likely to be initiated by the team leader than by any other team member. Furthermore, women were more likely than men to perceive the existence of team pressure on attitudes.

However, the importance of these differences is diminished when we consider two points. First, we need to take into account responses to the whole range of survey questions. There were no significant differences in responses to the majority of questions. Second, we need to examine the answers in rounds 2 through 4 to those questions that elicited significant differences in round 1. In the final three rounds, women's and men's responses converged, and it is interesting to note that this convergence was more the result of men changing their opinions than of women changing theirs.

The second grouping of responses that varied by sex pertains to differences in women's experiences with health and safety. In earlier chapters, we argued that RSIs are inextricably linked to certain features of lean production. While the overall level of injuries at CAMI was considered unacceptably high by both managers and the union, over all four rounds of our survey women were significantly more likely than men to report that their jobs exposed them to repetitive strains and other similar injuries. Half of the women (16 out of 32) in round 1 reported that their jobs exposed them to repetitive strains all of the time or often. This was almost twice the percentage for men, still high at 28 percent. Less than 10 percent of women said they were never exposed to such injuries, compared to 38 percent of men.[7] Perceptions of greater strain among women also showed in their responses to the question of how often they found their jobs physically tiring. Almost half of women in round 1 answered "all of the time or often," well over twice the rate of male workers. Similar differences were recorded in the final three rounds.

A number of factors complicate male-female comparisons of work injuries. Messing et al. (1994:95) identify four: "(1) gender differences in hours worked, (2) gendered task assignments within industrial classifications, occupations and job titles, (3) gender differences in age/seniority, and (4) gender differences in the interaction between equipment and tool dimensions and work activity." We could add the consideration that the double day of factory work combined with domestic labor in the home may make women more susceptible to injuries. Notwithstanding such complexities, the data still point to special problems for the health and safety of women workers that had not been resolved by round 4.

One woman union activist at CAMI suggested that gender differences in the data for work injuries might be partly explained by a reluctance on the part of men to report a developing work injury, especially symptoms related to carpel tunnel syndrome. The argument finds support in writings on masculinity at work by Willis (1990), as well as in the more specific observations by Gottfried and Graham (1993:618) on the way male workers at the SIA plant viewed some types of injuries.[8]

7. The confidence level for a significant difference in responses was 95 percent for the question on repetitive strains, and 90 percent for a question on muscle fatigue and strains. Forty-four percent of women reported that their jobs exposed them to muscle fatigue and strains all of the time or often, compared to 26 percent of men.

8. We would argue that the task of convincing male workers to recognize and report injuries is easier to accomplish in the unionized setting of CAMI than in the non-union SIA

After leaving the plant, we learned of a change in the way PAs were allocated to jobs. According to a union rep, "In the beginning there was a random draw. You just went wherever you went. Now they actually look at where the guy is going. They look at the physical person, you know, if he's six-foot-something they'll put him where he's suited. They don't put a five-foot-two-inch girl in the underbody team any more." The rethinking of the practice of job assignments may have had the desired effect of, as one committeeperson put it, "helping a little bit on the injuries," but it also meant more of a tendency to sex-type jobs and a return to elements of the scientific management tradition of selecting the most physically suited for a particular job.[9] Lean production, like scientific management, finds it easier (and cheaper) to fit workers to jobs than vice versa.

Teams and Gender

A local union leader acknowledged that some male PAs had expressed frustration and resentment over the deployment of women within teams. He conveyed the views of some men with the following harsh but not uncharacteristic assessment: "I think the men accommodated some of the women in some of the tougher jobs initially, and they finally said piss on it. They get paid the same; they can do the same work." A team leader on the truck line provided an example of how such tensions developed: "There's a lot of hard jobs in our area. We had four women on the team and the guys were getting pissed off because they had to pick up the slack that the women couldn't—nothing against the women—but it just seems to fall naturally for the guys to take up the excess."

When women and men experience different levels of difficulty at work, whether it be reports by women of finding the work more physically tiring, or higher levels of job-related injuries for women, there can be negative implications for gender relationships over and beyond

---

plant. The local union at CAMI placed great emphasis on encouraging all workers to pull the andons if they felt they risked injury, and to report any evidence of work-related injury.

9. In one of his most famous studies, Frederick Taylor (1947) relates how he carefully selected his experimental subject (described as "a human ox") to do the physically demanding job of loading bars of pig iron onto box cars.

sheer physical hardship. Teamwork under lean production is not necessarily conducive to an equitable solution. The problem of integrating workers into an environment that is sustainable for both women and men can be exacerbated rather than resolved by the institution of teamwork, as we observed on the seat install operation.

Everyone agreed that seat install, especially the back seat, was a tough job. Workers were unanimous that no one could work unassisted on putting in the back seat all day long—220 times on that operation would be too much. So they rotated the job every two hours. The men working on rear seat install complained that women were not rotating through this, the hardest, job. "The ladies aren't coming down here to do this job," complained one of the seat installers: "Hell, if they can't do it because they're women, then I sure as hell can't do it, because I'm too old for this."

Much changed in the seat install area over the course of our observations, but not the complex relationship among technology, job design, and social relations. The job itself was improved: on our fourth observation, two people instead of one had been assigned to the back seat. One installed the seat cushion and a decal on the next car in the line, and another PA installed the seat back along with some other tasks. It had improved in another way as well. The team for the first time was on full rotation.

But there was another obvious change: there were no women on the team. The issue, in one sense, had been "resolved." One male worker explained: "We don't want women. They can't do seat install." According to this worker, the presence of women on the team would disrupt the rotation schedule, would force some PAs into the harder jobs more frequently, and that in turn would increase RSIs, which would further limit rotation, and so on.

The tension on seat install, however, had more to do with the design of the jobs than with the relationship between men and women. Indeed, the relationship between automation and manual effort was revealing. Management had expended considerable effort and expense to get the seats to the line in the right sequence at the right time, and additional expense and effort to convey the seat automatically over the pit, but they had made no effort and no expense to make the jobs easier.

In most assembly plants, the seat install operation uses mechanized come-alongs that at least take the weight of the seat and make it easy to jockey the seats into the vehicle. In a few plants the seat install is robotized. Technological decisions are never neutral. CAMI could have introduced machine assists to reduce the physical demands of the job, with positive outcomes for the health and safety of all workers and for an improved relationship between men and women on the job.

The overlap between gender concerns and problems of team pressure became an issue at CAMI following the implementation of a clause in the 1995 contract that provided for workers who suffered work-related injury or disablement to return to work by trying out on multiple jobs, with a provision if necessary to stay on just one job. Of the four injured women and one injured man who have tried this option, three of the women reported that when they were unable to rotate through all the jobs on their team they were pressured by other team members to such a degree that they went on medical leave for stress. The three women PAs, in consultation with the union, subsequently lodged a complaint under the Human Rights Code. Part of their complaint charged that the concept of teams at CAMI was responsible for their predicament, since teams pitted worker against worker.

Other Gender Issues and Union-Management Relations

Management and the union at CAMI, as well as at other workplaces in Canada and the United States, have had to respond to public policy guidelines and some legislation designed to advance the status of women and minorities and bring about greater equity in the workplace. In the United States, for example, pressures placed on transplants included complaints to the Equal Employment Opportunity Commission (EEOC) concerning a 30-mile hiring radius that was alleged to have adversely affected the recruitment of black workers at the Honda plant in Marysville, Ohio. Fucini and Fucini (1990:117) report that Honda "has paid $6.5 million to settle various Equal Employment Opportunity Commission complaints since opening its American plant."

In April 1996, the EEOC launched a lawsuit over allegations of sexual harassment at the Mitsubishi plant at Normal, Illinois.[10] In this case, the U.S. federal agency sued the company for allegedly "creating a hostile and abusive work environment" for its female employees (Chappell 1996b:42). The suit was launched after "a 15-month investigation of sexual harassment at Mitsubishi found as many as 500 of the 893 women in the plant victims of 'unwanted groping, grabbing, and touching'; threats of job loss if they refused sexual favors or complained; 'sexually derogatory' comments; and sexual graffiti that sometimes named specific women" (Moody 1996:1).

The Mitsubishi case produced a storm of controversy over the role of the plant's management, both for its alleged failure to act in the past, and for the campaign of protest orchestrated by the company in response to the allegations. Also interesting was the suggestion that neither UAW Local 2488, the union representing Mitsubishi workers, nor the UAW International made any special effort to address this problem "despite knowing for two years that the EEOC was investigating an epidemic of sexual harassment cases" (Moody 1996:14). To date this is the most prominent case of sexual harassment to appear at a lean production auto plant.

At CAMI, both management and the union agreed on a definition of harassment that followed Section 4(a) of the Ontario Human Rights Code. The Human Rights officer of the union summarized the policy as follows: "The CAW and CAMI both have a zero tolerance policy towards human rights violations. When CAMI is made aware of situations of harassment, the discipline issued by Employee Relations can range from education of the individual to termination of employment" (*Off the Line,* Dec. 1996).

During interviews at CAMI, we asked if concerns had been raised over problems of sexual harassment and the policies in place. On both questions there appeared to be no difference in the responses of CAMI managers, individual workers, and the local union leadership. One work-

10. Mitsubishi Motor Manufacturing of America Corporation's car plant was formerly a joint venture between Chrysler and Mitsubishi and was known as Diamond Star, but Chrysler terminated the arrangement in 1991. The facility has since been Mitsubishi's only North American production source.

er recounted her experience: "It depends on the team leader and the guys on the team. You get jokes. I was getting harassed, but I talked to my union rep".

A woman area leader also acknowledged cases of harassment within teams: "I've had some problems. I had to talk to a team about harassment. I had to clarify it with them. I had to tell them what it meant, what it meant to them, and what it meant to the woman. You know, we had a team that hadn't had a woman for a long time, and she went into that team. So I've dealt with that. It's hard for a woman that's never worked in that environment to go into an environment and have it poisoned. Because it was a poisoned environment." The area leader reported that the union knew about the specific problem and proved helpful in resolving it. "They're very supportive on those issues," she added, confirming reports from both management and workers that in attempts to deal with sexual harassment the company and the union appeared to have a good working relationship.

Other special concerns to women workers, such as the difficulties of overtime for women with young children noted by both Fucini and Fucini (1990) at the Mazda plant and by Gottfried and Graham (1993) at the SIA plant, were found at CAMI. The last two authors relate an instance of a collective refusal when SIA management in the non-union plant scheduled overtime without advance notice. Gender-specific subcultures formed over the issue, since most of the men "did not experience overtime as a conflict with gender expectations or family obligations" (Gottfried and Graham 1993: 622). At CAMI both male and female PAs agreed that last-minute *cancellation* of scheduled overtime tended to affect women workers with children more adversely, especially single mothers, who may have made special childcare arrangements. A contract clause protecting CAMI workers from having to perform overtime without notice may help to explain why specific gendered subcultures do not appear to have developed to the same extent at CAMI.[11]

Female representation in CAW Local 88 leadership positions has increased gradually since the local was established in 1989. By the fourth

---

11. The collective agreement specifies that due notice must be given for required overtime, but it allows management the discretion to cancel previously scheduled overtime.

round of interviews one woman held a leadership position, with several women in alternate positions. In 1992, the union's national office began leadership training for women and visible-minority members, designed to complement the national women's conference and the conference on human rights that the union organized annually (Sugiman 1993:183). Such policies may have helped increase the number of women who have subsequently served on the local union executive and in-plant committee. Furthermore, the 1995 collective agreement provided for a part-time Employment Equity and Human Rights Representative to be selected by the union.

The Struggle for Sustainable and Equitable Work

Despite CAMI management's initial willingness to hire women, and despite the views of a clear majority of workers of both sexes that the company did not discriminate in allocating women to jobs in the plant, there is little basis to believe that lean production is intrinsically more favorable than mass production to the development of an equitable workplace. To the contrary, some evidence suggests that the more egregious features of work intensification under lean production may affect women more severely. Furthermore, the example of intra-team tension described in this chapter suggests that the model of teams fostered by CAMI may exacerbate tensions along gender lines whenever some work tasks become too difficult or overburdened for some members of the team. Such tensions might sometimes be resolved within the team, but many situations require an openness by the company to the intelligent redesign of jobs that may disadvantage women.

Although the workers we interviewed did not see gender-related tensions as a major problem at CAMI, a number of union and collective bargaining initiatives in support of employment equity appeared to be bringing about arrangements more compatible with the interests of both sexes. Although some observers have expressed reservations about the way seniority systems can operate against women (e.g., Creese 1995), at CAMI the institution of seniority was unequivocally supported by women and men. Other measures to improve the working conditions of both men and women that found union support included job redesign, the negotiation of production standards, and rotation schedules. According to their union, sustainable work for CAMI workers means jobs that are designed to be performed safely on an ongoing basis, with or without rotation, by men or by women, and by young workers as well as those closer to retirement age.

CHAPTER 9

The Kaizen Agenda

W HILE TAYLOR STROVE TO REMOVE ALL MENTAL COMPONENTS from a worker's job and Ford's ideal was to have one worker repeatedly perform a single operation, the Japanese are credited with rediscovering intelligence on the shop floor and reuniting the conception and execution of work through a process known as kaizen.[1] Wood (1989:454) views this "attempt to harness the tacit skills and latent talents of workers" as the "striking characteristic" of Japanese management, and Kenney and Florida (1993:15) call kaizen its "cornerstone." Kenney and Florida (1993:4) call the Japanese system "innovation-mediated production," a term that highlights the centrality of a kaizen process that produces a "powerful synthesis of intellectual and manual labor." "The central role played by worker initiative and the use of workers' knowledge contradicts the view that the Japanese model is simply an extension of Fordist mass production. It lends support to the alternative conceptualization

---

1. Kenney and Florida (1993:41) find the roots of kaizen in Japan in the post–World War II period, when employers implemented procedures to collect information on problems causing worker dissatisfaction and radical demands for reform. This initiative, so reminiscent of the extensive interviewing undertaken at the Chicago Hawthorne Works by Elton Mayo and his associates, was over time transformed into a process for soliciting workers' ideas on improving production.

that it is a new and potential successor model based upon harnessing workers' intellectual and physical capabilities" (Florida and Kenney 1991:388).[2]

Lean production adherents view kaizen not only as a source of continuous productivity and quality improvements but also as a process that empowers and motivates workers, who are given the opportunity to apply their know-how on a daily basis. Womack, Jones, and Roos (1990:102) describe the lean workplace as an environment where workers "think continuously of ways to make the system run smoothly and productively." When workers hold back their know-how and commitment, the MIT group argue, the major advantage of lean production is lost.

In discussing lean production in transplants, especially NUMMI, Shimada and MacDuffie (1987:15) write that "workers, rather than managers or engineers, have control over the specification of work methods, and revise them constantly, based on their daily production experience." They maintain (1987:16) that "workers are free to make revisions in work methods and modifications in equipment design and configuration which make the job easier for them to carry out, as well as changes which are more clearly related to boosting productivity." This turns workers into minor industrial engineers, breaks down barriers between engineers and workers, and transforms the contentious process of setting job standards into a consensual activity (MacDuffie 1988:16).

Adler (1993a, 1993b) describes NUMMI as a "learning bureaucracy" whose core is the win-win process of kaizen. Adler and Cole (1993:89) attribute NUMMI's excellent vehicle quality ratings to kaizen, arguing that "constant improvement is the key to productivity and quality in a product as standardized as an automobile." Workers benefit because they, not industrial engineers, are routinely involved in establishing and refining work standards. Kaizen, then, transforms "despotic Taylorism" into "democratic Taylorism" and can "humanize even the most disciplined forms of bureaucracy" (Adler 1993a:98).

Kaizen, then, allegedly empowers workers, increases their job satisfaction and morale, and encourages diligent work performance. Adler

2. These authors repeatedly describe kaizen as a mechanism that "harnesses" workers' know-how. This brings to mind a team of horses yoked together by a driver who limits the movement and direction of the beasts.

(1993b:165) maintains that kaizen is recognized by workers as a "productive technique . . . in their own collective interests."[3] NUMMI workers, we are told, quickly bought into kaizen, as evidenced by their high rate of participation in the suggestion program and by selected interviews. A NUMMI manager, for example, states: "They understood the technique because it [standardizing jobs] had been done to them for years, and they liked the idea because now they had a chance to do it themselves" (Adler 1993a:104). Kaizen "is not designed to squeeze more work out of employees . . ." Instead, it can "fuel a continuous improvement of efficiency and quality without intensifying work beyond workers' capabilities" (Adler and Cole 1993:90-91). Adler (1993b:160) qualifies this very favorable characterization of kaizen by acknowledging that "at least some employees" viewed the process and its results not as "alienating but as a motivating feature of their work environment."

Even reading these reports on their own terms raises questions about kaizen's liberatory impact on workers. The production process used in transplants is patterned after their Japanese parent companies', and the details are worked out in the front office, not on the shop floor (Wood 1989:19). How much space do NUMMI workers have, for example, to establish and refine work methods in a production system modeled after the one in Toyota's Takaoka plant? Shimada and MacDuffie (1987:15) acknowledge that kaizen operates within the boundaries of production standards and work methods established by engineering requirements: "Worker control is limited to the area of work methods and even there is constrained by the parameters of the production process as a whole." Self-management under lean production, the authors recognize, "means something quite different from workers' autonomy envisioned in blueprints for industrial democracy." It is also difficult to reconcile Adler's (1993b:176) praise for the humanizing impact of kaizen and his depic-

---

3. This assertion is based on workers' recognition that their job security depends on the firm's competitiveness and on the assumption that workers take pride in doing a job in the most effective way, even if this means reductions in team size. Adler echoes the pop psychology of Monden on this latter point. Reductions in the workforce might appear to be antagonistic to workers' human dignity, Monden (1983:131) opines. "However, allowing the worker to take it easy or giving him high wages does not necessarily provide him an opportunity to realize his worth. On the contrary, that end can be better served by providing the worker with a sense that his work is worthwhile and allowing him to work with his superior and his comrades to solve the problems they encounter."

tion of NUMMI as an emergent form of "industrial democracy" with his own admission that "workers at NUMMI did not have very much individual power over their own work, nor did production teams exercise much autonomous power . . ." If workers do not have much power individually or as a group, in what sense can kaizen be considered to have empowered them? One wonders how typical is the NUMMI worker who observed: "A lot of times the team simply isn't involved or even consulted on standardized work" (Adler, 1993b:153).

Adler (1993b:113) writes: "NUMMI's system of standardized work was very close to Frederick Taylor's ideals. Each gesture was analyzed as scientifically as possible, the optimum sequence was selected and everyone performing the task had to employ the prescribed sequence." Consequently, jobs at NUMMI are rigidly standardized with an average cycle time of 60 seconds. This standardized base is the starting point for kaizen, whose "resulting job designs are very Tayloristic in their narrow scope and gesture-by-gesture regimentation" (Adler and Cole, 1993:86).

Adler and Cole (1993:91) state that kaizen is not set up to squeeze more work from workers, but then they say kaizen does not intensify work beyond workers' capabilities. These are two very different statements. The second one is an admission that kaizen does indeed intensify work—only not beyond what workers can handle. In any case, one wonders how work that is beyond workers' capabilities could be completed under any system. It is to Adler's (1993a:100) credit that he does cite several critical NUMMI workers, one of whom underscores labor intensification as an outcome of kaizen: "We're supposed to go to management and tell them when we have extra seconds to spare. Why would I do that when all that will happen is that they'll take my spare seconds away and work me even harder than before?" Even Kenney and Florida (1993:271), whose praise for kaizen borders on the evangelical, acknowledge that under this process "workers are called upon to increase their own rate and pace of work."

As for kaizen's impact on productivity at NUMMI, Adler and Cole's (1993) argument lacks a firm empirical foundation. Berggren (1994) points out that a valid assessment of the relationship between kaizen and output requires a research design that entails collecting data over several points in time. Adler and Cole had no such information. Moreover, Toyota is known for producing vehicles that are easy to manufacture. The original vehicles (Novas) made at NUMMI were designed and previously produced by Toyota. Adler and Cole (1993:93) acknowledge in a footnote that NUMMI's high productivity and quality are "strongly influenced" by Toyota's superior manufacturability. How, then, are we to interpret the authors' claims for the integral contributions of workers to NUMMI's productivity?[4]

Several studies of transplants have challenged the view that kaizen is a democratic form of Taylorism that empowers workers. Based on their observations of transplants and interviews with key informants, Parker and Slaughter (1988:19) conclude that kaizen translates into super-Taylorism. They emphasize that management dictates "the processes, basic production layout, and techniques to be used. These in turn largely determine job requirements and design."

A participant observation study of the Subaru-Isuzu (SIA) plant near Lafayette, Indiana, revealed that management dominated the kaizen process from start to finish. Instead of empowering workers, involvement in kaizen reinforced their subordination. Management "tightly controlled the topics that could be raised for consideration," as well as when, where, and how suggestions were implemented (Graham 1993:148).

Studies of the Mazda plant in Flat Rock, Michigan, also exposed an underside to kaizen. Fucini and Fucini (1990:161) question workers' acceptance of kaizen as well as who benefits from the process. Mazda workers initially endorsed kaizen, but "when it became obvious . . . that their suggestions were only increasing their own workloads, enthusiasm for *kaizen* all but disappeared." Babson's (1993) survey of Mazda workers revealed that suggestions from the floor, which were carefully screened by managers and engineers, were approved only when they met productivity and cost-down objectives. As time passed, job standards increasingly originated with and were imposed by management with little or no consultation. This finding is consistent with the disclosure that special kaizen teams of engineers, supervisors, and team

4. Roughly 80 percent of the cost of a vehicle originates outside the assembly plant. Just as productivity is affected largely by vehicle size and design and by production technology and processes implemented by industrial engineers—not workers—so too is vehicle quality heavily dependent on the performance of parts suppliers. This is not to say that workers' kaizen efforts can make no contribution to increasing productivity, cutting costs, and minimizing defects. However, from an overall performance standpoint, assembly workers' kaizen contributions are relatively limited.

leaders were operating at Mazda (Fucini and Fucini 1990). Workers reported not only that management undertook job changes unilaterally but also that the changes made the work harder.

Cole (1979:201) indicated over a decade ago that these departures from "democratic Taylorism" are not simply North American aberrations. Looking at Toyota Auto Body in Japan, he described managers' "firm control of the innovative process." Management initiated the problem-solving agenda pursued by workers and rigorously controlled and guided their "activities into channels which flow toward the achievement of basic management goals" (Cole 1979:217). Cole (1989) maintains that participation enhances management power in Japan, whereas in Sweden unions use it to advance workers' interests.

In his study of 48 medium-size and large Japanese companies producing everything from textiles to cars, Marsh (1992) concluded that the much vaunted participatory decision making of the Japanese firm obscures the distinction between who submits and who decides to implement suggestions. Implementation is an *exclusive* management prerogative, and in most cases the sole preserve of upper-level managers. More importantly, recent research indicates that Japanese workers' involvement in kaizen is also minimal. Wood (1989, 1993), who once considered kaizen a partial transcendence of Taylorism, later concluded that foremen and supervisors in Japanese plants are the key figures in the kaizen process. This point is made even more emphatically in a paper by Nemoto cited in Nonaka and Sasaki (1993). According to Nemoto, in Japan 80 to 90 percent of all kaizen activity is undertaken by team leaders and foremen!

The lines of the debate are clearly drawn. Does kaizen democratize Taylorism, or is it a process whose parameters of participation preclude genuine worker empowerment? Do the outcomes of kaizen mutually benefit workers and the company, or do they serve only corporate interests? CAMI provides fertile ground for assessing these questions. CAMI's kaizen efforts probably rank at or near the top of North American auto transplants. After touring North American transplants, Berggren (1993) concluded that CAMI led all others in the submission of suggestions. As CAMI President Ikuma told guests and employees at Partners' Appreciation Day in May 1990, "Kaizen is forever, and this company value will guide our future activities." Whatever else might be said about CAMI's adherence to its own values, the company's dedication to the kaizen program is beyond dispute.

Kaizen at CAMI

The CAMI Training Manual makes the point that the only way to secure profits in the competitive world of vehicle manufacturing is to cut production costs (rather than raising car prices or increasing market share). In the language of Japanese production management, this translates into kaizen, or the continuous incremental improvement of the production process. Kaizen, the manual explains, is achieved through the "process of searching out waste, eliminating it, then deploying the resources made available to a more productive task." Waste is defined as anything not essential to the operation. Any activity that does not directly add value to the product is waste. Installing a bumper is value added, but walking to pick up the bumper is waste. Forms of waste are idle time, producing defective parts, and excessive transport, movement, inventory, inspection, and processing. It is not the dramatic innovations that CAMI counts on. As an instructor told a group of trainees, "Base hits win ballgames."

CAMI recruits, who have not yet had a taste of what it is like to make cars, receive classroom kaizen lessons. The instructor in one 1990 session (who was trained as an industrial engineer) informed the class that kaizen was a reversal of Taylorism because workers have input into their jobs and the way work is organized. Another instructor hammered home the theme that "kaizen comes from everybody's ideas." This notion is spelled out, explained, and practiced. The following exercise, representing a die change in a stamping press, was part of a kaizen training session.

Three brick-sized blocks of wood are stacked and fastened together with two long bolts and topped with washers and nuts. The middle block represents a die. Although it can be put in place in a variety of ways (left to right, top to bottom, etc.), there is only one correct way that allows all the blocks to align properly. The task is to dismantle the blocks, take the middle one out, and then reassemble them. The group of 12 students is divided into teams of two, with the exception of one person who is identified as a quality auditor and another who has a stopwatch. Each team comes to the front of the room and is given a few minutes to decide how to do the job.

A person from the first team initially unlocks both nuts with the wrench, then holds the assembly while the other worker uses both hands to spin the nuts off the bolts. The other teams watch, incorporate the good techniques, avoid the pitfalls, and add their own innovations. Team 1 comes in at 69.5 centiminutes: a round of applause. Team 2 makes a good time but needs a quality adjustment—a penalty of 15 centiminutes is imposed. Another round of applause and some good-natured jibes. Team 3 registers 77.25 centiminutes. The competition continues. The best time is 59 centiminutes. It is a good time that, under the circumstances, is probably impossible to beat.

But now comes the punch line. Their best was not good enough. The instructor says the goal is to get the time down to 15 centiminutes. Around the room are expressions of disbelief and some dismay. Their best time was four times that! This is the message of kaizen. No matter how well they did, they can and must do better.

In contrast to traditional factories, CAMI does not have an industrial engineering (IE) department. Kaizen is the responsibility of all employees. In theory, each work team serves as its own IE department. As one manager said, "Our philosophy is that engineers can't possibly know as much about the jobs as the people that are doing them." Another manager remarked: "We have 26 different competitors and the only way that we can get better than them is that we need the ideas of every individual in the organization. We need the ideas of the people on the floor. Otherwise, we're just not going to be able to make it down the road."

CAMI maintains that kaizen benefits both workers and the company. Management's reasoning goes beyond the claim that job security is linked to company profitability; kaizen is also said to make jobs easier and safer. However, the ultimate goal of kaizen is not safe, easy jobs, but to produce with the absolute minimum of workers. (In his exposition of the Toyota production system, Monden (1983:123) writes, "Remember that the purpose of any improvement is to reduce the number of workers.") The Kaizen Report Book kept by team leaders, area leaders, and production managers emphasizes the continuous reduction of cycle time through time study and line rebalancing. The book describes a hypothetical five-person team in which each worker needs a slightly different amount of time to complete his or her job. The team leader repeatedly times the jobs, discusses the results with and gets input from the team, and then evens out the workloads of four persons, leaving the fifth with little to do. The lesson continues: "Then, as a next step, improve E's [the fifth person's] operation so his man-hour is eliminated [that is, drop him from the team]. If not eliminated, he should be given additional jobs. What is important in assigning operations, each associate should be given jobs up to 100 percent cycle time."

This example reveals that line rebalancing, which is often done by teams, is part of a top-level strategy to reduce continuously the number of workers needed to handle a given amount of work. The objective of eliminating manpower is also illustrated in the CAMI Training Manual, which shows a group of workers waving good-bye to a co-worker, following what is described as a team effort at kaizen. After all, the manual reminds, "kaizen must always be tied to concrete cost reductions."

There is more to kaizen than reducing costs, however. When asked how CAMI evaluates the effectiveness of its suggestion programs, one manager maintained that there was no cost or quality measure of success. The only standard of success was the degree of participation. "This comes from the president, and I think it's pretty good counsel. You want to try to get people to feel their ideas are worth something, and it's very easy to say no all the time. So when you get a suggestion that might not be acceptable, what is a way that you can find so that you can make it acceptable, because that way a person will continue to participate and feel good about that."

As this statement suggests, kaizen is at the heart of CAMI's campaign to convince workers that they have the capacity to make important decisions. The kaizen process (including the QC circle and suggestion programs) is a means of instilling in the workforce a sense of empowerment, an attitude that can reduce workers' likelihood of resisting, stimulate their initiative and effort, and commit them to the company. The programs CAMI has implemented to realize continuous improvement, a manager declared, are "part of the empowerment process"[5]: "We've hired

5. Monden (1983:126) believes the real purpose of many suggestion programs is to nurture company loyalty and pride among employees. However, he argues that the primary objective of Toyota's suggestion programs is to tap know-how on the shop floor, although the company, Monden says, is not oblivious to the psychological import of these programs.

people for their brains as well as their brawn. Nowadays the workforce is not going to feel fulfilled if you just come in and tell them what to do. Our philosophy is that the engineers can't possibly know as much about the jobs as the people that are doing them. If you feel you really are empowered, you have some ability to control what you do and how you do it, you're going to walk out of this place feeling a lot better about yourself at the end of the day."

This statement is consistent with human relations theory, which holds that workers' participation in decision making eliminates potential resistance and develops identification with and commitment to the company. Participation, then, is a way of manufacturing consent in the workplace.[6]

The Suggestion Programs

Vehicles for the realization of kaizen include the informal passing of ideas to team leaders, team discussions, and formal suggestion (teian) and QC circle programs. CAMI recruits learn about QC circles as part of their classroom training, but only team leaders and area leaders receive more intensive instruction on QC circles. They are taught, in the words of one manager, "how to sell problem solving."

The aim of the QC circle program, the Employee Handbook states, is to make work easier and safer, remove mistakes, increase efficiency, and reduce costs. The handbook also says teians can contribute to building morale, improving human relations, and strengthening team spirit. The handbook makes it clear that PAs engage in QC circles on their own time—before work, during lunch, or after work. (This practice differs from that prevailing in Japan, where QC circles generally meet on company time.)

6. Employers' attempts to cultivate committed workforces through worker participation are not peculiarly Japanese. This was an objective of the North American employee representation plans (company unions) and works councils that appeared in the early twentieth century, as well as of the human relations studies conducted by Elton Mayo and his associates in the 1920s and 1930s at a branch of AT&T in Chicago. In 1948, an influential experimental study by Coch and French helped persuade "progressive" executives of the link between worker participation and commitment. The study found that prior consultation with workers muted their resistance and committed them to heavier workloads with no extra pay. The manipulative thrust of the study is suggested by its title, "Overcoming Resistance to Change." For a critical discussion of the participative management school see Rinehart (1996:167–171).

The handbook provides guidelines on how to conduct meetings, how to interact in a group setting, and what steps to take in detecting and resolving problems. These guidelines originated with Toyota, were borrowed from NUMMI, and given a Suzuki twist. The handbook says good QC goals are clear, explicit, and measurable in terms of efficiency improvement, attendance improvement, and defect reduction. The experience of a QC circle in a Suzuki plant in Thailand is used as an example, showing the steps circle members took to solve a cost problem, the procedures they followed, and the outcomes of their deliberations. The resolution of the Thai problem involved workers pressuring each other to use their gloves longer, take better care of them, and spend time cleaning them.

Like other QC circle training formats, CAMI's examples are aimed at persuading workers to view workplace problems from the company's perspective (Parker 1985; Rinehart 1984). Workers are urged to think in terms of cost-cutting, to share their ideas with the company rather than using them to lighten their own workloads, and to press their coworkers to attend work faithfully, be cost conscious, and so on. Ideally, QC circles are driven by workers, but workers and one manager told us that area leaders, assistant managers, and department managers do push certain themes and sometimes provide the solutions.

CAMI goes to great lengths to cultivate participation. This emphasis is consistent with President Ikuma's conviction that these programs will assure the success of the plant's operation. While the teian program is voluntary, every employee below the level of assistant manager is expected to submit at least five teians a month. It is commonly believed on the shop floor that active involvement in CAMI's voluntary programs is necessary to receive privileges and to get ahead. A team leader said one of the most frequent complaints he receives from PAs "is the push and shove and guilt trip on voluntary items such as QC circles." Even a manager complained that "you're judged on how many teians are put in your department, how many QC circles."

On CAMI teian forms, employees state the nature of the problem (what, where, when), the suggested solution, and its effects (including cost to implement). There are also teian approval forms, teian record transfer sheets, monthly teian report forms, departmental team summary sheets, teian audit sheets, and one form on which each individual's teian activity is recorded, complete with number, savings per month, and point awards.

A worker who submits a teian gets 50 cents (or a coupon worth this amount), and if the teian is approved (but not necessarily implemented) the submitter receives an additional 50 cents or a coupon. Coupons can be exchanged for cash or used in the company cafeteria. Teians that save CAMI money are slotted into 10 classes, ranging from monthly savings of $5,000 or more down to less than $100. For each of the 10 classes the team receives a cash award, ranging from $500 to nothing, and the individual suggester receives teian points ranging from 500 to five. For teians that are implemented but do not save money, the team receives no prize money, but the individual submitter receives 50 points for an "outstanding" idea, 25 points for an "excellent" teian, and five points for a "good" one. Teian points can be accumulated and traded for products listed in a popular retail store catalog. For 186 points—the equivalent of 37 "good" suggestions—one can, for example, purchase a Bulova wall clock. If a worker amasses 10,000 points, they can be turned in for a CAMI car.

Each month, the company president personally awards the teian cup to a department, based on the number of suggestions submitted. And at the end of each year, people with the highest (implemented) teian point totals receive bronze, silver, gold, or platinum plaques and cash awards up to $1,000. Five of the year's top 10 teian submitters are selected for a two-week study trip to Japan.

Management continually invents new incentives for handing in teians, giving the program the appearance of a workplace lottery. Teams with excellent teian records are treated to free pizza at the end of the month. Team recognition dinners are held. In one department, at the end of each month the person with the most teians gets the use of a Tracker for a weekend. And teian points may now be exchanged for a microwave oven for the team rest area.[7]

Potentially valuable teians (savings of $1,000 or more a month) must be approved by high-level managers, but minor suggestions (small, cost-free changes in work sequence, for example) can be quickly reviewed by

---

7. Using microwaves as an incentive was inspired by skilled tradesmen who brought their own oven into the plant. Management objected, but the workers prevailed. Instead of continuing to contest this issue, management incorporated microwaves into the teian incentive system.

low-level managers and implemented by teams. This fast-track implementation of teians distinguishes CAMI's system from standard suggestion programs.

CAMI sponsors an annual rally for QC circles, at which circle members present their best innovations and compete for cash prizes. The winning circle gets a free trip to Japan, where it vies with QC circles from Suzuki plants around the world.

CAMI has instituted an elaborate set of procedures and programs to encourage workers to continuously improve operations and to give workers a feeling of empowerment that will commit them to the company and its objectives. The next chapter discusses workers' evaluations of and involvement in the participatory programs, the number and character of workers' suggestions, and some conflictual consequences of kaizen.

CHAPTER 10

Kaizen: Shop Floor Responses and Outcomes

Levels of Participation

*A*CCORDING TO COMPANY RECORDS, CAMI'S OFFICE AND SHOP FLOOR employees submitted 106,451 suggestions in 1990. This averaged out to 68 teians per employee, or over five per person each month. The company claimed to have implemented about three-quarters of these teians, and another one-fifth were approved or under evaluation. Between December 1991 and May 1992, the same monthly average of five teians per employee was maintained. Between May 1990 and April 1991, 1,230 office and production workers were active in 149 QC circles, although for the entire year of 1991 the participation rate on the shop floor was only 35 percent. Survey data throw additional light on these figures.

In round 1, 55.6 percent of workers in our sample said they belonged to a QC circle, and a remarkably high 84.9 percent reported involvement in the teian program. By our second visit, people had less time to spend writing up teians or attending meetings because the plant was running at full capacity; participation in the QC circle and teian programs dropped to 45.5 percent and 71.3 percent respectively. The level of circle involvement dropped off to 38 percent in round 4 (see Figure

FIGURE I. Percentage of respondents who belonged to a QC circle.

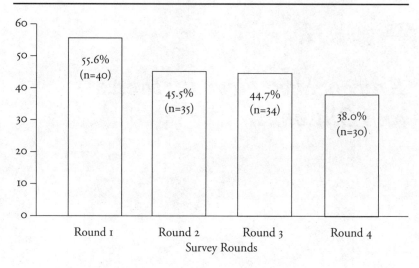

1).[1] Support for the teian program continued to erode, and by the final round participation stood at 45.6 percent (see Figure 2). Growing disenchantment with teians was also shown by answers to the question, "Do you think everyone should participate in the suggestion program?" In the first round, over half (58.6 percent) thought everyone should hand in teians. This percentage dropped sharply to 28.9 in round 2, and by the final interview only 17.6 percent felt everyone should participate (see Figure 3).

Statistics on numbers of participants do not reveal reasons for workers' involvement. Is participation related to a sense of empowerment and commitment to CAMI, or is it reluctant, half-hearted, or cynical? When asked in the first round, "Is there any pressure to participate in QC circles?" Forty percent replied yes. One worker said her team was paid $1 for attending QC meetings during lunch, and "if you're not there, there is trouble." Another worker said that when the line goes down, you have a choice—attend meetings or clean the area. Team and area leaders were

1. The apparent discrepancy between company statistics and survey results regarding participation can be partially explained by the fact that the company tallied suggestions of both office and shop floor workers, and there was no indication of declining office worker participation in the programs. Moreover, since the company figures were based on number of teians submitted rather than on number of participants, it is possible that a declining number of participants could have submitted an increasing number of teians.

FIGURE 2. Percentage of respondents who submitted suggestions.

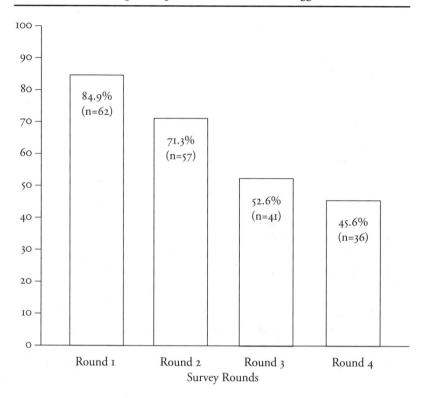

FIGURE 3. Percentage of respondents who thought everyone should submit suggestions.

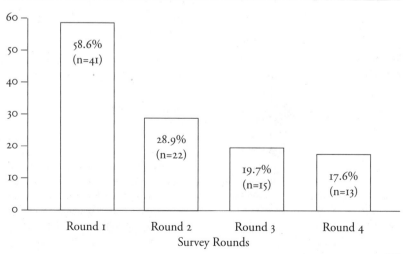

cited as the source of the pressure. In round 2 we asked those who participated in QC circles if they did so a) because they thought it was a good idea, b) due to pressure, or c) for other reasons. Reports of pressure had declined substantially in round 2, and by the fourth round only 11 percent cited this as a reason. As time passed, pressure to hand in teians also dropped off. When asked, "How often does your team leader pressure you to submit suggestions?" 38.7 per cent in round 1 and 86.3 per cent in the final round said "never." The decline in pressure probably reflected assurances from the local union and the union newsletter that participation was purely voluntary and the union would stand behind those who refused. In addition, the union's clarification of the team leader role and its insistence that team leaders not assume managerial duties, which would include pressing participation on workers, undoubtedly contributed to easing the pressure.

The percentage of participants who took part because they felt the circles were a good idea dropped from 46 in the second round to 35 in the last round, while "other reasons" were cited by 41 and 54 percent of the participants in rounds 2 and 4 respectively. When we asked respondents for clarification of their reasons, over half in round 2 and just under a third in round 4 said circles solved problems important to workers, such as infrequent job rotation and unbalanced, difficult, unsafe jobs. In round 4, 12 percent said they participated because there was nothing else to do or just to go along with the team (down from 31 percent in round 2). As one worker explained, "I'm sitting at the table playing cards and it [circle meeting] happens to go on around me." By the final round, the most frequent explanation for participation was the lure of cash and prizes (56 percent in round 4 compared with only 15 percent in round 1). While a core of workers participated based on the conviction that QC circles were useful and solved important problems, for an increasing number the rationale shifted to one that entailed calculation or, as one worker put it, "using the system."[2]

2. Burawoy (1979) would interpret playing the system in this manner as having the effect of generating workers' consent to their own exploitation. Workers who perceive *they* are making decisions, however limited, acquire a sense of empowerment that obscures their subordinate position, and this binds them to the company and its objectives. It was our impression that workers who used the system to achieve their ends were under no illusions about their subordination, and they expressed little or no commitment to the company.

The following exchange between a team leader and an interviewer sheds light on what happens at some circle meetings and workers' reasons for participating.

Q: What do you do with the QC circles?

A: Mickey Mouse things.

Q: Only Mickey Mouse? Why do you have them?

A: It's the money [$1 per person per meeting]. It's like the teians.

Q: So what do you talk about at QC circles?

A: Like I said, we do stupid ones, like changing team names. That's to up the morale.

Q: Who sets the agenda in QC circles?

A: We don't. They [management] have an agenda that's already set. But we don't follow it. We have a meeting, write the meeting up, and that's what they get for their QC circle.

Participation and Empowerment

Companies set up QC circle and suggestion programs to cut costs and raise productivity and to develop in workers a sense of empowerment that will commit them to the firm. QC circles, Lincoln and Kalleberg (1990:95) state, are "clearly aimed at increasing the workers' sense of participation in shop floor decisions and control over operations and through these mechanisms commitment and morale." Several questions allowed us to draw conclusions about the relationship of participation and empowerment.

In round 1, 89.5 percent of PAs in our sample said they had a say in the way they did their jobs all the time or often. By round 4, the percentage who answered this way had declined to 60.7. When asked to state in what way they had a say, the most common reason given was the ability to perform the job in one's own way. The percentage who advanced this reason increased from 39 in round 1 to 63 in round 4. Only a small minority in any of the four rounds attributed job control to the teian or QC circle programs. (This capacity to individualize the way one did the job ran counter to CAMI's emphasis on strict enforce-ment of work standards, as discussed later in this chapter.)

Another question asked, "Are you actively involved in making deci-sions at work?" The percentages answering yes in rounds 1 and 4 respec-tively were 54.2 and 33.8. When asked to explain why they said yes, a steadily increasing proportion of respondents referred to decisions re-lated to their immediate jobs (31 percent in round 1 and 69 percent in round 4). Less than 10 percent in round 4 considered teians or QC cir-cles as the sources of their capacity to make decisions.

These responses indicate that most workers' sense of empowerment is quite limited. When there is some perceived discretion, it takes the form of having the capacity to make small-scale adjustments to one's immediate work area, or to perform a job in one's own way. It is ironic that workers' sense of empowerment, however limited, was based not on their involvement in kaizen but on *deviations* from the lean pro-duction ideal of total adherence to standards. It appears, then, that one of the objectives of participation is not being met at CAMI. The sug-gestion programs have enlisted a relatively high level of involvement. However, if workers do not regard teians and QC circles as empow-ering, these programs can hardly be expected to commit workers to CAMI and its objectives.

The very limited feeling of control that CAMI workers get from par-ticipation is based on a realistic assessment. QC circle and suggestion programs are implemented by management for management's purposes. Even Lincoln and Kalleberg (1990:14), who are advocates of the forms of participation associated with Japanese management, acknowledge that QC circles "diffuse responsibility and commit workers to organizational decisions, *without producing significant alterations in the governance struc-ture of the firm*" (our emphasis). Although CAMI's programs appear to be more flexible than most, they remain firmly under management con-trol. Like other participatory programs in North America and Japan, CAMI's give workers a voice but not a vote. Workers can make sugges-tions, but what happens to the suggestions is entirely in the hands of management. Of course, workers can join together to pressure man-agement to accept their recommendations, as has sometimes happened at CAMI, but this takes determination, solidarity, and organization. In contrast, management's capacity to determine the disposition of suggestions ordinarily is taken for granted, automatic, and effortless.

Shop Floor Evaluations of Kaizen

Only a minority of team leaders we talked to wholeheartedly endorsed kaizen and the associated participatory programs. One enthusiastic leader reported that his team had had 40 circle meetings over a 12-month period. He proudly described how a QC circle had reduced the time required to perform an operation. Another team leader said, "Speaking for my team, we know where the true sense of security lies and that's in how this place runs. If we're going to compete with Ford and Chrysler, that's how you do it." The comments of a team leader from Assembly indicated he was sold on kaizen: "For us it's no matter how good we have it, we always think we can make it better, which we do." This team leader described how he was always rebalancing the line. Sometimes this involved trades of tasks with other team leaders. "You're constantly negotiating. 'We'll give you this and we'll take this.'" He admitted that his team members were not always pleased with the results and viewed the practice as meddling with their jobs. Still another team leader equated kaizen with working smarter:

> We pretty well have an outline of how many people there are supposed to be at each work station and how many people are supposed to be on each team. Sometimes we might try and reduce steps in a particular job . . . because over an entire day production will be higher if your steps are less and in some cases the production associates won't have to go through so much; they won't get as tired in a full day. Everybody in the team is interested in that. If they create less steps and make the job easier, then your time is more productive. Let's say they were to speed the line up—speed the process up—if you had fewer steps it's going to even out.

The remarks of several other team leaders revealed a qualified acceptance of kaizen, i.e., they endorsed it only when the outcome was unequivocally in workers' interest: "[My team] wasn't really into it [QC circle meetings]. And we got into the rotation, because people were getting hurt. Then everybody got involved, because it was something really to do with everybody. The others [other issues addressed in QC circle meetings] were—how come studs were breaking, or how can we repair them? So like, who cares?"

Some team leaders appeared to be sold on the idea of suggestion programs but believed CAMI's were poorly conceived. A common criticism was too much emphasis on quantity and not enough on quality. As one team leader complained, "We have people who hand in 50 teians a month, and once you start looking at them closely they're ridiculous, stupid." This feeling was echoed by a team leader who said: "I write maybe one every three months. There's other people who write 80 a month, but they're stupid ones . . . If you say, 'put the garbage pail over there' you get 50 cents, so they do it."

In the union newsletter, CAMI was criticized for buying pizzas each month for teams whose members turned in five teians each. This, the article maintained, only generated absurd suggestions: "The buck for these teian and pizza extravaganzas must stop. We are all familiar with the outrageous management-approved teians, such as rotating a garbage pail, removing the dead fish from an aquarium, or everyone's favorite: if it's a hazard, tape it. This has driven our fellow workers to write dozens upon dozens of the most stupid teians imaginable in an effort to milk the system." The solution: greater monetary rewards for good ideas. "Any idea that really reduces costs or prevents accidents is surely worth more than a slice of pizza" (*Off the Line,* Aug. 1990).

The majority of team leaders and union leaders were critical of, or not interested in, the suggestion programs. One team leader viewed the QC program, and particularly the contest for the teian cup, as creating divisions within the workforce. A disillusioned team leader told us that management took two years to act on a suggestion to remedy a problem with an assembly component. Another team leader expressed concern only with production. In his opinion, teians made no contribution to this task.

When asked about QC circles, one team leader remarked: "We don't do any because we hated them. It's like exercising in the morning. We stopped. We said, 'Sorry, no more unless you're going to pay us for it.' They [management] tried to kick up a bit of a stink about it, but we just kept saying, 'You're not paying us for it. It's our free time.'" Another team leader denied that anything got accomplished with QC circles: "To tell you the truth, if we had to get through QC circles to solve everything, we'd be back in the Dark Ages. It just takes too long. People aren't willing to give up their lunch periods, you know, more than once a month. You don't get much accomplished in a half an hour."

A local union official viewed the suggestion programs as beneficial only to the company: "This empowerment, when it's cost saving or quality problems, okay, but when it's human problems, a comfort issue, there's no empowerment. It's one-sided. That's the bottom line." Rob Pelletier, president of Local 88, attacked kaizen in the union newsletter:

> Kaizen is a great idea which is practiced in some form in everybody's life. Whether we're working in our homes or in our yards, pursuing continuing education, reading—improvement is as natural to us as life itself. However, we must always be wary of how easy it is for management to fill up the time we save with our improvements. This sort of continuous redistribution of work costs us jobs and eventually puts such a burden on us that we risk injury from trying to work too quickly, forgetting about safety . . . When practicing kaizen, or writing teians, attack the cost of parts, consumables, or floor space, or improve the safety of your area. If you can figure out a way to do something in less time, keep your secret within the team! This is your time, you've earned it! (*Off the Line,* Feb. 1991).

This advice violates the CAMI-CAW contract, which commits the union to supporting continuous improvement activities.

The union newsletter ran a poem warning that teians benefit only the company and can eliminate jobs. The poem ends with this message:

> Every time we write a teian,
> We only do their work.
> Smarten up, I say—
> Don't accept their JUDAS PAY! (*Off the Line,* June 1991)

A set of survey questions tapped respondents' attitudes and behaviors around kaizen. While CAMI expected workers to use periods when they were not working to deal with production issues, most workers drew a clear line between their time and company time. We asked respondents

TABLE 6.   If you find a way to do your job easier or faster than the specified way, what do you do?

	Round 2		Round 3		Round 4	
	N	%	N	%	N	%
Keep it to yourself	2	4.2%	4	7.4%	5	8.6%
Share it with no one other than a few co-workers	15	31.2%	20	37.0%	29	50.0%
Tell the team leader	13	27.1%	17	31.5%	14	24.1%
Submit a suggestion	18	37.5%	13	24.1%	10	17.3%
Total	48	100.0%	54	100.0%	58	100.0%

Note: Numbers are small because many workers reported they had not found an easier or faster way to do their jobs.

if they regarded lunch break as their personal time or as a good time to go over things and solve problems.[3] In round 2 the great majority (80.8 percent) defined lunch period as personal time, and by the final round the percentage who felt this way had risen to 92.9.

When asked, "If you find a way to do your job that is easier or faster than the specified way, what do you do?" 35.4 percent in round 2 reported that they kept it to themselves or shared it with no one other than a few co-workers, while 64.6 percent said they told the team leader or submitted a suggestion (see Table 6). The first two responses constitute clear deviations from CAMI's expectations, while the second two are consistent with the company's kaizen objectives. By round 4 nearly six of every 10 (58.6 percent) of those who had discovered shortcuts were not sharing their ideas with the company.

When asked, "Which of the following best describes CAMI's efforts at reducing waste and increasing efficiency?" 51.8 percent in round 2 and 60.3 percent in round 4 chose "working harder" over "working smarter"; 82.5 percent in round 2 and 92.3 in round 4 opted for "reducing jobs" over "increasing jobs"; and 77.1 percent in round 2 and 89.9 percent in the final round selected "a more demanding work pace" instead of "a more comfortable work pace" (see Table 7). These figures

3. One manager objected to this question, arguing that it would put ideas in workers' heads.

TABLE 7. Which best describes CAMI's efforts at reducing waste and increasing efficiency?

	Round 2		Round 3		Round 4	
	N	%	N	%	N	%
Working harder	44	51.8%	43	57.3%	47	60.3%
Working smarter	41	48.2%	32	42.7%	31	39.7%
Total	85	100.0%	75	100.0%	78	100.0%
Reducing jobs	66	82.5%	62	84.9%	72	92.3%
Increasing jobs	14	17.5%	11	15.1%	6	7.7%
Total	80	100.0%	73	100.0%	78	100.0%
A more demanding work pace	64 ·	77.1%	62	82.7%	71	89.9%
A more comfortable work pace	19	22.9%	13	17.3%	8	10.1%
Total	83	100.0%	75	100.0%	79	100.0%

reveal that early on a majority of workers were skeptical about the outcomes of kaizen, but as time passed this majority became even larger. More and more people on the shop floor had come to sympathize with the worker who said she regretted kaizening (eliminating) a job from her line, and to share another worker's definition of kaizen as "a polite way to get more out of us."

Kaizen Outcomes: Circle Suggestions

On our first visit to CAMI, a manager described one circle's suggestion as "an incredible win-win situation for them and for the company." This suggestion improved installation of the rear gate on the sports utility vehicle. "It's a big piece of metal. You've got to maneuver it into place and fit it on the hinges. It was causing a lot of back problems for people because it was an awkward job." The QC circle decided to build a small, lightweight aluminum and wood tool to install the door. This eliminated the physical problems and saved production time.

At the 1991 rally, nine QC circles gave presentations. Their documents contained written descriptions and rationales, elaborate fishbone diagrams, bar and pie graphs, and precision drawings of tools, dies, jigs, components, and pallets. Several documents concluded with the words, "We are CAMI. Yosh!" A few examples of the presentations will illustrate their character.

A QC circle from Assembly set their problem as accommodating to an impending increase in line speed. A series of modifications—moving jigs, replacing components, changing tools, and transferring some tasks to another team—enabled the team to handle the new speed. According to the circle's calculations, these changes would save $368,000 in the following year and reduce defects by 72 percent.

One circle reduced paint usage and eliminated two of four paint sprayers (workers) for a projected savings of about $150,000 per year. The solution involved splicing the air line into four pieces and then attaching air lines and guns.

The winning circle from Stamping solved the problem of metal slivers that marred metal finishes and required stopping the presses to clear the dies. A combination of improvements, including a technique to blow the slivers away, new modes of cutting (recommended by engineers), and a revised method of greasing dies, was projected to save the company nearly a quarter of a million dollars annually.

The finalists' reports in the QC circle competition were remarkable for their technical sophistication, thoroughness, and projected results. These outstanding presentations, however, were not typical. Several examples illustrate the character of ordinary suggestions. An assembler suggested using an apron rather than one's hands to carry parts to the line. Problems with gluing a gasket to a car mirror were resolved by a worker's teian that recommended having the supplier firm do it rather than an assembler. On the truck line one worker handled and sorted parts and then attached them to the vehicle. As a result of the team leader's suggestion, the handling and sorting were assigned to one worker, while a second worker simply attached them.

Managers said that the great majority of suggestions (from both programs) did not lead to cost reduction or had no significant impact on cost. Despite this, the company claimed to have saved $10,840,121 as of March 1990 from the ideas of employees.

Local union activists were skeptical of these reported savings. For example, the prize-winning suggestion from Stamping described above turned out to be a dud. Central to this proposal was a modified cutting edge of the trim die. Initially, the adjustment worked, but when the operation reached the required speed, the cutting edge kept breaking, and the slivers returned. We were also told that CAMI's announcements of cost savings arising from suggestions are based on projections, rather than on calculations after a period of time.

Kaizen Outcomes: Standardization

"Adopting standardized operation is the trigger of Kaizen," according to CAMI's Training Manual. "If everyone performs the operations in the same way, potential problems or waste will be easily identified." But according to workers and managers, both codification of standards and adherence to them deviated from CAMI'S prescriptions. As time passed, team leaders increasingly failed to update or enforce the CAMI Operating Standards (COSs), and fewer respondents reported that they performed their jobs in the prescribed manner "all the time" or "often" (60.6 percent in round 1 and 45 percent in round 4). During a third round observation of the truck line, a PA who put in the rear axle said there was a COS for the job, "but I've never seen it." At another work site in Welding, a worker who put the main bracket on the front end and installed the hatch said he had no idea where the COS for this job was located. He had devised his own method of installing the hatch so that it was flush with the right side of the car (otherwise the hatch protruded a bit). He manually put pressure on the left side of the hatch as he installed it. This minor but important adjustment was not recorded on the phantom COS. One team leader referred to COSs as "the silliest things." Another team leader elaborated: "We don't use them [COS standards] that often. I've found that what's good for one person might not be good for another, so I don't expect them to stick to the COS. Like there are some jobs, I know when I do them, if I went by the COS I'd be dead by the end of the day just from the way they are. So I try and keep it so that they do it in the same order, but they can move around within that and do it whatever way they feel more comfortable with. It's totally personal . . . It's fairly close but, like I said, it's not followed to the letter anymore."

Interviews with managers and team leaders suggested that the frequent rotation cycles and relatively large size of teams inhibited the codification of and adherence to standards. Since over a dozen workers (from two shifts) may regularly rotate through the same job, there are individual variations in the way the jobs are performed. Repeated time-studies yield variable standards because the calculations are based on the performance of different workers. Moreover, each team member (on both shifts) must agree to changes in COSs. This makes changing written standards a tedious process that team leaders tend to avoid. Large teams make it difficult for team leaders and area leaders to exercise control over how each person performs a job. Finally, the designed responsiveness of the Suzuki system to changing conditions, product demand, breakdowns, etc., means that "standards" is an empty concept; conditions change so frequently that nothing is ever standard very long.

In response to the drift away from standardization, management had begun, as of our last research visit, a campaign to have teams register all job changes on COSs and to use these specifications as the basis of job performance. In the fall of 1994 CAMI introduced a course on teaching workers how to perform jobs. Based on the assumption that there is one best way to train, the course emphasized worker adherence to standards. As the instruction manual pointed out, "Changes in operation, standards or additional work due to emergencies or accidents" required the training of veterans as well as recruits. Given the importance CAMI attributes to kaizen, the company's renewed emphasis on standardization—the "trigger" of kaizen—is understandable.

Kaizen Outcomes: Conflict

In the early stages of our research, before production reached its peak and as new lines and systems were being developed, there were a series of "leaning" or kaizen periods when teams were involved in industrial engineering tasks—reducing idle time, rebalancing jobs, and sending redundant workers to other teams. A manager boasted that staffing levels of his area were approaching the lean levels of Suzuki's plant in Kosai, Japan, and he was determined to surpass them. A team leader described the emulation process: "We know how many people it takes in Japan. Say we've got four and everything is working well. They [management] come to me and say, 'This time we're going to try it with three.' We [the team] talk about how to do it with three, and if the team says that's okay, then it's okay."

During our second visit, we were told of roving kaizen teams (similar to those operating at the Mazda plant) comprised of team leaders, area leaders, and trainers from Suzuki. One such team tried and failed to eliminate one person from a team in Assembly, but they did manage to increase the workloads on most of the jobs. According to one member, "they kaizened everybody." This "left a bad taste in everybody's mouth." The team complained there was no time between one job and the next and insisted they needed another person. Of the 14 workers on the team, four were "going for ice" (victims of RSIs) and one was off on workers' compensation.

On our third and fourth visits, we learned of intense kaizening and workload increases accompanying the introduction of the 1992 models. This was especially true with the addition of the so-called "soft shifts" on the truck line. There was not enough demand for two full shifts working at full staffing levels, but there was too much demand for one shift. This prompted a reassessment of job standards and staffing levels. It was decided to reduce the number of workers per shift, lower the line speed, and increase the workloads of each assembler. (Since demand for cars was picking up, surplus workers were moved to the car line or Welding.) A time-study expert was hired to evaluate the jobs for the soft-shift change. This person timed jobs throughout the plant, resulting in a further "leaning" of the work process. A team leader described the activities of this industrial engineer: "He actually came to the floor and he did a time-study of all the teams . . . He does it with a stop watch . . . they already have figured out how much time it takes for a movement, so all he does is write down the part and then he'll circle a little number on his sheet for degree of difficulty of moving that part. And then all he does is he consults a chart and tells you how much time it takes for a human being to go like that."

This development and others suggest that the kaizen process cannot, and perhaps never was intended to, rely entirely on ideas emerging from the shop floor.[4] A manager reported that these departures from "democratic Taylorism" were commonplace in Suzuki's Japanese plants. There, production managers regularly take matters into their own hands when workers fail to line-balance properly, a condition which is endemic.

In the above cases, kaizen was used to adapt teams to the requirements of continuous cost reduction and to workloads that were being increased. In other instances, the outcomes were not as one-sided, as workers appropriated the kaizen process to achieve their own objectives. Many suggestions dealt with safety or making the workplace more comfortable. For example, a QC circle remedied an air quality problem by replacing fans blowing solvent out with fans that sucked it in. A worker's teian got a ramp lowered so jobs could be done without bending. A QC circle replaced uncomfortable rubber boots with boots worn over shoes. Teams, especially in Assembly, have used QC circles to achieve more frequent job rotation. As one worker remarked, "We used it [QC circle] to force the company to rotate us." The company may not have anticipated the two-hour rotation pattern in Assembly, but it appears that CAMI is prepared to implement suggestions that benefit workers as long as they do not conflict with cost and production goals.[5]

Work station observations during our first two visits revealed that some teams had used kaizen to make work easier and more bearable. In some cases heavier jobs were eliminated and the time saved distributed to other work stations. A team in Assembly formed a circle and managed to unburden some of their jobs. They also proposed their workloads be reduced further and one person added to the team after the implementation of an impending line speed increase. Five team leaders from the truck line "kaizened one job per team" to create an off-line subassembly area; this allowed workers to rotate off the more physically demanding main line. Teams throughout the plant began to redistribute their work tasks between jobs to free up a position to carry out off-line duties. These positions, known as floaters, were incorporated into

4. When we were in the plant there were about 10 industrial engineers, and they were not so named. By 1995 there were about 30 of them, and CAMI made no attempt to euphemize their title.

5. As discussed in Chapter 5, management subsequently had second thoughts about rotation, especially its presumed negative impact on vehicle quality. Consequently, after we left the plant the company began to place limits on this practice.

the team rotation schedules and were intended to offer workers a break from the main line. But developments exposed the vulnerability of gains made through kaizen.

On our third visit we discovered that management had unilaterally eliminated the off-line subassembly positions and incorporated the jobs back into the teams on the truck line. Management was also temporarily moving workers from teams with floater positions to other teams or areas when there were staff shortages. So workers in teams that took on added work to create off-line positions got stuck in their line jobs, with little else to show for their kaizen efforts. A union leader related an incident on the car line: "They kaizened their area . . . to create a floater among the team. The guy was moving around, helping everybody, unpackaging stuff, and then the company turned around and started taking the person away when there were head count problems. The team busted their ass to create the position within the team to make it a little easier for themselves. And then as soon as they did it, the company started fucking them by taking it away all the time. And the team exercised its right to refuse unsafe work a couple of times as a result of that." In this instance the refusals succeeded in getting the floater returned to the team.

Kaizen as Liberator?

In much the same way that Braverman (1975) viewed Taylorism as an omnipotent force that thoroughly routinized jobs and removed from workers all remnants of conceptualization, lean production advocates have attributed to kaizen an almost mystical capacity simultaneously to liberate workers and to commit them to the company and its objectives. Allegedly, kaizen harnesses workers' know-how, democratizes Taylorism, synthesizes manual and intellectual labor, induces an empowered workforce to participate voluntarily in the continuous improvement of operations, and generates job satisfaction and commitment. However appealing such imagery might be to managers on the lookout for ways to harness workers democratically, it represents an idealized version of kaizen.

Proponents of lean production also claim that the outcomes of kaizen mutually benefit workers and the company. Adler (1993b), for example, argues that workers recognize kaizen as being in their collective interests because a) they take pride in doing a job the most effective way, and b) job security depends on their plant's competitiveness. But it is misleading to advance as a premise the obvious link between a plant's viability and job security, and then simply allege that workers, as a consequence of recognizing this link, buy into kaizen.

We do not deny that workers may have an interest in cutting costs and making operations more efficient that goes beyond whatever monetary rewards they may receive. It is not unusual to hear workers complain about managers' and engineers' ignorance of shop floor operations or their refusal to listen to workers' suggestions on how to improve them. Workers take pride in performing jobs in the most effective way, are frustrated by defective, ill-fitting components, and are committed to making quality products. If kaizen addressed these concerns without negative side effects and led to working smarter, workers would have no reason for skepticism. There were instances at CAMI where kaizen did have win-win results. QC circles were used to increase the frequency of job rotation, adjustments made jobs easier and safer, and rebalancing did sometimes lead to more equitable workloads.

Having said this, it is important to realize that management implements suggestions that benefit workers only when they do not conflict with the cost-down criterion that drives kaizen and renders it problematic from the point of view of workers. Companies' long-term support for participation is contingent on workers' continued submission of cost-down, productivity-up ideas. As Nobel Prize winner Herbert Simon (1957:111) so candidly put it: "The employer can tolerate genuine participation in decision making only when he believes that reasonable men, knowing the relevant facts and thinking through the problem, will reach a decision that is generally consistent with his [the employer's] goals and interests in the situation."

The supposed convergence of worker and management interests is called into question whenever continuous improvement translates into an increased pace of work, heavier workloads, the loss of a team member, a greater risk of injury, or the inability to get relief or take a day off work. To the extent that "smarter" ways of performing jobs are accompanied by such side effects, workers will, as they did at CAMI, become dissatisfied and withdraw from kaizen activities. Lean production advocates are acutely aware of workers' capacity to improve operations but fail to credit them with the intelligence to recognize the purposes and limitations of kaizen.

Certainly, workers understand the connection between plant viability and job security, but this recognition does not necessarily lead them to endorse kaizen. Most workers understand that many of the factors that lead to a plant shutdown, e.g., outmoded equipment or lack of consumer demand for their product, are beyond their control. It also is unrealistic to think that workers are not cognizant of kaizen outcomes that make work more difficult and stressful, and that this recognition will not condition the nature and level of their participation. CAMI could claim a measure of success in enlisting workers' participation in the kaizen programs. However, workers' involvement, which declined over time, was based more on calculation than on a conviction that their job security was at stake.

If shop floor participants see kaizen as a rigged game that is weighted heavily in favor of the company, they will be reluctant to divulge their trade secrets. This contradiction was manifested at CAMI. Workers on occasion shaped their participation to facilitate the achievement of *their* goals, but these gains were vulnerable to being overridden by management. Management removed floaters and employed special kaizen teams and an industrial engineer to ensure that kaizen outcomes met corporate objectives. This produced more cynical attitudes toward kaizen, the participation programs, and the company. If this pattern continues, more graffiti like that on a whiteboard in an assembly area—"GET OFF YOUR KNEES. THIS IS A TEIAN-FREE ZONE"—are likely to appear, and current levels of participation will decline further.

Kaizen does allow workers to assume some of the functions of industrial engineers. However, the parameters of workers' involvement are established by the initial job and operations designs installed by industrial engineers, as well as by management's objectives for kaizen. The *process* of kaizen does constitute a departure from Taylorism, but the *outcomes* of the process generally conform to Taylorist dictates. To describe kaizen as a win-win democratization of Taylorism is to ignore that its liberatory potential is limited because the disposition of suggestions is controlled by management and because its goal is cost reduction rather than workers' safety, satisfaction, or skills development.

Kaizen programs do differentiate lean from traditional mass production plants. But mass production workers too had opportunities to use their experience and knowledge while on the job. Workers in traditional auto plants regularly used their "trade secrets" to make jobs easier and to create breaks, but these improvements were rarely shared with the company. The major differences, then, boil down to a) lean production's systematic and *formal* appropriation of workers' knowledge, and b) the different ways workers' knowledge is used, by management for management's purposes in lean plants, and by workers for workers' purposes in mass production plants.

We witnessed few signs at CAMI of the revolution in workers' consciousness required for kaizen to operate as described by those who romanticize it. Our results suggest that to characterize kaizen as win-win idealizes the process and overlooks its adverse effects on workers.

CHAPTER 11

Commitment

JAPANESE WORKERS ARE COMMONLY DEPICTED AS DEDICATED, LOYAL, and committed to their companies' success. These attitudes are regarded as a major ingredient of Japan's rise to industrial prominence. Shimada (1983:7), for example, posed a question asked by many other researchers: "Why are Japanese workers so earnest and dedicated in their efforts to increase the productivity of their companies?" Early explanations emphasized the peculiarities of Japanese culture and personality—a strong work ethic and sense of duty, deference to authority, selflessness, collective orientation, and other traits linked to the country's religions and pre-industrial past (Ouchi 1981; Vogel 1979).[1]

Current interpretations give less weight to culture, stressing instead special organizational, management, and production practices. These practices range from lifelong employment guarantees to genuine opportunities for workers' participation and intrinsically satisfying jobs (Womack, Roos, and Jones 1990). Lincoln and Kalleberg (1990:80), for example, concluded from their study of large samples of Japanese and American workers that commitment among the former arises from

1. In his book, *Japan as Number One: Lessons for America,* Vogel (1979:131) remarked (wondrously) that Japanese workers take pride in their work, are loyal to the company and "actually seem to work even without the foreman watching."

a constellation of factors: "Decentralized and participatory decision-making, flexible division of labor, internal labor markets, along with welfare, training and social programs translate at the individual employee level into more interesting, challenging jobs, greater freedom and flexibility, and warmer, broader relations with workmates and managers."

Japanese workers' commitment is taken for granted by many lean production advocates, who maintain that North American workers must be similarly devoted if the Japanese system is to be diffused here. One of the keys to transplant success, according to Kenney and Florida (1993:124), is corporate practices designed to motivate workers and commit them to the employer. Although some proponents of lean production suggest commitment may be contingent on iron-clad employment security or what Womack et al. (1990) call "reciprocal obligations," most are satisfied that the transplants have reproduced enough of the motivational environment of the Japanese firm to realize this objective. Presumably, transplants provide meaningful worker training, participation, challenging jobs, and enlightened managers which, in conjunction with selective recruitment, extensive training, and corporate indoctrination, constitute powerful motivational forces. Because lean production is defined as a win-win system mutually beneficial to workers and company, some adherents project a sanguine vision of worker commitment and labor-management harmony in the transplants.

Some argue that even if the managers of a lean production transplant are not particularly enlightened about human resource management, the fragility of a lean system obligates them to use practices that commit workers to the company and its objectives. JIT delivery systems, for example, can be easily disrupted by disgruntled workers anywhere along the chain—at enormous expense. MacDuffie (1995b:60) observes: "Lean production relies heavily on the contributions of a skilled and motivated workforce . . . to make workable such production practices as just-in-time inventory systems, small lot production, quick die changes, workers self-inspection of quality, and a flexible production mix." A motivated workforce, then, is viewed as a necessary condition for the realization of lean production efficiencies; if lean gets mean it loses its competitive advantage over mass production. Babson (1995:16) refers to this notion as lean production's self-correcting "hidden hand."

Again, NUMMI surfaces as the paragon. Adler (1993a, 1993b) attributes NUMMI's record of superior productivity and quality partly
to a committed workforce, citing as evidence low absenteeism and a
survey in which over 90 percent of workers described themselves as "satisfied" or "very satisfied" with their jobs. Adler singles out three factors
responsible for workers' commitment (intrinsically gratifying work is
not one of them). The first, which he calls the "desire for excellence,"
comes from the pride workers feel in building a quality product. The
second is a mature sense of realism. The evidence suggests that at least
some workers at NUMMI are powerfully motivated by the simple recognition that international competition now forces them 'to earn their
money in the old-fashioned way'" (Adler 1993a:106). (Logically, such
realism is conducive not to commitment but to compliance, a distinction we address below.) The third source of commitment and motivation is the mutual trust and respect that prevails between workers,
the union, and management. Adler gives a glowing description of joint
decision-making, of managers who are experts but not dictators, and
of the democratization of Taylorism. To punctuate the point, Adler
(1993b:130) cites a worker who says, "The interesting thing about this
place is that they never stop making you feel important."[2]

All the auto assembly transplants have tried to select and nurture
committed workforces. Committed workers make no distinction between
"them and us," see their interests as identical to those of the employer,
show up for work faithfully, and are willing to toil assiduously to ensure
the company's success. Committed workers display initiative rather than
indifference, cooperation rather than resistance. Committed workers see
no necessity for unions or strikes. They trust management and uncriti-
cally accept company policies and practices. Commitment, then, entails,
"identification with an organization and acceptance of its goals and values as one's own" (Lincoln and Kalleberg 1990:12).

2. This remark is not typical of the handful of workers Adler interviewed. In fact, what
is striking about both his papers is the jarring inconsistency between the author's thesis and
the often bitterly critical comments of the workers he cites. He parries their remarks by spec-
ulating that they may have been due to growing pains.

Declining Commitment at CAMI

Each of CAMI's four values—empowerment, kaizen, open communications, and team spirit—is ideally an integral element of CAMI culture, and each of the values is related to the company's goal of developing a cooperative, hard-working, and committed workforce. The lengthy recruitment process is designed to select applicants whose attitudes and capabilities are compatible with CAMI values and culture. CAMI values are transmitted through Nagare training. Classroom instructors emphasize that CAMI is dedicated to more than the manufacture of quality vehicles. Students are taught that their ideas will be valued, they will have the opportunity to develop their abilities, and they will receive fair and respectful treatment. As the trainees head for the shop floor, many look forward to working in a unique environment, one that is not only different from but better than traditional plants.

Workers told us they wanted to work in an organization that could deliver this package of promises. Many were willing to give CAMI the benefit of the doubt, wanting to believe what they had learned in Nagare training. However, disillusionment gradually set in among more and more workers, as they were exposed to conditions on the shop floor that belied what they had been led to believe. With the passage of time, enthusiasm waned. This growing disenchantment was shown vividly by the responses to our questions on policies and practices associated with CAMI values.

Table 8 shows changing attitudes toward CAMI and its values. A substantial minority, and in some cases a majority, of respondents were initially skeptical of CAMI's values and practices, and with each subsequent interview this attitude was expressed by a growing proportion of workers. By the final round 88.3 percent of the sample viewed CAMI as no different from other companies; over 90 percent felt common cafeterias, uniforms, and parking areas were a smokescreen that masked differences in power; almost three-quarters regarded CAMI as undemocratic; and over 80 percent viewed it as competitive and stressful.

CAMI goes to great lengths in orientation and training sessions to convince employees they are part of one big team, whose members, independent of their positions in the organization, respect and trust one another. How do workers feel about this? When asked, "Do you

TABLE 8. Attitudes toward CAMI

	Round 1	Round 2	Round 3	Round 4
CAMI is a special kind of experiment, designed to change the way people work in Canada. I am enthusiastic and excited about it.	44.4% (32)	31.6% (24)	18.2% (14)	11.7% (9)
There is really nothing special about working at CAMI, and, in fact, all things considered, CAMI really isn't any different than other corporations.	55.6% (40)	68.4% (52)	81.8% (63)	88.3% (68)
Total	100.0% (72)	100.0% (76)	100.0% (77)	100.0% (77)
Which of the following statements comes closest to your feelings about common cafeterias, dress codes and parking areas?				
It's a good thing, it's starting to make managers and workers more equal.	42.4% (28)	24.7%(19)	11.7% (9)	6.4% (5)
It is nothing but a smokescreen. The reality is that management still has all the power.	57. 6% (38)	75.3% (58)	88.3% (68)	93.6% (73)
Total	100.0% (66)	100.0% (77)	100.0% (77)	100.0% (78)
CAMI is democratic	55.4% (41)	53.2% (42)	42.1% (32)	27.3% (21)
CAMI is undemocratic	44.6% (33)	46.8% (37)	57.9% (44)	72.7% (56)
Total	100.0% (74)	100.0% (79)	100.0% (76)	100.0% (77)
CAMI is cooperative and helpful	59.2% (42)	45.2% (33)	32.4% (24)	16.9% (13)
CAMI is competitive and stressful	40.8% (29)	54.8% (40)	67.6% (50)	83.1% (64)
Total	100.0% (71)	100.0% (73)	100.0% (74)	100.0% (77)

think management at CAMI would 'put one over' on workers if they had the chance?" only a tiny minority in any of the four rounds indicated trust in management. Eight out of 10 respondents in round 1 felt managers would put one over on them, and 98 percent did by the final round. Many regarded this as a silly question because the answer was so obvious. Comments such as "Come on, you've got to be kidding," or "You better believe it" were not uncommon.

Workers' evaluations of management were also reflected by their opinions on the need for a union. Most respondents apparently entered CAMI with a pro-union bent. When asked in round 1 what they thought of the following statement—"We need a union at CAMI because no matter how cooperative the relationship, there will always be differences between workers and management"—41 percent agreed and 57 percent agreed strongly. But by the final round, the percentage who strongly agreed had risen to 81 percent (with all the rest agreeing).

To provide an overall picture of how successful CAMI has been in transmitting its philosophy and developing a workforce committed to the company and its objectives, we constructed a "Commitment Index" based on each respondent's answers to five questions.[3] From these responses we distinguished three categories of workers. Those who scored high on the index believe in the reality of CAMI values and are com-

3. The commitment index consisted of the following five questions:
1. Some people say that when team concept has been tried at other plants the teams work more for the good of the company than for the good of workers. Based on your experience at CAMI would you (agree to disagree)?
2. Do you think everyone should participate in the suggestion program?
3. Choose one: CAMI is a special kind of experiment designed to change the way people work in Canada. I am enthusiastic and excited about it. Or, There is really nothing special about working at CAMI, and, in fact, all things considered, CAMI really isn't any different than other corporations.
4. In your opinion, how interested is CAMI management in the welfare of the workers (very to not at all interested)?
5. Which of the following statements comes closest to your feelings about common cafeterias, dress codes and parking areas? It's a good thing, it's starting to make managers and workers more equal. Or, It is nothing but a smokescreen. The reality is that management still has all the power.

Each of these five items showed a reasonable amount of variance, and each was internally consistent with every other item. In other words, all items measured the same concept, as indicated by a Cronbach alpha of .74. An alpha value of less than .70 indicates that at least one item of a scale is not measuring the same concept as the others. This version of the commitment index was developed and its reliability confirmed by Andersen (1994).

mitted to the company and its objectives. These people we labeled highly committed. Respondents who scored in the middle range—the moderately committed—expressed ambivalent attitudes toward CAMI, holding some negative and some positive opinions. Those who scored low viewed CAMI as just another factory and indicated no identification with the company and its values. These people we called uncommitted.[4]

As Figure 4 indicates, the proportion of highly committed and moderately committed workers in the sample declined through each of the four interview periods. By the final round, 50.6 percent fell into the moderately committed category, while only 1.3 percent indicated high commitment. The percentage of uncommitted respondents grew steadily from 11.8 in round 1, to 24.7 in round 2, and to 48.1 in the final round. Despite a highly selective recruitment process, the ideals taught in Nagare training, and the company's professed commitment to a labor-management partnership, workers' disenchantment with CAMI grew steadily. The number of workers who indicated no commitment to CAMI's objectives quadrupled over the two-year research period.

Commitment was not significantly associated with age, gender, department, or previous union membership. For round 4, we ran a series of cross-tabulations to determine the relationship between scores on the commitment index and responses to questions tapping five potential commitment sources—training, challenging work, participatory programs, empowerment, and team working. For these analyses we broke commitment into high and low; depending on their index scores, medium commitment persons were assigned to one of these polar categories.

Where statistically significant relationships were present, a greater proportion of high commitment than low commitment respondents indicated involvement in participation programs and satisfaction with training, teams, jobs, and empowerment. However, because of the preponderance of low commitment respondents in the overall sample, more low commitment than high commitment workers indicated

4. The term "uncommitted" does not imply that workers who were so labeled did not care whether or not they were employed by CAMI, that they were not interested in making CAMI a better place to work, or that they took no pride in doing a good job. The comments of a worker who was cynical about CAMI, its culture, and its kaizen programs are instructive: "I come here to do a good job and then go home and forget about it."

FIGURE 4.   The Commitment Index:
Respondents' degree of commitment to CAMI.

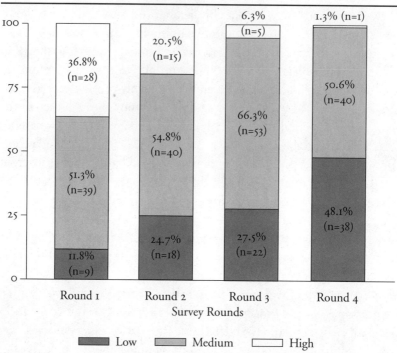

participation or satisfaction. The pattern of results can be illustrated by a question on job satisfaction. For round 4, more high than low commitment workers expressed some degree of job satisfaction (substantial majorities in both cases). Looked at from another angle, however, of those workers who reported some degree of job satisfaction, 76.8 percent were in the low commitment category and only 23.2 percent were highly committed (see Table 9).

It is clear from these results that worker commitment cannot be inferred from positive responses to a broad, fixed-choice question about job satisfaction. This is not surprising considering the many possible meanings that can be read into the question. When workers answer, do they have in mind wages, employment security, their co-workers and bosses, job content, or the length of time it takes to drive to work? Moreover, it is likely that positive responses simply mean that people

TABLE 9. Cross-tabulation of job satisfaction and commitment

Commitment	Job Satisfaction		
	Very Satisfied/ Satisfied	Dissatisfied/ Very Dissatisfied	Total
High	23.2% (13)	14.3% (3)	20.8% (16)
Low	76.8% (43)	85.7% (18)	79.2% (61)
Total	72.7% (56)	27.3% (21)	100.0% (77)

are satisfied relative to the job opportunities available to them. Given high unemployment and the jobs open to most workers, their present jobs may be the best of a poor lot.

What conclusions can be drawn from this exercise? First, eight of the 14 variables showed statistically significant relationships with commitment. Favorable evaluations of training, job and team working satisfaction, involvement in the teian program (but not in QC circles or kaizen in general), and perceived empowerment were significantly associated with high commitment.[5] Second, these are cross-sectional data,

5. The relationship between commitment and answers to the following questions was examined. Single-starred items were statistically significant at the .05 level and double-starred items at the .01 level.
1. As a result of [your] training, would you say you are more skilled or are all the jobs about the same?**
2. I have been provided with the opportunity to continually upgrade myself and learn new skills.
3. The opportunity for training at CAMI makes it easy to get the skills you need to get a better job.
4. There is too much on the job training and not enough classroom training.*
5. Would you best describe your job as interesting and challenging, boring and monotonous, or somewhere in between?*
6. How satisfied are you with your job?**
7. Do you participate in the suggestion program?*
8. Do you belong to a QC circle?
9. Have you ever been involved in kaizen?
10. How often do you have a say in the way your job is done?*
11. Do you think workers are empowered here?**
12. How satisfied are you with the amount of decision-making power you have?
13. How much do you like the idea of working as part of a team?**
14. How much do you like being a member of your team?
These and other correlates of commitment at CAMI were the focus of an M.A. thesis by Andersen (1994).

so we cannot tell which is cause and which is effect. For example, it may be that job satisfaction is a source of commitment, but highly committed workers may be prone to report high job satisfaction. Similarly, is involvement in the teian program conducive to high commitment, or is high commitment conducive to participation? Third, *assuming* that commitment is the dependent variable, even in those cases of statistical significance the preponderance of low commitment workers in all response categories suggests that sources of motivation and commitment are provided in homeopathic doses and/or are not powerful enough to outweigh the multiple sources of discontent associated with lean production at CAMI.

Interviews: Descriptions of Plant Culture

Team leaders, managers, and union reps echoed the attitudes we found in the surveys. A team leader observed: "When I first came here I thought it was going to be the greatest place on earth . . . Nagare really pumps you up really good. They know how to do that. But once you get out on the floor and start working for a while it's a lot different." Another team leader remarked, "A lot of the enthusiasm the people had when they'd come here, you know, it's supposed to be so different than every place else. There's been a lot of things go on that made people realize that it is no different . . . and I think the novelty's kind of wearing off the place now that we've been running for a couple of years . . . People came in here with a lot of enthusiasm because of their training before they actually get onto the floor—leads them to believe it's really going to be different."

This team leader said CAMI doesn't practice what it preaches. When asked to illustrate, he said, "The perfect example, for our department, anyway, is one thing they preach is 'never use a defective part' . . . but when push comes to shove, do we stop the line because these parts are no good, or do we use them? Well, it's 'use them, keep the production line going.' When it comes down to money, where it's costing them money, well, 'we'll let these substandard parts go. We've only got a hundred of them; we'll use them up because we can't afford to be down.' And they're driven by production in a lot of respects."

A union rep observed: "We're here to build cars. We're not here to hear some bullshit smokescreen all the time about how happy and great this place is. It's just another factory just like anywhere else, and a factory that's somewhat regressive."

A team leader described CAMI in much the same language: "People are certain to come to the realization that regardless of how highly they talk of this place or make it sound, that basically it's just another auto plant."

A team leader described the drift away from the CAMI philosophy: "I'm becoming a factory worker just like everyone else. I mentioned that to the assistant manager just today. You know this is turning into just a factory, and if that's what it is, tell people. Don't make something that doesn't exist."

A worker told us she was upset by the changes that had taken place in the plant: "We were . . . getting awards and getting this and getting that. And it's gone downhill, seems that we're going the way that every other factory goes. That is a letdown. That's why I came here . . . I thought it would be different, everybody'd have a good time."

A skilled trades worker gave a graphic description of changing conditions in the plant: "When the plant started you just sat about and talked about how you were going to do things better tomorrow. Now? Don't stand in the doorway [at the end of a shift] or you'll get knocked over in the rush."

Recognition of the disparity between ideals and reality was not restricted to workers. A manager stated: "One of the concerns that we had heard—this is already over a year ago—is that what's being taught at the training sessions is not necessarily the same as what's practiced on the floor. So we've tried to tone down some of the segments of the program."

Not everyone believed that CAMI had failed to deliver on its promises. During our third visit a staff manager could still refer to CAMI as unique. When asked to amplify, she replied:

I think in the values that are expressed in the company and I think in the level of open communication. I think when you talk about communication, people always want more, but realistically there's a level of involvement in the decisions made here and a level of knowledge about what's happening in the company that I don't think you find in most organizations. I think the other value—kaizen—when you look at the opportunity people have here to improve their work area and that their suggestions are not put on a shelf for a year or two—everything is responded to fairly quickly and people do have an impact on the areas that they work in, and I think that's fairly unique as well . . . I would say those are the two [values] that we're particularly strong in at this point.

In the early rounds, an area leader felt CAMI was living up to its ideals as much as could be expected in an environment where "production . . . is the backbone of what we're doing." During our final interview, however, this area leader did admit that CAMI values were not operative: "As far as . . . the environment, I think it's getting more traditional as the days go on. You don't want that to happen."

CAMI's failure to deliver its package of promises had become so obvious that in mid-1991 management initiated a "back to the values" campaign.[6] Admitting that the CAMI values were not being practiced, one manager said, "I'm not naive enough to say that every area leader or manager practices the same way, but one of the objectives that we have for this organization for this year is to again get clearly focused on the values; to not drift from the way we tried to set up the organization . . . I think it's important to keep working at it, especially as we get more into this routine of building vehicles. It's not the same as what it was when we started out the organization when there was more time."

A union rep was less enthusiastic about the company's attempt to reaffirm its values: "They came out with a piece of paper, and that's about it . . . said they wanted to get back to the basics, you know . . . just like something right out of Nagare. The guys are down there building cars. The last thing they want to hear about is open communication, kaizen, empowerment, especially when the management doesn't practice it themselves."

6. A June 7, 1991 memo sent to all employees from the Vice-President for Production stated that the company president, Mr. Ikuma, had declared the CAMI theme for that year "a re-dedication to the CAMI beliefs and values."

Social Relations on the Shop Floor

The opinions expressed by workers in the sample were reflected in behavior on the shop floor. With production in full swing, there were growing signs of discontent and conflictual labor-management relations. The win-win, partnership outlook had given way to a "them vs. us" attitude and a belief that it is workers who pay the price for lean production. Workers had more and more complaints about disciplinary actions and management's tendency to dictate to rather than consult with workers. Indifference or resentment grew, and workers increasingly attended only to absolute necessities. Interest and participation in QC circle and teian programs declined. Few workers did taiso, fewer still shouted "yosh." Grievances increased, work slowdowns and stoppages became more common. The erosion of CAMI values and growing distrust of management were accompanied by conflicts over issues that might seem trivial but took on significance because they were a large part of daily life on the shop floor. Playing radios, reading newspapers, wearing shorts, washing up before the end of the shift—issues like these became contested at CAMI.

A union rep said during our final visit: "We're getting guys written up for the most moronic things, like they think we're in high school or something. You go down to the principal's office—that's ER [Employee Relations]—we have to discipline you, you know." Another union rep lamented the petty enforcement of CAMI's dress code: "All the lip service about a CAMI family is just a total crock . . . I've got one assistant manager walking around issuing an Assembly-wide policy that pants aren't to be rolled up, it's against uniform policy. Meanwhile, we've got 2,000 damn cars sitting outside waiting missing parts. And the only thing he's worried about is whether somebody's rolling up their pant legs."

A team leader described the growing indifference among his team members: "I see it every day, people pulling together really helping each other out. But then there comes a breaking point where one says, 'Heck with the team concept. This is my job, that's all I'm going to do.' Once that takes hold, then I think we kind of get back into the real traditional kind of factory work." An area leader told a similar story. "When the line goes down for up to half an hour or 40 minutes . . . people just stand around. Whereas, when I was a team leader . . . a couple of years ago, everyone kept busy, and they'd do things, improve things."

Thinking about Commitment and Lean Production

These reports should lay to rest the notion that there is an invariable, organic connection between lean production and committed workers. They also raise questions about the contention that to operate optimally, lean production requires a committed workforce. This was a subject our research group spent hours debating.

As Braverman (1975) recognized, the distinct interests of capitalists and workers give rise to one of management's most pressing problems—how to translate purchased labor power into labor performed in accordance with the employer's standards. Without this translation, management would be unable to pursue successfully the continuous reduction of necessary labor time. Braverman emphasized one solution—the progressive elimination of workers' skills, knowledge, and discretion via Taylorism and advanced machinery. That there are other remedies is obvious (Burawoy 1985; Edwards 1979; Friedman 1977). That there are no perfect solutions is also obvious.

The ideal answer is to construct a workplace that is conducive to the voluntary commitment of workers. This is what lean production enthusiasts say their preferred model does—either due to enlightened management or because the fragility of the system demands it. In the absence of ideal structures and social relationships, however, a range of conditions outside and inside the workplace can serve as functional alternatives to commitment, alternatives that produce *compliance.* These include widespread joblessness, underemployment, the absence or erosion of a state social safety net, growing wage polarization, and, as a consequence, employment *insecurity.* As Wells (1995:199) points out, the relatively high wages and job security of transplants represent "a last best hope for many to enjoy the 'middle class' lifestyle that forms the basis of full citizenship in much of Canada and the United States." Added to the insecurity are technical controls and direct supervision with punitive sanctions for nonconformity, peer pressure in the context of understaffing, stringent absenteeism policies, and, in most transplants, no union to defend and advance workers' independent interests.

In their zeal to promote lean production as the one best way of manufacturing, advocates tend to ignore or assign little importance to these more coercive sources of worker motivation that operate to varying degrees in both Japan and North America. Consequently, advocates choose commitment over compliance in explaining worker diligence and the relative absence of conflict in Japan and in the transplants. The former term denotes identification with the company and willing, voluntary cooperation. The latter simply denotes an attitude born of powerlessness, dependence, and lack of alternatives. Adler (1993b), for example, asserts that NUMMI workers are highly committed, but he does not consider that what he is describing may be compliance and gives little explanatory weight to the motivational impact of their extended period of unemployment. Similarly, impressed by Japanese workers' diligence, long hours of work, and strike-free record, Lincoln and Kalleberg (1990) ignore coercive elements of Japanese companies and attribute these actions to workers' commitment.

Little independent evidence exists to support this inference. In fact, the two most comprehensive comparative attitudinal surveys ever undertaken found that Japanese workers were less committed to their jobs and employers than Americans (Cole 1979; Lincoln and Kalleberg 1990). It is true that the authors in both instances attempted to explain away these results, but we take their data at face value and find their circumventions unconvincing.[7] Since committed and compliant attitudes may produce identical behavior, all that lean production needs to operate as its designers intended is a compliant workforce.

Explaining the Decline

What accounts for the drift from CAMI values and workers' declining commitment? What lies behind workers' now prevalent belief that CAMI is just another factory?

---

7. For a critical discussion of the data interpretations of Cole and Lincoln and Kalleberg see Besser (1993). Evidence to support the argument that Japanese workers are compliant rather than committed can be found in Dohse, Jürgens, and Malsch 1985; Kamata 1982; Kanawashi 1992; Okayama 1987; Price 1994, 1995.

Faulty Execution

The conventional explanation for problems in transplants is that the lean system has been inadequately or only partially implemented;[8] the authors of this failure are "unreconstructed" North American managers. Florida and Kenney (1991), for example, maintain that American workers have adapted well to lean production. Where problems have surfaced, as at Mazda, they attribute them not to lean production itself but to managers who are too inflexible or threatened by the new participatory environment to allow it to operate properly. American managers, we are told, are used to the unilateral exercise of authority, have difficulty taking orders from foreign nationals, do not understand the importance of workers, and can neither comprehend nor tolerate a system that gives workers so much discretion (Kenney and Florida 1993:117, 291). Adler (1993a:14) found that NUMMI workers also attributed shop floor problems to American managers. "The criticisms were, with very few exceptions, directed at what workers saw as avoidable flaws in the implementation of the system, not with the system itself." A Nissan plant manager in Sunderland, England, advanced a slightly different version of the thesis: "In the pressures of automobile manufacturing it is easy to revert to type and top management must constantly reinforce the philosophy it holds. Particularly first line supervisors . . . if not properly trained and fully committed, can easily turn lean production into mean production" (Wickens, 1993:21).[9]

How applicable is this explanation to developments at CAMI? Some attributed the drift from CAMI ideals to the arrival of hard-liners from the GM system and the departure of managers who lived and breathed CAMI values ("torch-bearers [who] waved the banner," in the words of one manager). Indeed, the managerial ranks have seen considerable move-

8. Scholars who advance inadequate implementation as an explanation for problems in the transplants have also argued that to operate effectively a lean production system must be accompanied by "enlightened" human resource and labor relations practices, but these practices need not be identical to those prevailing in Japan. According to this view, lean production can be effectively diffused to North America without, for example, individualized remuneration or enterprise unions (Florida and Kenney 1991; Womack, Roos, and Jones 1990).

9. A very different view of the Nissan Sunderland plant is provided by Garrahan and Stewart (1992), who report that the plant is inherently mean—operations are driven by coercion and manipulation, and workers run on fear.

ment and turnover. Of the initial group of managers we interviewed, few have remained in their original positions, and others have left CAMI. Management priorities and styles also changed.

A former plant manager was often cited as a "torch-bearer" of the CAMI way. Another manager described him as a "charismatic" person who "had an uncanny knack for knowing everybody." The first generation of managers acted as cheerleaders on the shop floor and tried to short-circuit complaints. When workers were dissatisfied with the actions of an area leader, they might appeal directly to the vice-president in charge of production. Having someone at the top intervene to resolve a problem tended to reinforce belief in CAMI's philosophy and good intentions and lead to the conviction that problems stemmed not from the system of lean production but from lower-level managers who stubbornly continued to behave in the "old way." One member of the original management group described his style: "I purposely sit there at breaks and lunches and chew the fat, find out what's going on . . . I was holding quite a few line-side chats with teams. And they'll come up with stuff, and I'll just call about two or three people and say, 'get this thing fixed, take care of this,' and my managers are starting to do it . . . I have to cascade my style to other people so it's transparent, so if I ever left or when I leave, that somebody else can do it the same way."

Such "open communication" and consultation gave way to a more sober, no-nonsense approach. Management is now "more product-oriented," according to one manager. There is more emphasis on "institutionalizing procedures and processes, more concern with putting systems in place," according to another. As time passed there was much talk, even within management ranks, of reality setting in, of less cheerleading, of less time spent on the floor, and more on getting the product out. Had some of the first-generation managers remained at CAMI to experience the escalating pressures that arose from implementation difficulties and the push for production, it is likely their management styles would have become more hard-nosed.

It also appears that CAMI made an effort to replace departing managers with people who were open and flexible. A second generation manager stated: "It was said to me several times during the interviews that they did not want a traditional manager. They did not want a manager that had any bad habits. They wanted someone who had a history of being a little different even within the General Motors organization and hadn't established any bad habits as they think General Motors has."

Kenney and Florida (1993) reported that their interviews in transplants pointed to American managers as the cause of deviations from the humane and harmonious Japanese model. Our interviews at CAMI revealed just the opposite: American and Canadian managers described their Japanese counterparts as hard-nosed, an attitude formed, in part, through their visits to what they considered regimented and authoritarian Japanese firms. According to an ex-vice-president of production at CAMI, "You do not approach your boss and disagree with him. If you are a manager you talk with people on your own level, but you do not speak to peons. They [Japanese executives] are completely flabbergasted that I would deal with production associates on the line. But in North America we are trying to eliminate such hierarchies and deal with the person you need to deal with" (Walmsley 1992:22).

Japanese managers were determined to implant holus bolus the Suzuki system in Canada. Only the wise counsel and interventions of the Canadians, we were told, tempered Japanese rigidities and headed off confrontations with employees and the union.[10] One manager is worth quoting: "We consciously realized right from day one that if we didn't have a Canadian presence in terms of managing people that they would try to manage people like they do in Japan. We can cite all sorts of examples. We've done away with a bell in the office to tell people to pick up their pens and start working and a bell that goes at lunch . . . In Japan I'll tell you you're going to work tonight until 9:00, and they tell you that at the last minute, and you just do it. And that's not appropriate [in Canada]."

This manager recounted a debate over workers' requests to have reading material in team areas: "It took a while to convince the Japanese that it wasn't going to turn the place into a pig sty. It took some time because they don't do it in Japan." He also mentioned workers' requests to be allowed to wear blue rather than the standard, easily soiled white uniform shirts: "It took me six months to convince them that was appropriate."

10. We could not get the other side of the story, since we were denied interview access to Japanese personnel. We were allowed to present in writing a series of questions to which we received from the Japanese terse written comments that were not particularly informative.

Managers who had visited the Suzuki plant in Kosai commented on the heavy workloads, workers' diligence, the absence of job rotation, and a cavalier approach to health and safety. One manager said he was astonished by how lax Kosai management was on safety issues and gave as an example the standard (and dangerous) practice of repairing robots while they were running. "When I was over there I was kind of shocked. We don't do that in Canada because it's not safe and we're required by law to lock out [turn off] the equipment."

Another manager who was in Japan for a month said: "A lot of things go on over there that we'd never allow over here. Whether it's safety-oriented or RSI-type things. Job rotation over there is almost nonexistent, for example."

Growing Pains

There is another version of the inadequate implementation thesis, one that might be called the "growing pains" explanation. CAMI was a greenfield operation. All the elements of a lean system had not yet been put in place or perfected. Tremendous effort and resources were devoted to this task, and unavoidable crises kept emerging. As with other new plants, there were unanticipated developments, much had to be ironed out, or, to use managers' terminology, the system required a great deal of "tweaking." As a consequence, work was stressful, and there was no time to attend to human relations matters.

When we first entered the plant in March 1990, CAMI was approaching full production on a single shift. In a year the company had gone from 383 workers making a few vehicles a day to just over 1,000 production workers building about 370 vehicles each day. By our last research visit in November 1991, CAMI had added a second shift and was producing 700 vehicles with nearly 2,000 workers. During this time the company experienced a series of severe problems, many of which had not been resolved when we completed our study. Equipment breakdowns, defective parts, and suppliers' failure to meet delivery deadlines were common. Missing or defective components complicated production scheduling, and all too often there were long runs of high-option content models. According to management, between the second and third research periods unanticipated turnover, recruitment problems, and the escalating incidence of RSIs caused serious staff shortages. The addition of second shifts compounded these problems.

The growing pains explanation has some validity. Many of the *kinds* of difficulties CAMI faced during its first several years of operation undoubtedly are experienced at all greenfield sites. But there is one major exception—persistent understaffing. Personnel shortages at CAMI magnified the normal range of problems associated with getting the plant up and running at full production. In other words, the *severity* of difficulties CAMI faced was exacerbated by the company's dedication to implementing a lean system. This production system, as CAMI candidly acknowledged, strives constantly to achieve maximum output with a minimum number of workers. Adherence to these dictates of lean placed a heavy burden on workers as well as managers, strained relationships between the two parties, undermined CAMI values, and produced declining worker commitment.

It's the System

While growing pains and problems with management style cannot be discounted entirely, a more realistic explanation for the drift from CAMI ideals is that the promises collided with a production system oriented to maximum output with minimum workers. As a thinly spread workforce scrambled to keep up with a full production schedule, Nagare ideals, of necessity, were increasingly ignored. We maintain that it is the system of lean production itself that shapes management styles rather than the reverse.

An area leader tells an Assembly team they will need written passes to go to the washroom; a worker can't get away from the line to take his insulin; roving kaizen teams pare away staff; overtime is scheduled arbitrarily; inter-team transfers cause complaints; floaters are routinely removed from teams; RSIs escalate; workloads and staffing levels are continuously disputed; overwork is blamed on injured workers, causing dissension within teams. Both managers and workers told us over and over again that CAMI's practice of operating with a minimal workforce makes it impossible to realize CAMI ideals, leading to employee attitudes and actions similar to those in traditional auto plants.

A team leader located the source of worker disenchantment in an understaffed workforce that had no time to spend on the kinds of work practices drummed home in Nagare training:

> We generally work quite a bit of overtime in our area and [an area leader] wanted us to work till four in the morning. All the lines would be done at two, and this particular area leader thought it was insulting that we wouldn't stay till four o'clock in the morning to help clean the plant up, so when the manager got there in the morning it would be nice and clean. Who are you trying to bullshit? Let him walk through and see how this place looks. Give us some more people and we'll clean the place. Put some more people on the line and we won't be so busy in this area. And that is generally the bottom line. There are not enough people on the line to do the work.

This team leader looked back wistfully to a more relaxed period when workers had time to do their jobs and would voluntarily pitch in to deal with problems and glitches. "When I started here, guys would go out of their way to repair something that was broken. Now they say, 'the hell with it,' and I don't blame them. They just don't have the time to do it."

One manager echoed the team leader's views: "When you're not at full production you have the luxury of a lot of things—a slower line or downtime. There was time for people to work on suggestions, head over to repair to work on a quality program . . . Now that we're at full production we have to run at maximum speed and everyone is assigned to their teams, and that's pretty much it. So, as a result, they probably are less content with their jobs."

Another manager gave the following explanation for the drift from values: "I personally think that because of our push for vehicles, our push for quality, our push for numbers, because of the overtime we've had to work, because of their schedules, that our use of the values has suffered . . . I'm not saying that it's worse than other plants and, in fact, it may be better than other plants, but to me it's a bit of a disappointment."

The union local was not an innocent bystander to these developments. Union officials and a few rank and file activists were familiar with statements on work reorganization and lean production put out by the CAW national office, though it is unlikely that most members had seen them. The union newsletter carried criticisms of management and the system of lean production. Union committeepersons brought workers' complaints to management's attention or filed grievances. In some instances the union pursued highly charged departmental or plant-wide issues at the insistence of the membership. In other instances the union assumed a leadership role only after worker protests had become potentially explosive. These highly visible actions served to demonstrate the union's relevance and commitment to the membership.

It is impossible to determine the extent to which the union contributed to deteriorating labor-management relations and declining worker commitment. However, apart from the steady stream of criticism printed in the newsletter, the role of the union local was both reactive and proactive; initiatives originating on the shop floor were as likely to spur the union to action as the reverse. Accordingly, it is not unreasonable to conclude that company practices weighed much more heavily on workers' attitudes and behaviors than the perspectives and activities of the union.[11]

Over the course of this study labor-management relations deteriorated and workers' commitment to the company declined markedly. That CAMI was able to maintain high levels of productivity during this period raises questions about the allegedly necessary connection between the success of lean production and a committed workforce. All that lean production appears to require is compliant workers.

The partial implementation thesis purports to explain production or labor-management problems that arise in lean production transplants. When applied to CAMI, the most popular version of this thesis would attribute shop floor problems and declining worker commitment to the arrival of tough GM bosses who circumvented the prescribed management style of lean production. A second strain of this thesis would view CAMI's difficulties as quite normal for a new company struggling to get into full production. Both explanations undoubtedly have some rele-

11. This and other issues related to the union are taken up in more detail in the next chapter.

vance, but do not sufficiently explain the CAMI case. CAMI managers perceived themselves to be more tolerant, democratic, and flexible than their counterparts they had observed in Japan. To the extent that this view is valid, and a good deal of research on Japan suggests that it is, it lends support to an alternative interpretation of what happened at CAMI. We maintain that it is the system of lean production itself that shapes management styles rather than the reverse. As for the second version, we argue that the structures of lean production, especially those related to staffing, compounded the problems CAMI experienced as it moved into full production.

The partial implementation explanation of problems in the transplants is perhaps the most misleading of all misconceptions about Japanese production management. It allows lean production enthusiasts to explain away operational or labor relations problems in actually existing factories. In effect, this rationalization insulates lean production from criticism, since assertions of the system's superiority along any number of dimensions can never be empirically disproven. At CAMI, all the elements of lean production were not in place and many that were needed refinement. But company practices were driven by the principles of a lean system single-mindedly dedicated to maximum output with minimal labor. Rigid adherence to this lean model, not its partial implementation, is at the heart of the dissatisfactions workers voiced.

❋ CHAPTER 12

The Union

U NIONS FACE MAJOR CHALLENGES IN THEIR ATTEMPTS TO
organize transplants in Canada and the United States. In its birth-
place in Japan, lean production ordinarily functions without overt labor-
management conflict due to the absence of a union or the presence of a
compliant enterprise union. Union independence is a challenge to managers of lean, who attempt to align the goals and activities of workers with
those of the company by creating a corporate culture in which all employees define themselves as part of one big team. So far, transplants wholly
owned by the Japanese have actively and successfully resisted unionization. Union certification has been impeded by locating plants in rural
areas, selective recruitment, indoctrination of employees, outright intim-
idation of pro-union workers, and other blatant forms of anti-unionism.
Pro-union applicants have been screened out by Nissan and SIA in the
U.S. and by Honda and Toyota in Canada. Shortly before workers were
to vote on unionizing at Nissan, the company transmitted anti-union
messages on television screens throughout the plant and stopped the line
to allow managers to address workers. Prior to the CAW's certification
at CAMI, only three North American transplants, all joint ventures—
Mazda, Diamond Star (now Mitsubishi) and NUMMI—were unionized (Green 1995; Green and Yanarella 1995; Parker and Slaughter 1988).

Unions in the transplants are peripheral to the analyses of most lean production advocates.[1] If the union does surface, it is made clear that the effectiveness of lean production may be compromised by an independent labor organization (Shimada and MacDuffie 1987:27). In his discussion of the Toyota production system, Monden (1983:51) has little to say about organized labor, but he does argue that the only barrier to the successful worldwide diffusion of this system is union opposition. Kenney and Florida (1993:285) argue that Japanese employers are not anti-union as such; they oppose unions that adopt an adversarial stance and provide an independent source of worker identification. In other words, transplant employers can live with unions as long as they are similar to Japanese enterprise unions.

In the early 1950s, militant industrial unions in Japan fought pitched battles with Nissan, Suzuki, and Toyota. After extended lock-outs and sweeping purges of union activists, the industrial unions were defeated and replaced by enterprise unions. A pattern of labor relations was established, as other automakers followed suit. Born out of defeat, the enterprise unions' early years were marked by an utter subordination and a collaborationist bent that have persisted to this day.[2]

Enterprise unions are plant-specific and have only loose ties with one another. This isolation pits workers in one plant against those in others and breeds among the workforce an enterprise consciousness. Workers understandably are prone to believe their well-being depends on the economic performance of their plant and to identify with plant management. Collaboration is reinforced by the internal structure of the enterprise union. Each union represents office employees, core production workers, and several layers of front-line management. Foremen and

1. There are only two brief references to unions in *The Machine that Changed the World*. One is to the concessions of the UAW in the 1930s and one to the UAW's inability to organize transplants wholly owned by the Japanese.

2. There are, however, signs that all is not well in the heartland of lean production. Workers and unions have come to realize the price they have paid for their companies' success. Surveys indicate that auto workers are discouraging their children from taking jobs in the car plants, and the automakers are finding it increasingly difficult to recruit young workers. Auto unions in Japan have called for a major reduction in working hours, restrictions on overtime, fewer model types, and extended life spans of models (the normal life span of a model made in Japan is four years) (Confederation of Japan Automobile Workers Unions 1992).

182 * *Just Another Car Factory?*

their supervisors ordinarily monopolize union leadership positions[3], and non-management union leaders frequently end up in the ranks of management. Consequently, the union lacks independence, affords workers little protection from management power, and promotes cooperation. The enterprise union has been characterized as an administrative arm of management (Kanawashi 1992), a partner in Japanese capitalism (Kenney and Florida 1993:33), and a subordinate organization that allows unfettered management domination (Turner 1991:217). This translates into constant pressure on the shop floor to work fast and hard (Dohse, Jürgens, and Malsch 1988; Glaberman 1983; Kamata 1982; Okayama 1987; Turnbull 1988).[4]

With this background, it is understandable that the unionized transplants have labored mightily to cultivate cooperative unions. Their efforts were facilitated by the national UAW's disavowal of adversarial unionism and endorsement of labor-management cooperation. Again, NUMMI served as a model. As Berggren (1993:180) points out, "The labor-management collaboration and teamwork at NUMMI was heralded by Solidarity House [UAW headquarters] as the future, and an embodiment of central union aspirations."[5] At NUMMI joint union-management committees discuss issues that unions traditionally have not wanted to discuss or that management has not felt the need to discuss. Adler (1993a:108, 1993b:156) views this "jointness" as a source of union power, although he does acknowledge that it also inhibits the union's capacity to protect and promote workers' interests. Similarly, Turner (1991:52), who advocates greater union-management cooperation as a way of revitalizing the U.S. labor movement, argues that the union

3. Such management involvement in a labor organization is illegal in Canada and the United States.
4. Kenney and Florida (1988; 1993) show a certain ambivalence on the ability of enterprise unions to defend workers' interests. While they admit that Japanese industrial unions were completely defeated in the late 1940s and early 1950s, they regard the outcome of this victory of capital as a compromise settlement in which corporations had to make numerous concessions to workers. This interpretation stands in sharp contrast to that of scholars such as Dohse, Jürgens, and Malsch (1985), Halliday (1975), Kanawashi (1992), Moore (1983), Price (1995), Woodiwiss (1992), and Van Helvoort (1979).
5. In the *New York Times* (December 25, 1988) UAW Regional Director Bruce Lee praised NUMMI: "The workers' revolution has finally come to the shop floor. The people who work on the assembly line have taken charge and have the power to make management do their jobs right." Lee was responding to a *Times* article by Parker and Slaughter (1988a).

at NUMMI has a voice in areas that traditionally were the sole preserve of management. However, he maintains that the union has no independent vision, is dominated by management, and has taken on many of the characteristics of Japanese enterprise unions. This evaluation mirrors the criticism of lean production opponents Parker and Slaughter (1988). Union compliance in U.S. transplants, however, cannot be assumed, as indicated by developments at Mazda (Babson 1995, Fucini and Fucini 1990).

A major question for our research group was: what happens when a lean production system is faced with a national and local union that rejects close collaborative ties with management? Is the union able to establish an independent presence and make substantial encroachments on lean production principles and management practices? Can the union maintain standard wages, benefits, and work arrangements across the auto industry in the face of lean production's preference for enterprise-specific bargaining?[6] Developments at CAMI provided some answers to these questions.

A Foot in the Door

The CAW's first challenge was to get a foot inside CAMI's door. After initial discussions with union officials, the new company agreed not to oppose a CAW campaign to organize the plant, and the union signed up 90 percent of the workforce. The large percentage of sign-ups made a vote unnecessary, and the CAW was certified by the Ontario Labour Relations Board.[7] As at other unionized transplants, the quid pro quo for certification was an agreement to give up certain standard work rules and practices and to cooperate with management.

The first collective agreement at CAMI was signed January 23, 1989, prior to the start of production. The 36-page document departed from standard agreements in the auto industry. It committed the union to

---

6. For a discussion of lean production's challenge to North American unions see MacDuffie (1995b).

7. In 1995 the Conservative government of Ontario made sweeping changes to the province's labor laws, and now union certification requires a vote—as in the United States.

support some of the principles that came to be associated with lean production, including team concept, workers' participation in the continuous improvement of operations, elimination of job classifications,
"multi-job workers" and job rotation, and considerable management
flexibility in the allocation of work and workers. Suffused with references
to labor-management harmony and cooperation, the preface to the contract states: "This agreement between CAMI and the CAW was negotiated and will be administered in the spirit of mutual trust and in support
of CAMI's values." In addition, the union agreed to an economic package on wages and fringe benefits that fell below the industry norm.

In keeping with standard auto industry contracts, this one contained
a management rights clause as well as important union principles such
as union security, recognition of union committeepersons, a grievance
procedure, and minimal shop rules. It also included provisions for moving in the direction of parity with Big Three wages and benefits.

The CAW was formed out of a split with the UAW in December
1984. The decision to break away from the UAW was based, in part,
on the Canadian section's opposition to concessions and collaborative relations with employers. This policy was officially adopted at a
District Council meeting in 1981.[8] The gist of the union's position was
to hold the line on master agreements and pattern bargaining and to
advance a set of independent union demands backed by the readiness
to strike. This course of action diverged from the American wing's tendency to yield to corporate demands for profit sharing and bonuses (in
lieu of customary wage increases), QWL programs emphasizing cooperation with management, and the relaxation or elimination of standard work rules and shop floor practices (Yates 1993:206).[9]

8. The District Council (later renamed the Canadian Council) is a policy-making body
composed of delegates elected from the plants. The Council serves as a forum for debate and
facilitates communication between union leaders and the rank and file. The UAW has no
comparable structure. In fact, as Herzenberg (1993:315) points out, "UAW leaders [have] mar-
ginalized their critics through their control over union resources, staff positions, and forums
for internal debate..."

9. The divergent paths of the CAW and UAW emerged from a constellation of socio-
historical, political, and economic conditions, union structures, and rank and file actions that
took distinct forms in Canada and the United States. Concessionary bargaining in the auto
industry began in 1977 when a nearly bankrupt American Motors departed from the pattern
settlements across the industry. But the real turning point was the 1979 Chrysler negotiations
that wrung concessions from workers in both countries. It was after this point that the Cana-

Given this orientation, the second challenge faced by the CAW was how to deal with a new form of management and production that featured teamwork and labor-management cooperation. There was some disagreement within the union as to whether the CAW's departure from standard Big Three contracts and its agreement with CAMI to support aspects of lean production like teamwork and kaizen was a tactical compromise or an acceptance of the new system that signaled a change of direction for the union. This debate was aired at a meeting of the CAW Council in 1989. The Council adopted and widely circulated a "CAW Statement on the Reorganization of Work" that presented a distinctively union alternative to a vision of workplace restructuring driven by corporate criteria and objectives.

The doctrine of competitiveness, the statement declared, is not about productivity and quality but is an ideology that pits workers within and across nations against each other in a race to see who can provide the cheapest labor. Moreover, management aims to supplant worker solidarity with total identification with the company and its objectives. The document raised questions about labor-management partnership, arguing that "management's agenda is not about surrendering its power, but of finding more sophisticated ways to extend it" (CAW 1989:22).

> As we mobilize against regressive taxation, the weakening of unemployment insurance or plant closure legislation, we are reminding our members that the "team" they are on is not the same team as their employer, and the "adversary" is not other workers but those who are on the other side of these issues. Similarly, as we take on other collective bargaining issues—like opposing profit-sharing, or demanding indexed pensions or insisting on some movement towards reduced worktime, the message that the needs of working people are quite different from those of management is constantly articulated (CAW 1989:24).

The statement allowed that there was nothing inherently bad about teams, collapsed job classifications, job rotation, or kaizen. However, if

---

dian UAW began to generate a distinct no-concessions policy. The catalyst for the split was the 1984 GM negotiations in which UAW President Owen Bieber tried to impose a concessionary settlement on the Canadians (Benedict 1985; Edwards and Podgursky 1986; Gindin 1989, 1995; Herzenberg 1993; Holmes and Rusonik 1991; National Film Board 1984; Yates 1993).

these practices jeopardized workers' rights, degraded working conditions, and eroded union independence, they should be contested. The document stated that rigid work standards must be rejected because they inhibit worker discretion. Kaizen should be resisted if it intensifies work and makes it more stressful. And if lean production translates into a company's inability to accommodate older or injured workers, it should be opposed.

The document indicates support for productivity and quality improvements, as well as more rewarding jobs and a democratic workplace. However, the means to achieve these ends must come not from a partnership with management but from the pursuit of a specifically union agenda in which workers' interests are paramount. The statement declared:

> We support efforts to involve and empower workers, to increase worker dignity, to produce quality products with pride, to make jobs more rewarding and the workplace more democratic. These objectives will be achieved through our own agenda for change, our own demands around training, technology, improving jobs, improving the work environment, guaranteeing health and safety, strengthening mobility rights, strengthening affirmative action and strengthening the union. (CAW 1989:25)[10]

CAMI and Local 88

The union local occupies, or more accurately shapes, the space between a collective agreement that accommodates aspects of team concept and the policy statement of the national union that raises many questions about lean production. The history of CAW Local 88 involves both adjustment to the lean system and the promotion of workers' rights and interests.

CAMI teaches recruits that management and workers have a common interest in continuously reducing costs to undercut competitors in the dog-eat-dog world of vehicle manufacture. They are told that if

10. See Kumar and Holmes (1996) for a discussion of the evolving relationship between the CAW and the auto industry in Canada. These authors characterize the CAW's position as a mixture of ideological resistance and pragmatic willingness to negotiate reforms that are mutually beneficial to workers and companies.

they do not follow the new lean production route, CAMI will be forced out of business. Underlying this message is the company's insistence that lean production is a system with no losers. In an era of mounting plant closures, high unemployment, and a business ideology of competitiveness that justifies a downward spiral of wages and working conditions, CAMI's philosophy is powerfully seductive. The company's indoctrination and Canada's troubled economy make it difficult for a union to pursue an independent course of action and to generate among rank and file members strong commitments to the union and its objectives. To achieve independence Local 88 has had to engage in a tug of war with CAMI management for the hearts and minds of the workers.

The local wasted little time in establishing an independent presence. While CAMI was in start-up mode, the union had a desk in the Employee Relations office.[11] Its only written communication with members was through several paragraphs in the company bulletin. Workers were hesitant to call the union and complained about the failure of union reps to get back to them if they did call. As often as not, union reps sought informal solutions to settle workers' complaints, and only four grievances were filed in 1989. In our first round of interviews a team leader said: "It was obvious you had a union there [at his previous workplace]." He felt the union's presence was not so obvious at CAMI.

Over time, the union began to demand changes. Independent space was an important issue, and union reps skirmished with the company over the meaning of the collective agreement's provision to furnish space for the union. Local 88 wanted an area to itself; management wanted shared accommodation, presumably to portray the union as an arm of the company's Employee Relations Department. By our second visit, the union had taken over a workroom and called it the "Union Work Center." In February 1990, the local began publishing its newsletter, *Off the Line,* and committeepersons were now devoting all their time to union business.[12] These kinds of developments prompted one manager to criticize the union for its aggressiveness, attributing this to the

11. Union representatives and employee relations personnel at Mazda and NUMMI also shared the same office. Mazda workers sometimes confused the two groups, while at NUMMI workers' confusion was so great that they unwittingly brought complaints to company personnel. In several instances the complainants were fired as a result (Fucini and Fucini 1993:119–121; Kenney and Florida 1993:278).

12. The union newsletter was a sore point for managers, some of whom told us they regarded it as nothing more than propaganda reflecting the opinions of the militant minority.

leadership's inexperience. "They [local union reps] can't see the forest for the trees and realize some things don't get solved instantaneously. They sometimes have to evolve over time."

The relationship between local union officials and the rank and file involved a great deal of back and forth influence. In some instances, union reps acted proactively by defining issues, galvanizing the membership, and spearheading struggles. More often than not, however, the union took up issues only after complaints or collective resistance had reached a critical stage. For example, a union rep described a work slowdown in the paint shop that quickly resolved a problem. He remarked: "It was great. I wish I could orchestrate something like this." In the final round a team leader observed: "We're hearing some very serious complaints about committeepeople not pushing hard enough, indicating the membership is becoming more militant than the union." On a day-by-day basis, then, the actions of the union were powerfully shaped by the membership.

As production got into full swing, accelerated line speeds and increasingly heavy workloads came to occupy much of the union reps' time. Survey respondents and workers throughout the plant complained about managers acting in a heavy-handed and arbitrary manner, the strict absenteeism policy, the difficulty of getting an authorized day off, overtime and overtime equalization, pressure to submit teians or do taiso, understaffing, the dress code, and hassles over prompt washroom relief. Many workers viewed these conditions as a betrayal of CAMI's promises of empowerment and openness and urged the union to do something about them. As one union rep pointed out, "People are now starting to realize on the floor CAMI's not this great place to work that they [management] portray it. The bottom line is it's an automobile plant." Another union rep explained: "We started making cars. It became a factory, and it changes people's attitudes. A lotta people have got burned or screwed around, and they're bitter." Sometimes an effective union response was straitjacketed by contract wording or by management inflexibility. At other times, the union was able to reach a settlement or to set the stage for the company to reevaluate and relax its policies. Even a partial list of union actions gives a sense of the kinds of issues taken up and their outcomes.

The union assured workers that refusals to do pre-shift exercises, to hand in teians, or to participate in QC circles would not lead to grief or punishment. The local supported a collective andon-pull to protest understaffing on the door line, and won two extra workers in the area. (One team pulled the cord 169 times, 97 of which stopped the line.) The local pushed unsuccessfully for workers' right to listen to radios and won the right to have reading material other than that distributed by CAMI in team areas. The local's support of workers' demand to wear poppies on Remembrance Day or shorts and sweatshirts led the company to relax enforcement of its strict dress code. A supplier's mistake led to missing seats. When the seats arrived the supplier's employees began installing them on vehicles parked outside the plant. The union vigorously maintained that the jobs belonged to the members. The company relented and even agreed to "armchair pay" (wages for not working) for CAMI's seat installers.

The local put a stop to CAMI's policy of arbitrarily determining cross-training moves between teams in different departments. The demotion of a team leader was grieved and settled by arbitration in favor of the union. The local formulated a set of guidelines that clearly distinguished team leaders' responsibilities from those of management.[13]

Local 88 was involved in a protracted struggle over health and safety. The local presented CAMI with a detailed proposal to train PAs in the nuts and bolts of ergonomic analysis. This would allow workers, rather than an arm of the company, to redesign unsafe jobs. CAMI flatly rejected the proposal. The company was also reluctant to recognize workers' legal right to refuse unsafe work. Workers were sometimes threatened with discipline for exercising this right.[14] At other times, managers pressured workers to cut corners to minimize downtime, such as failing to lock out machines. In response to mounting concerns, the union safety

13. In January 1991 Local 88 met with the leadership of UAW Local 3000 from Mazda. Representatives of the two locals learned that the operations, working conditions, and shop floor relations in their plants were similar in many respects, as were many of the issues they took up on a daily basis. Out of this discussion emerged a document that outlined the common problems faced by the two locals. "A Shared Struggle" rejected labor-management partnership and emphasized that adversarial relationships are both natural and positive.

14. Some managers believed workers were abusing their rights. One of them observed, "I think some of the work refusals out there have an underlying cause more than just safety. I think they're using it, sometimes at least, as a method of addressing another situation." In June 1996 the Ontario Labour Ministry charged CAMI and a supervisor for taking disciplinary action against a worker who refused to work with a pneumatic device used to install the wheel assembly on cars. The charge was called "unprecedented," since most health and safety disputes are settled within companies (*London Free Press,* June 8, 1996).

reps called in the Ministry of Labour, which forced the company to recognize workers' right to refuse unsafe work. As at other plants represented by the CAW, the union distributed to CAMI workers wallet-size
cards that specified the procedures to follow in refusing unsafe work.

Local 88's record of challenging CAMI's philosophy, policies, and
practices strengthened the influence of and support for the union. The
survey results confirmed this trend. Despite the fact that a little over 40
percent of the respondents had no union experience before coming to
CAMI, in the final round of interviews 81 percent strongly agreed and
19 percent agreed that a union was needed at CAMI (the corresponding round 1 figures were 53.4 and 43.8 percent). Participation in local
elections has been high. More and more workers looked to the union
to resolve their problems. In round 1, 37.3 percent of survey respondents
said that if someone in their team was subjected to harassment or unfair
treatment they would most likely contact their union rep. The other
respondents said they would approach their team leader, area leader, or
someone from Personnel. By round 4, 60.8 percent said they would
turn to their union rep in a case of harassment or injustice. This survey
result was reflected by comments of union reps, one of whom said, "I've
found that a lot of [workers] have turned to us for their problems, where
before they were trying to get them fixed by management. Our workload's gone up quite a bit." Another rep observed: "The mistrust of a
lot of area leaders and assistant managers has caused people down on
the floor to request us a lot more. . . . [As] the company pisses them off,
they turn to us." These comments were consistent with the expanded
grievance load, which reached 150 in October 1991. By September 1992,
just before the strike, the number of unresolved grievances had bal-
looned to over 400.

After the strike CAMI hired a new Vice-President of Production
from Toyota, adopted a more stringent absenteeism policy, and tight-
ened up on enforcement. The Joint Attendance Committee, which was
composed of one rank and file worker, one union rep, and one person
from Employee Relations (ER), was disbanded by the company when
both union members began to regularly outvote the ER member on
questions of discipline. The company also announced a get-tough policy on unscheduled washroom breaks, making it difficult for assemblers
to leave the line when the need arose. For a period in 1994 CAMI was
posting supervisors at selected work areas to track workers who left the

line. The union's vigorous opposition and several exposés in the *London Free Press* led the company to back off this practice.

Contracting out, about which we heard little during our time in the plant, has become a volatile issue. Some work in Material Handling has been lost to a nearby firm that uses temporary (and much cheaper) workers. The jobs—opening and unpacking shipping cartons—were among the worst in that department but still preferable to line jobs. CAMI managed to chop these positions without too much backlash from the floor, but in March 1995 the company, with no prior notification, contracted out TPM tasks (e.g., cleaning robot tips and the lines) in Welding. Workers responded immediately. Upon hearing of the company's move, the entire second shift (about 1,000 workers) joined the Welding workers and refused to enter the plant. For 45 minutes all three entry gates to the plant were jammed. The work stoppage was called off when management agreed to negotiate, mete out no discipline, and pay workers for the 45 minutes. The company agreed to use eight CAMI "weekend workers" to handle TPM. For six weeks these PAs worked 12 hours on Saturday and Sunday for 40 hours' pay. Subsequently, TPM in Welding was handled by the midnight shift.

Contractual Gains

The 1992 strike settlement narrowed the wage gap between CAMI and the Big Three and brought COLA (cost of living adjustments), SUB (supplementary unemployment benefits), health care, insurance, and pensions up to the industry standard in Canada. This economic package was significant not only because it raised the living standards of the members, but also because it represented a setback to CAMI's (and the Japanese system's) goal of tailoring wages and benefits to the economic performance of the individual enterprise. By rejecting the company's preference for tying collective bargaining to the unique conditions of the single enterprise and holding out for the principle of wage parity across auto plants, the CAW avoided getting caught up in the concessions game.

The new contract incorporated several important encroachments on lean practices (which were discussed more fully in earlier chapters). First, CAMI agreed to establish a permanent crew of relief workers for each department, to cover absenteeism. This clause went directly against the lean axiom that team members should cover for each other, to keep head-count down. Second, the contract committed the company to consider the "reasonable working capacity of normal experienced operators" in setting workloads. Again, by introducing the concept of "reasonable" capacity, this wording chipped at the lean principle of never-ending speed-up. Third, the agreement provided for the election rather than management selection of team leaders.

The contract required CAMI to contribute to the CAW Paid Education Leave Program to upgrade employees' trade union skills, through a one-cent-an-hour payment. This was intended to strengthen Local 88 members' involvement in the CAW and reinforce the union's independence. A joint Training Review Committee, a joint Environmental Committee, and a joint Employment Equity Committee were established. The union achieved improved language on advance notice of technological change, including full discussions on the effects of such change. The contract also contained a host of specific improvements, including more opportunities for leaves of absence, relaxation of attendance rules, assurance that employees who appropriately used the andons would not be disciplined, regular posting of seniority lists, strict limits on transfers to and from the bargaining unit, limits on work done by supervisors, improved language on overtime equalization, and provision for the reconsideration of "impulsive resignations."

The 1995 contract was ratified without a strike by just over two-thirds of the voting membership. As discussed in previous chapters, the contract called for additional paid time off, which necessitated the hiring of more workers. The contract also created a full-time union production standards rep, established a mechanism to regulate and place limits on workloads, and provided union resources to fight excessive workloads. This was a major accomplishment in a lean environment, since it directly attacks the principle of kaizen. The union got wage and benefits gains, economic security in case of permanent layoffs or a plant closure, improved job posting procedures, and health and safety improvements. The union also got the company to acknowledge in a "best efforts letter" that work historically done by CAMI workers in the plant should remain in the plant. This was a step toward restricting outsourcing, but the union was unable to secure a firm contractual commitment. As a symbolic gesture, the union insisted that the words "in support of CAMI values" be dropped from the preface to the contract.

The literature on lean production has raised, but not answered, two important questions. Under lean production, is it possible to build a strong union capable of representing the independent interests of workers? Second, can that strength and independence be used to modify substantially the terms and conditions of lean production?

Garrahan and Stewart (1992:19) observed that workers at the Nissan plant in Sunderland, England, have no coherent alternative to the company's vision of reality: "There is no real absence of conflict [at this plant], but an absence of a particular type of conflict—the conflict of organized oppositional world views." A similar level of corporate hegemony has been noted in the nonunion auto transplants of North America. In contrast, CAMI's attempts to cultivate a workforce with a corporate identity committed to cooperation on management's terms has been effectively contested by the union. Local 88 has given workers a distinct point of reference, one that stands in sharp contrast to and challenges the philosophy and actions of the company. The union alternative to CAMI ideology and practice has played a crucial role in reflecting and influencing the attitudes and activities of the members. The local has established itself at CAMI as an independent voice, one that has allowed workers to translate their individual discontents and grievances into a collective and more effective effort to protect and promote their rights and interests. These actions allow an affirmative answer to the first question on union independence.

In light of the 1992 and 1995 agreements a qualified yes can be given to the second question. Both contracts challenged key practices of lean production, and these revisions are a step in the direction of more extensive and more binding union limits on the operation of the system. However, not only is contract language open to different interpretations, but the translation of written clauses into restructured shop floor relations and practices is rarely uncontested. Even when agreements on work rules and practices are implemented, they are subject to challenges, evasions, and gradual erosion. Like other complex organizations, those based on the lean model never stand still. If there is one constant in an auto assembly plant it is constant change. Vehicle models are altered; market demand fluctuates; management introduces new procedures, programs, and directives; contracts get rewritten; and shop floor relations are a negotiated order whose boundaries are constantly shifting.

CHAPTER 13

Is CAMI Exceptional?

P ROPONENTS OF LEAN PRODUCTION MAY WANT TO DISMISS THE findings of our study, especially those that belie the lean system's alleged harmony and humane, empowering environment. We anticipate several modes of criticism. First, we expect the critique that since ours is a case study, generalization must be limited. Second, we expect critics to define CAMI as exceptional by stressing its Canadian context and the militancy of the CAW. Finally, it is likely that lean production adherents will try to explain away our results by invoking the partial implementation thesis.

We will begin with the last concern. Since "partial implementation" was thoroughly discussed in Chapter 11, we will be brief here. We maintain that the drift from CAMI values, the declining levels of worker participation and commitment, the growing resistance, and the strikes did not arise from the inadequate implementation of lean procedures. CAMI managers did become tougher—less observant of "CAMI values"—over time, but certainly no more so than their counterparts in Japan or in other transplants that have been systematically studied, such as Mazda and Subaru-Isuzu. And CAMI did face a host of problems getting the plant up and running at full capacity. Both of these conditions undoubtedly contributed to manifestations of worker indifference and discontent. However, the shift in management style and CAMI's "growing pains" were driven or magnified by the demands and pressures associated with implementation of more and more elements of leanness. In short, many of the problems we detected were rooted in and inherent to a lean system.

Wherever it operates, lean production strives to operate with minimal labor. It is a system that aspires to eliminate all production buffers save one—an understaffed workforce that is expected to make up for production glitches, line stoppages, unbalanced production scheduling, and injured or absent workers through intensified effort and overtime. The true buffers in this system are the workers. During 1992 each CAMI worker logged an average of 1,903 hours in the plant; 2,169 hours in 1993; 2,298 in 1994. Based on the first five months of 1995, the projected total for the full year would be 2,354 hours.[1] While there are substantial differences between traditional mass production plants and lean transplants, including CAMI, these differences do not make shop floor life under lean more humane. They make it more arduous and stressful.

CAMI exceptionalism and the limited generalizability of our results will be addressed together. Our findings on the labor process and the ways CAMI workers and their union have responded to lean production do not stand alone. Other reports of working conditions and shop floor relations in lean plants, whether union or nonunion, have paralleled our findings at CAMI in important respects. It is true that labor-management relations in North American transplants have been remarkably stable if the measure is the absence of strikes and the failure of union organizing drives. However, this surface calm is not tantamount to ideal working conditions and labor-management harmony. The handful of transplant studies undertaken from the vantage point of the shop floor have challenged the popular notion that working conditions under lean are superior to those that prevailed in traditional North American plants. Lean staffing, rigidly standardized jobs, and a grueling work pace are commonplace, as are strict attendance policies, dress codes, and rules of conduct (Babson 1993; Berggren 1992; Fucini and Fucini 1990; Graham 1993, 1995; Junkerman 1987; Kendall 1987; Parker and Slaughter 1988, 1994). These are not the conditions out of which harmony is fashioned.

1. CAMI workers were moving away from Western Europe's average of 1,800 annual hours of work and approaching Japan's 2,500 (in 1991). This trend is occurring in the North American auto assembly industry in general.

The transplants' surface stability, we submit, is partially a response to current economic and political conditions. Workers across North America presently are relatively immune to unionization and reluctant to strike. Militancy is inhibited by massive employment losses in manufacturing in general and the auto industry in particular, declining union density (especially in the United States) and political influence, whipsawing and outsourcing by the auto companies, and the threat of plant closures and relocations to low-wage regions of the world (Huxley, Kettler, and Struthers 1986; Turner 1990; Wells 1995). Economic pressures are accentuated by the auto transplants' tendency to locate in areas where wages are low and jobs scarce, with no history of unions. Moreover, transplants wholly owned by the Japanese have actively opposed unionization (Green and Yanarella 1995; Kenney and Florida 1993; Parker and Slaughter 1988). These conditions may curb union drives and strikes, but they cannot produce labor-management harmony.[2]

The evidence suggests that labor-management relations inside transplants are fraught with conflict. Graham's (1993, 1995) participant-observation study at nonunion SIA in Indiana revealed considerable strife and worker resistance.[3] The unionized transplants' efforts to nurture worker consensus and transform local unions into junior partners have been supported by the national UAW's endorsement of team concept and cooperation. Despite this, labor-management relations at the local level in all U.S. auto plants, including the transplants, are decidedly uneven (Turner 1991). At Mazda working conditions and shop floor relations are similar in many ways to those at CAMI. The initial group of appointed, pro-cooperation local union leaders was replaced through elec-

2. It would be foolish to maintain that these conditions will permanently prevent unionization. Babson (1993), for example, argues that unionists should not view the one-third pro-union vote at the Tennessee Nissan plant in 1989 in a totally pessimistic light. He bases this observation on the very young age of the Nissan workforce. As workers age, the rigors and pace of work demanded of them will become increasingly intolerable, and it is not unreasonable to think that at some point they will look favorably on a union solution.

3. Selected interviews with Nissan (Smyrna, Tennessee) workers revealed working conditions similar to those at SIA (Slaughter 1989). Little is known of other nonunion transplants, since researchers have not managed to get inside them. Likewise, little has been written about the unionized Diamond Star plant in Illinois (subsequently Mitsubishi), although Berggren (1993:181) was told by the local union president that workers' attitudes had shifted from trust to distrust of management. Widespread complaints of sexual harassment in this plant provide further evidence of poor relations in transplants.

tions by a more militant slate. The plant has seen recurrent in-plant demonstrations, work stoppages, work-to-rule actions, and boycotts of the suggestion program. In 1991 the membership gave a 94 percent strike mandate. The strike was averted just before the deadline (Babson 1993). A few minutes more and Mazda, not CAMI, would have become the first transplant to go on strike.

This leaves NUMMI as the ostensible model of harmony in a unionized transplant. The bulk of the literature on this plant is a paean to its labor-management harmony and operational efficiency. While lean production adherents attribute this state of affairs to union cooperation, management's emphasis on building high-trust relations, and workers' participation, they do not discount contingent conditions. Few observers of this plant, including those who wholeheartedly endorse its lean system, fail to mention the severe trauma experienced by NUMMI workers, many of whom were thrown out of work for several years by the closure of the GM plant that now houses NUMMI (Adler 1993a, 1993b; Parker and Slaughter 1988; Turner 1991). It is not unreasonable to assume that these workers are still haunted by the fear of a shutdown, or what Adler (1993b) calls a "mature sense of realism," and that this fear influences their attitudes and behavior.

If NUMMI's stability is contingent, it is also relative. NUMMI workers, particularly those in assembly, have taken actions that indicate deep discontent with working conditions and management. In 1988 1,000 workers signed a petition to protest understaffing and the strict absenteeism policy. In that same year many candidates of the opposition People's Caucus were elected. In the 1991 elections dissatifaction with speed-up and favoritism propelled People's Caucus candidates to victory in a majority of important union positions throughout the plant (Berggren 1993; Turner 1991). In 1994 the Administration Caucus played on workers' fears of job loss as an election issue, suggesting that an opposition victory could cause the plant to close. Despite this tactic, the People's Caucus, which campaigned on the issues of favoritism, heavy workloads, and a high rate of RSIs, won half the union positions, including chair of the bargaining committee (Parker 1994). In August 1994 NUMMI's 10-year no-strike record was broken by a two-hour walkout over management's demand for the ten-hour day at straight time and a free hand to change work rules. Management handed out flyers encouraging workers to resign from the union and cross picket lines. But the company withdrew its demands, and seven days later a new contract was ratified (Lund 1994, Parker and Slaughter 1994).

CAMI is unique in only one sense—its workers staged the first and only sustained strike of a North American auto transplant. While the strike defines CAMI as exceptional, the conditions that produced it are not exceptional, since they appear in both union and nonunion transplants. To the extent that these onerous conditions are the norm in transplants, events at CAMI cannot be explained by reference to the militancy of the CAW. The divergent policies of the CAW and the UAW are important but not decisive. At the end of the day, local militancy or cooperativeness cannot be imposed from the top by national union officials. Local union politics reflect economic conditions, national union policies, shop floor relations among workers and between workers and managers, and the actions of local union leaders. The CAW has rejected concessions and labor-management cooperation. It has raised questions about the impact of lean production on workers and encouraged the CAMI local to promote workers' interests actively. But apart from the strike itself, developments at Mazda are quite similar to those at CAMI, and Mazda workers have manifested great shop floor militancy. Perhaps NUMMI is the most distinctive unionized transplant. NUMMI may lie toward the harmonious end of a continuum, but the distance between NUMMI and the more combative locals of Mazda and CAMI is not all that great.[4]

Across North America the Big Three automakers are incorporating more and more elements of the lean model. The Ford plant in Hermosillo, Mexico, which began production in 1987, exhibits striking operational and organizational similarities to CAMI (Huxley, Rinehart, and Robertson 1994). Hermosillo was ranked high by the International Motor Vehicle Program's worldwide survey: "The best plant in terms of quality, Ford at Hermosillo, Mexico, in fact had the best assembly plant quality

---

4. The differential militancy and effectiveness of the Mazda and NUMMI workers' challenges to the lean system reflect in part a) the bitter rivalry between the NUMMI local's Administration and People's Caucuses, and b) the pressure on NUMMI workers from the UAW Regional Office to accede to management demands. Internal divisions within the Mazda local are less pronounced, and their UAW Regional Office has supported worker militancy and organized supplier plants in the region (Parker and Slaughter 1994:286).

in the entire volume plant sample, better than that of the best Japanese plants and the best North American transplants. The best developing country plant was also surprisingly efficient, particularly given its modest level of automation" (Womack, Jones, and Roos 1990:87). The MIT group attributed this sterling performance to the plant's lean procedures.

Despite the fact that the Confederación de Trabajadores de Mexico union (CTM) has little presence on the shop floor at Hermosillo and a reputation for containing dissent, labor-management relations there have been highly conflictual. The CTM led a wage strike in 1987. When the company fired the strike committee, the workers responded with line stoppages, boycotts, and a high level of absenteeism. Workers did not get the wage settlement they sought, and opposition groups denounced the CTM. A more militant slate of local union officials was elected, but they too were fired. Eventually, Ford conceded bonuses and wage increases. Since the strike, resistance has taken more passive forms, such as workers wearing red arm bands and quitting (the turnover rate ranges between 25 and 44 percent) (Shaiken 1993; Sandoval and Wong 1994). While a legitimate case might be made for the unique conditions under which Ford Hermosillo operates, events there do raise questions about the alleged organic connection between lean, peaceful labor relations, committed workers, and superior performance.

The case against CAMI exceptionalism is further strengthened by developments at several General Motors plants in Canada and the United States where unions have vigorously challenged lean methods of working.

In October 1994 workers at the Buick City complex in Flint, Michigan, walked out over speed-ups, overtime that sometimes required 66-hour work weeks, and health and safety. The four-day strike ended when GM agreed to hire 779 new workers, settled thousands of grievances over workloads and health and safety, agreed to a rehabilitation center for injured workers, and ceased workshops on synchronous manufacturing (GM's term for lean production) unless approved by the union (Braid 1994; *Globe and Mail,* Oct. 3, 1994).

Similar conditions at GM's AC Delco plant in Flint prompted workers to strike in January 1995. Work resumed when the company announced it would hire 663 workers (the total workforce was 6,600) and invest $90 million to avoid contracting out—a move that would save 244 jobs in the plant (*Globe and Mail,* Jan. 23, 1995). Also in January 1995, workers at GM's assembly plant in St. Thérèse, Quebec, wildcatted over a foreman's actions. The CAW argued that the underlying cause of the walk-out was understaffing and speed-up. The workers were ordered back to work by the courts, under threat of severe penalties.

The 17-day strikes at two Dayton, Ohio, GM brake plants in March 1996 led to the closure of many independent parts plants and 26 of 29 GM assembly plants in North America.[5] The central issue in these strikes was outsourcing—a key component of the lean system. However, the settlement included concessions to the UAW on issues of the internal lean regime—hiring several hundred workers to alleviate excessive overtime and exhausting work and spending $6.5 million on ergonomic improvements to reduce injuries (Chappell 1996a; Charles and Sedgwick 1996).

These developments are significant because the issues in dispute are intrinsic to lean production—understaffing, contracting out, heavy workloads, excessive overtime, and RSIs. To the extent that conflicts such as these continue to plague lean facilities, it will be increasingly difficult to single out CAMI as exceptional.

It may be, as Womack, Jones, and Roos (1990:278) conclude, that "lean production will supplement both mass production and the remaining outposts of craft production in all areas of industrial endeavor to become the standard global production system of the twenty-first century." However, their claim that this will make the world "a much better place" has been and will continue to be regarded by many, most notably workers in lean workplaces, with a healthy skepticism. As lean production finds more and more sites of application, we are more likely to witness manifestations of discontent and unrest than a new post-Fordist era of industrial peace and harmony.

---

5. Ironically, NUMMI—an alleged leader in JIT inventory—was one of the three plants not affected by the strike. NUMMI had a substantial stockpile of anti-lock brake systems; in this instance just-in-case turned out to be superior to JIT (Chappell 1996a).

CHAPTER 14

Just Another Car Factory?

DOES CAMI REPRESENT A TRANSCENDENCE OF FORDIST MASS production? Is it just another car factory? The answer to the first question is an unequivocal no, but the second one has no categorical answer.

To designate lean production as postFordist is to claim that it represents a qualitative advance over mass production in two workplace spheres. First, the system must operate with manufacturing procedures significantly different from those used under mass production. Second, it must be distinct in the areas of job design, the labor process, and labor-management relations.

At first glance, lean production appears to meet the initial criterion. JIT, kanbans, leveled production, quick die changes, and related techniques constitute departures from the procedures employed in traditional auto plants. CAMI's operations sometimes deviated from the lean ideal, but the company constantly strove to perfect them. But even if they are functioning optimally, these techniques do not constitute a transcendence of mass production. They are more appropriately regarded as supplements to or refinements of Fordism. At CAMI, as at other lean auto plants, the conveyor remains the heart of production. The logic and pace of the line set the tone and tempo of work for the entire plant. This combination of conveyor-based production and the technical and operational procedures unique to lean production may best be described as neo- rather than postFordist.

Lean production also falls short on the second criterion. Only if lean plants afford the kind of humane work environment described in the early literature on the subject would they qualify as postFordist. The lean environment is characterized by standardized, short-cycled, heavily loaded jobs. It is remarkable that, in a period when the writings of scholars are saturated with references to postFordism, one of the most contentious issues at CAMI centers around time-study, workloads, and job standards. These issues figured prominently in union organizing drives in the 1930s and 1940s, and were an endless focal point of disputes in auto plants. To see them resurfacing in a lean facility speaks volumes about the validity of labeling this mode of manufacturing postFordist.

The early literature on lean production extolled the progressive personnel practices, committed workforces, and harmonious labor-management relations of Japanese firms and transplants. We found nothing at CAMI to suggest that the Japanese management system or Japanese managers were any more enlightened, or any less authoritarian and arbitrary, than North American managers. In fact, North American managers at CAMI said they acted as mediators between workers and Japanese executives and softened the rigid policies of the latter. Moreover, we found a low and declining level of worker commitment and forms of resistance ranging from indifference to collective andon pulls, work stoppages, and strikes. We see little reason to believe that lean production cannot operate effectively without a committed workforce. The only requirement is workers who competently perform their jobs and keep a plant running without frequent and major disruptions. This is not to say that lean companies do not prefer and actively seek to recruit and nurture committed workers, or that they welcome a "third party" (a union).

When used to designate lean production, postFordism is a misnomer. It is one part rhetoric, one part rush to judgment, and one-third wishful thinking. We suggest that the term be put under wraps until, we hope, a production system arises that is worthy of the appellation. To reject the applicability of the term postFordist is not to deny substantial differences between lean and mass production, however.

Team concept, which has ideological, social, and operational components, invariably is associated with lean auto plants. While work teams and job rotation facilitate the elimination of the multiple job classifications typical of traditional plants, we detected little in the lean production process that necessitated teams per se. Most of the technical operations in the plant could be conducted without teams. Standardized jobs, short-cycled, line-based work, JIT pull processes, and several layers of production management precluded any but the most routine kinds of team discretion. The most important functions of teams lie in the social sphere. On the one hand, working in teams facilitates sociability and mutual support. On the other hand, they operate as a lateral control system and create cleavages among workers. We found little in the writings of either critics or proponents of lean to alert us to the complexity of team dynamics. At CAMI teams were simultaneously sources of support for and resistance to management authority and expectations.

Team leaders at CAMI assume many of the tasks performed by foremen in traditional plants, but they have no managerial authority. They face the often contradictory expectations of team members and management. Team leaders are central to the aspirations of the company in as much as they may identify with and support either the team or management. It is not surprising that the selection and role of team leaders are contentious issues at CAMI.

Lean production's encouragement of worker participation in continuously changing jobs via kaizen and associated programs clearly sets it apart from traditional plants where formal job design was monopolized by industrial engineers. However, no evidence suggests that the production knowledge of workers under lean production is any greater than that of their mass production counterparts. The latter engaged in what may be described as an *informal* kaizen process. Workers continuously modified their jobs to make them easier to perform, but ordinarily these improvements were not shared with the company.

We found little evidence at CAMI of a reunification of mental and manual labor. While workers are encouraged to improve operations, the parameters of kaizen are defined by the criterion of cost-reduction, not safer, easier, or more interesting jobs, and the disposition of suggestions—other than the most trivial ones—is in the hands of management. When practices workers instituted through kaizen conflicted with the cost-down dictates of lean production, they often were torpedoed by management. Over time workers evinced greater skepticism of kaizen, their participation in QC circle and teian programs declined, and the corps of industrial engineers grew. Because of these developments and the narrow scope and degree of worker input, kaizen in no way can be construed as a democratization of Taylorism.

The early literature on lean production repeatedly referred to workers as multiskilled and the work as challenging. At CAMI, some jobs were better than others, and there were preferred work areas and departments. But the same is true of traditional auto plants. We didn't discover many challenging jobs at CAMI. Most of them were quickly learned, highly standardized, and repetitive. The only break from monotony was job rotation, but that was a matter of multitasking, not multiskilling. Nor did the assumption by workers of indirect tasks augment skill. Workers learned some soft skills not taught in traditional plants. However, training was brief, much of it was ideological, and opportunities for continuous skills development were few.

Most adherents of lean production acknowledge that work under this system is arduous and intense. We found that lean production means lean staffing, a penchant to load more and more work onto jobs, and an unquenchable thirst for overtime. Not surprisingly, given CAMI's design of jobs, we found a high incidence of repetitive strain injuries. This discovery did not challenge the findings of lean production advocates, since they had little or nothing to say about RSIs.

The 1992 strike against CAMI was only the most visible manifestation of worker discontent. Workers and union representatives regularly contest and constantly change CAMI's policies, work rules, demands, and working conditions. The company wants maximum flexibility in the scheduling of production, the design and rebalancing of jobs, and the use and deployment of the workforce. Workers want tighter, more specific contract language so that management policies and actions can be more effectively challenged and grieved. The union at CAMI is integrally involved in this give and take. It provides a distinct perspective on work, politics, and society. It is an alternative source of worker identification. The union defends and promotes the interests of workers, and it both leads and reflects workers' struggles against those elements of lean production and management practice that are inimical to these interests. In the 1992 and 1995 contracts CAMI agreed to some substantial modifications of lean practices. These agreements and the daily activities of Local 88 provide a clear answer to questions about the viability of an independent union in a lean plant. In regard to everyday resistance and union practice, not a lot distinguishes CAMI from traditional plants.

In some ways CAMI is similar to, but in many important respects it is different from, an ideal typical mass production plant. It uses a number of distinct technical, operational, and organizational procedures and practices. Vehicles are made by workers who rotate jobs and are organized in teams headed not by a foreman but a team leader. The system relies on elaborate programs to encourage workers to use their production knowledge to constantly refine their jobs. These and a constellation of related practices mark CAMI and lean production as distinct, but they do not make for a better, more humane workplace.

On more than one occasion workers described CAMI as just another car factory. We never asked them to amplify, but it seems clear these opinions were based on the activities that occupied most of their working day. The everyday routines under lean are more rigorous and demanding than those of traditional auto assembly plants. When it comes to how workers spend most of their time on the job, the contrast between lean and mass production becomes blurred. PostFordist, no; different from traditional auto plants, in some ways; better than traditional auto plants, not according to most CAMI workers.

Methodology

THE CAMI PROJECT RAISES A NUMBER OF METHODOLOGICAL ISSUES. This appendix provides an account of the research process, along with some technical information that the reader may require to assess our procedures.

Initiation of the CAW Research Group on CAMI

Labour Canada (a department of the federal government now called Human Resources Development Canada) wanted to fund a study of a lean production plant, but failed to persuade CAMI to open its doors to a professional research team. Subsequently, the CAW initiated this study of CAMI with the encouragement and funding of Labour Canada. Access to the factory by the CAW researchers was negotiated through senior level meetings between the union and the company. The union's hand during negotiations with the company was strengthened by holding the company to its stated goals of open communication and cooperation. Refusal to permit the research would have implied that the company was not prepared to live up to its stated values, and the union was quick to emphasize this point. CAMI agreed to our research group's access on the condition that it had the right to provide a written response to the report that would be submitted to Labour Canada. We were able to develop a good working relationship with CAMI management that extended over the entire in-plant phase of the study.

Funding was secured from Labour Canada with the understanding that the union would assume responsibility for administrative and secretarial support. Most of the grant of approximately $100,000 was used to pay release time for the CAW members of the research group, and a good portion was spent on travel and subsistence during the four research visits to the plant. Chris Huxley and Jim Rinehart received several small research grants from their universities.

In August 1989 Huxley and Rinehart met with the CAW Director of Research. They learned of the union's intention to conduct a study of CAMI and were introduced to David Robertson, who recently had been given overall responsibility for coordinating the project. Huxley and Rinehart observed the October 1989 meeting of the union's Canadian Council, which discussed workplace reorganization. In January 1990 the two academics accepted the union's invitation to serve as members of what was to become known as the CAW Research Group on CAMI.

Research collaboration between union and academic researchers is rare, and our research group was unusual in this respect. It consisted of seven persons: the research coordinator and a researcher from the CAW national office, two academics, and three CAW members with long-standing industrial work and union experience at their places of work.

David Robertson and Jeff Wareham, the two CAW staff members, had conducted several detailed workplace studies for the CAW Research Department (Robertson and Wareham 1987, 1989). In addition to an interest in workplace research, Rinehart and Huxley had long shared an interest in issues of new forms of work organization debated both in the labor movement and by industrial relations practitioners.[1] Herman Rosenfeld, Alan McGough, and Steve Benedict had many years of work experience at CAW-organized factories.[2] In addition to holding elected positions at their workplaces, all three had served as local

1. Both authors had previously explored related topics. For example, Rinehart is the author of a widely used book on the labor process in Canada that is now in its third edition. He has researched quality control circles at a General Motors plant (1984) and quality of work life programs (1986). Huxley has investigated strike activity in Canada and has written on the factors underlying divergent trends in union density in Canada and the United States (Huxley, Kettler, and Struthers 1986; Kettler, Struthers, and Huxley 1990).

2. Rosenfeld worked for almost two decades at the General Motors van plant in Scarborough, on the outskirts of Toronto. He was a union committeeperson for CAW Local 303. He was also enrolled part-time in the Ph.D program in political science at York University. McGough, a skilled tradesman, was CAW plant chairperson at Northern Telecom's London plant prior to its closure. Benedict worked at de Havilland Aircraft and was a union committeeperson for CAW Local 112.

union discussion leaders (LUDLs) for the CAW educational program on work reorganization.

The academics' relationship to the research group was never codified. They were not offered, nor did they seek, any honoraria for their efforts.[3]

The Nature of the Inquiry

Questions are often raised about the objectivity of research on work and industrial relations. Traditionally, much mainstream research in industrial sociology has been accused of a bias toward management (Sheppard 1949; Mills 1949, 1959; Baritz 1965). Some might argue that, following the same logic, investigations sponsored by a union are subject to similar accusations of bias.

The potential for bias will be addressed in three respects. First, we consider the general issue of objectivity. Second, we respond to CAMI's criticism that the research was geared to support the union's position. Third, we consider whether either the known union affiliation or association of the interviewers, or the wording of questions in the questionnaire, was responsible for contaminating the interview process.

On Objectivity

The philosophy of social science perspective held by the research group can best be summed up by C. Wright Mills's aphorism (1962:10): "I have tried to be objective, but I do not claim to be detached." Mills pointed out that objectivity in industrial relations research was often absent, and he gave the example of human relations studies in which "the manager and the scholar have carried on the dialogue—a discussion between elites, about the worker, who is the prime human object of . . . research" (Mills 1949:207).

3. One of the authors' colleagues in economics expressed astonishment at the informal, unpaid nature of the collaboration. Curiosity about the academics' status on the project was not restricted to their university colleagues. For example, a staff member at the union headquarters jokingly inquired as to whether the two academics were, in union parlance, "double dipping" by receiving payment over and above their regular professorial salaries.

We follow Mills in seeing no contradiction between an attempt to achieve an objective dialogue that involves workers and a willingness to champion certain moral and social ideals, such as improving conditions at the workplace. While it may be at odds with both human resource management writings and contemporary currents of postmodern thought, the idea of combining the search for objectivity with a recognition of the researcher's own values has a long tradition in social science.

Potential Bias from Union Association

While granting the validity of many of our findings, CAMI management criticized our report submitted to Labour Canada in 1992 on the grounds that we were unduly influenced by the union.

> Certainly, it would be naive to have expected that the results of the study would not be geared to support a union perspective and agenda. From the outset, the CAW Council paper on the "Reorganization of Work" and the timing of this report (immediately prior to the commencement of CAMI/CAW Local 88 contract discussions) were signals that the potential existed for a biased set of results. The objectivity of the study group appears to have been strongly influenced by the CAW positions on team concept ("Comments by CAMI" reprinted in Robertson et al. 1993:61).

How is the reader to interpret our research findings in light of the strong positions taken by the CAW on many of the issues that our research addressed? In assessing bias, a major consideration is whether or not the CAW's perspective on lean production influenced our presentation, analysis, and interpretation of data. The CAW's support for this project arose from an interest in monitoring a mode of manufacturing about which it had little knowledge and which was rapidly being implemented not just at CAMI but in many other plants represented by the union. The study, then, was initiated not to reinforce any preconceptions of lean production the union leadership may have held but to provide first-hand information on the concrete operations of the system and its impact on workers. Accordingly, our research group and the present authors operated with complete autonomy from the union. In keeping with the initial agreement for research access, the results of all data runs were made available to CAMI, Labour Canada, and the union.

Another indication that our results were not predetermined by national union policy is that they are consistent with a growing body of research on the transplants. Several studies of Mazda (Babson 1993, 1995; Fucini and Fucini 1990), a tour of North American transplants (Berggren, Bjorkman, and Hollander 1991), and a participant-observation study of SIA (Graham 1993, 1995), all of which drew conclusions on lean production similar to ours, were conducted by persons who neither collaborated with nor were affiliated with a union. We addressed this issue in greater depth in Chapter 13 under the rubric of CAMI exceptionalism.

The Questionnaire

The original questionnaire instrument used in the survey of workers included 111 questions. The great majority of questions remained the same through all four rounds, but we did add and drop some questions over the course of the study. Appendix II lists all questions to which we make reference in the text. No questions allowed for one obvious answer, and clear alternatives were presented whenever respondents were asked to express their opinions.

In accordance with the understanding between CAMI and the union, company representatives perused our questionnaire, and after round 1 David Robertson discussed it in a long meeting with the Vice-president of Personnel. The Vice-president strenuously objected to our question on whether respondents liked using lunch time for QC circles or whether they thought lunch should be their own time. He also objected to some questions on team leaders that he thought encouraged workers to evaluate them in a negative light. We compromised and added some questions drafted by the company. Thus CAMI management provided some check of how others perceived the objectivity of our questions. At the very least, we would expect that managers would have detected questions marred by blatant bias.

Interviewer Bias

Apart from the understandable refusal by some managers to discuss some issues or provide sensitive information, we had no sense that our association with the national union influenced interviewees' responses.

Answers given by workers often did not fit either the researchers' expectations or the union's position. For example, the local union leadership was vociferous in objecting to lean staffing and heavy workloads. Yet, as we reported in Chapter 6, workers were less likely than we expected to identify these as problem areas. Workers did not hesitate to express support for particular management policies and practices, to criticize the local and national union, or to give answers that they probably knew contradicted the position of the union.

Even if an attempt had been made, it is unlikely that interviewers could have influenced individual respondents. Like other unions in North America, the CAW has been less than successful in influencing its members on political issues. For example, like other major Canadian Labour Congress unions in Canada, the CAW has often had difficulty in persuading a majority of its members to vote for the New Democratic Party, a social democratic party with which the union has long been affiliated. On a host of issues, including gun control and affirmative action, there have been sharp cleavages between the national CAW (it should be noted that the research group was associated with the national office, not the local) and the rank and file.

If our study had been based entirely on the responses of workers in the survey, accusations of bias might have had more bite. However, our analyses, interpretations, and conclusions were grounded in several modes of data collection and multiple sources of data. Many of our most important findings—for example, declining worker commitment and its sources, workers' growing disillusionment with the kaizen process, fear of RSIs—were acknowledged by CAMI and corroborated by interviews with managers, who could hardly be accused of identifying with the union. On this and other methodological questions we must leave it to the reader to decide.

Research Protocol

Our research design can be summarized briefly. In order to overcome the problems of findings based on a one-time snapshot of the workplace, the study was longitudinal. The in-plant phase entailed one-week research visits to the plant every six months over nearly a two-year period. We employed a triangulation of methods. Neuman (1994:141) defines triangulation as the use of "different types of measures, or data collection techniques, in order to examine the same variable." We did a panel study of several categories of employees, using several interview formats.[4] We also observed work stations on the shop floor and used union as well as company documents, statistics, bulletins, and newsletters. All steps and facets of data collection were carried out by members of the research group, without reliance on research assistants. After leaving the plant, we continued to collect data, albeit less systematically, until July 1996.

We were taken on a tour of the plant in January 1990. During the first two months of 1990 regular meetings of the research group, often weekly and all day, were held at the union headquarters in North York near Toronto. Meetings reviewed previous research on work reorganization, drafted questions for the survey, and identified key questions for the open-ended interviews. These sessions prepared the way for the on-site phase of the research.

The most intensive investigation was conducted between early March 1990 and mid-November 1991. Four separate five-day periods were spent in the plant. Time spent each day was divided between observations of selected work stations, open-ended interviews, and survey interviews. All interviews took place during work hours in the training area. Interviewers were assigned a large room with room dividers allowing for some measure of confidentiality.

The Survey Sample

The worker sample was randomly drawn from the CAMI/CAW seniority list as of January 31, 1990. Each worker on the list was assigned a number from one to 1,126, and a table of random numbers was used to generate a list of 128 workers for potential inclusion in the sample. This list included 14 team leaders. As described below, they were interviewed using a different format.

4. "The *panel study* is a powerful type of longitudinal research. In a panel study, a researcher observes exactly the same people, group, or organization in different time periods. In other words, he observes the same thing at multiple times. Panel research is formidable to conduct and very costly . . . Nevertheless, the results of a well-designed panel study are extremely valuable" (emphasis in original) (Neuman 1994:27).

TABLE IO. Survey Sample and Plant Population Distribution
by Department (Round 1)

Department	Plant Population	Sample
Car Assembly	194 (19.3%)	26 (25.5%)
Paint	192 (19.1%)	24 (23.6%)
Truck Assembly	220 (21.9%)	19 (18.6%)
Truck Welding	127 (12.7%)	9 (8.8%)
Car Welding	102 (10.2%)	8 (7.8%)
Material Handling	73 (7.3%)	7 (6.9%)
Inspection/QC	62 (6.2%)	6 (5.9%)
Stamping	33 (3.3%)	3 (2.9%)
Total	1003 (100%)	102 (100%)

The final sample of 102 workers was drawn from the group of 128 minus the 14 team leaders. To ensure representative numbers of women in the sample, and to allow for meaningful analysis, women were slightly over-sampled. Of the 100 who participated in round 1, 68 were male and 32 were female. The 102 workers dropped to 100 actual participants in the first round of interviews.

Table 10 shows that distributions of the sample by department closely matched the distribution of the plant population.

The workforce at CAMI, along with the round 1 sample of 100 workers, had changed by our second visit in November 1990. Of the original sample, 24 workers had left the company, changed status, or were otherwise not included in the second sample. In other words, only 76 of the original 100 participants from round 1 were included in the second survey sample. The following is a list of reasons for the deletions:

- Three PAs quit the company.
- Two PAs were injured and off work on Workers' Compensation during the second interview.
- One PA was off work on Sickness and Accident benefits.
- One PA was on maternity leave.
- Seven PAs became team leaders prior to the second visit.

They were interviewed as team leaders during the second visit and were not included in the second survey sample of PAs.

- All seven of the skilled trades included in the first round sample were dropped from the sample.

- One worker had become a skilled trades apprentice by the second visit.

- Two PAs interviewed in the first round did not show for their scheduled interview in round 2.

To deal with the problem of a shrinking sample size, 11 new PAs—chosen randomly from the January 1990 seniority list—were added to the survey sample for the second interview. When added to the original 76 from round 1 and the three team leaders from round 1 who subsequently became PAs, the size of the second survey sample increased to 90. Two persons missed their interviews, for a final N of 88.

The sample underwent further change after round 2. A total of 13 workers from the sample of 90 in round 2 were not available for interviews in round 3 in March 1991: one had quit CAMI, two were on maternity leave, five were off work because of injuries, and five were absent or missed their scheduled interview and could not be rescheduled. The sample size from round 3, including three PAs who participated in round 3 but missed round 2, was 80.

The sample size for round 4 remained constant at 80 PAs, but the composition of the sample again changed: two PAs from round 3 became team leaders; three were off work with injuries; two were on maternity leave; one took a position in management; one was on holiday; and two missed the interview. However, 11 PAs who missed interviews in round 3 were interviewed in round 4. Although we completed 100 interviews in round 1, statistical comparisons across rounds were based on the responses of only those interviewed in rounds 1 *and* 2 and any other round. This yielded effective Ns of 75, 88, 80, and 79 for rounds 1 through 4 respectively. The majority of workers in the sample (N=70) were interviewed in all four rounds. In those few instances where we report survey results for round 1 only we used an N of 100.

All indications suggested that the sample of respondents used in our longitudinal analysis was soundly based. The participants were selected randomly and replaced randomly. A t-test, used to determine the difference between round 1 mean scores on the Commitment Index (see Chapter 11) of respondents who were interviewed in all four rounds and of those who dropped out after round 1, showed no statistically significant difference between those who remained and those who left (Andersen 1994:64–65.).

Team Leaders and the Trades

Fourteen team leaders were included in our initial sample. There were sound reasons for excluding team leaders from the sample. While they are union members, team leaders occupy a special position and have special responsibilities. To include them in the worker sample would have required separate statistical analysis of their responses, and their number was too small to allow for meaningful statistical comparisons. Second, many of the survey questions were not geared to team leaders. Finally, we felt it important to examine the role of team leader in depth, which would not have been possible had they been included in the survey sample.

We interviewed 13 of the 14 team leaders from the initial sample. We tried to interview the same team leaders over the course of the study, but this was not always possible. By the second visit the composition of the team leader sample had changed. Ten team leaders from the original group of 14 were interviewed during the second visit. Three team leaders interviewed during the first visit had returned to their positions as PAs prior to the second visit. Each of these ex-team leaders was interviewed as a PA using the survey questionnaire in the second and subsequent rounds of interviews. Seven PAs from the original sample had become team leaders prior to the second visit, four of whom were interviewed using the open-ended format, making for a total of 17 team leader interviews in round 2. A total of 14 team leaders were interviewed both in round 3 and round 4.

Team leaders were interviewed during the half-hour lunch break. The interview format was open-ended, with a focus on changes in their team over time, the content of their jobs, attitudes toward their jobs and CAMI, and special problems and frustrations they experienced. These interviews were audio recorded and subsequently transcribed.

Since the survey questions proved unsuitable for the tradespersons included in the original sample, they were replaced with PAs for survey interviews after round 1. Starting with round 2, open-ended interviews were carried out with these seven skilled workers. Interviews with the trades lasted about 45 minutes, were audio recorded, and later transcribed.

Union Representatives

The local in-plant union representation structure at CAMI included a chairperson, a skilled trades representative, and four members of the in-plant committee. With one exception, these persons were interviewed four times. Interviews lasted between 30 and 45 minutes and were recorded and transcribed. Between the second and third round a new union committeeperson was elected to replace one of the committeepersons previously interviewed. This new representative was interviewed in rounds 3 and 4. In addition, two local union health and safety representatives or, when they were unavailable, their alternates—appointed between the first and second visits—were interviewed in rounds 2 to 4.

Managers

Pairs of researchers interviewed senior and junior managers from every production department and from a range of central and support operations. Seven managers were interviewed in round 1, nine in round 2, 14 in round 3, and 11 in round 4. Not all managers were interviewed more than once. Whenever it was discovered that a manager's responsibilities had changed as a result of promotion or a transfer to another department, the replacement manager was interviewed and re-interviewed on subsequent visits.

The interviews were open-ended and relatively unstructured. One hour was scheduled for each interview, with some running longer. Except for an occasional request to depart from the practice (and then only for a few asides), all interviews were audio recorded and later transcribed. The initial interviews elicited job descriptions and responsibilities, views on how CAMI compared with other assembly plants, the extent to which the manager and CAMI were achieving their objectives, and managers' frustrations and satisfactions. We also sought information on the rationale behind staffing and other policies such as the kaizen program. Subsequent interviews provided further clarification and focused on changes in operations since the previous visit. In each round we sought to elicit opinions on the extent to which the company was realizing its objectives and living up to its stated values.

On the final visit to CAMI we requested interviews (through a translator) with three ranking Japanese members of the management staff. The request was denied, but CAMI did ask the Japanese managers to provide written answers to a series of our written questions. The carefully scripted replies did not provide much new information other than some interesting (and envious) reflections on what the managers felt was the ability of Canadians to differentiate clearly work and non-work life and to enjoy leisure pursuits.

Work Station Observations

Eighteen work site observations, ranging from 30 minutes to over an hour, were completed during the course of each visit. Whenever possible a person with production experience was paired with one relatively unfamiliar with auto plants. Working in pairs allowed for the cross-checking of observations and a more thorough exchange of ideas. Whenever possible the same pair of researchers returned to work sites they had previously observed.

We observed sites throughout the plant, with somewhat greater emphasis on heavily populated areas in Welding, Paint, Material Handling, Assembly, and Stamping. Work stations were selected on the basis of the pre-site tour, the experience of the research team, comparability of operations elsewhere, and consultations with management and the union local leadership. We observed the following work stations:

- Truck chassis
- Car line stations 1–5
- Sealer line, Paint
- Battery install, Truck
- Engine subassembly, Car
- Frame assembly, Truck Welding
- Body weld, Car

- Instrument panel subassembly, Car
- Instrument panel install, Car
- Engine subassembly, Truck
- Door assembly, Car
- UBC masking, Paint
- Engine lift/drop, Car
- Seat install, Truck
- Seat install, Car
- Engine install, Truck
- White body, Car Welding
- Material Handling.

We conversed as much as possible with PAs, team leaders, and area leaders. A main focus was to track changes over time in team composition, work site condition, and the work process (cycle time, job content, etc.). Sometimes we joined teams on their rest breaks and lunches to continue discussions. Reports were read and discussed by the whole research group.

Data Analysis

Responsibility for supervising data entry, computer runs, and transcription of interviews was jointly handled by one union staffer and one academic. At various points four university-based research assistants were hired to work under academic supervision using university facilities. Data were entered into and stored on the university mainframe computer and the SPSSx program was used for data processing.

Research Subsequent to the On-Site Phase

Our final report was submitted to Labour Canada in March 1992. In accordance with one of the conditions under which the company had originally agreed to allow research access, it was acknowledged that an addendum by CAMI management would constitute part of the final report. The addendum was included in a four-page appendix to a subsequent version of the report published by the CAW in 1993 for union members (Robertson et al. 1993).

Various methods were used to follow developments at CAMI after we left the plant. Some members of our research group talked with workers on the picket line during the 1992 strike. We met with the local union leadership during a CAW Council meeting in Windsor, Ontario, in December 1993. The lengthy discussion was recorded and transcribed. Starting in 1994, David Robertson's new responsibilities as Director of Work Reorganization and Training at the union headquarters required that he continue to monitor developments at CAMI. The authors read each issue of the local union newsletter, had ongoing, informal discussions with workers and local union officials, and were given key union and company documents and statistics. We closely followed the 1995 bargaining between Local 88 and CAMI, and conducted several days of formal recorded interviews with local union reps in June 1995. Our last interviews with local union officials were done in June 1996.

Questionnaire Items Referred to in the Text

Chapter 2

1. How old are you?
2. Gender?
3. Is this your first full-time job? If no, where did you work before?
4. Did you move to take this job?
5. Have you been a member of the union before?
6. What department do you work in?

Chapter 4

1. Think back to the orientation session you had when you first started at CAMI. Which of the following best describes that session:
   A. Useful, or A waste of time
   B. Effective Training, or Indoctrination

2. As a result of training, would you say you are more skilled, or are all the jobs about the same?
   1. More skilled
   2. Jobs about the same

3. How long did it take you to learn your job? (open-ended)

4. Would you agree or disagree with the following statements about training at CAMI:
   A. There is too much training on QC circles and not enough training that develops my skills.

    B. I've been provided with the opportunity to continually upgrade myself and learn new skills.

    C. The opportunity for training at CAMI makes it easy to get the skills you need to get a better job.

    D. There is too much classroom training and not enough on-the-job training.

    E. There is too much training on teams and problem solving and not enough technical training.

5. Are you satisfied with the amount of training you receive for jobs in your team? Yes or No

Chapter 5

1. How many different jobs on your team do you rotate through regularly?
   All the jobs
   Most jobs
   Some jobs
   A few jobs

2. Who determines the rotation schedule?
   Members of the team
   Team leader
   Area leader or other manager
   Don't know

3. Do you like the idea of job rotation or would you prefer to stay on one job?
   Prefer rotation
   Prefer to stay on one job

4. How many jobs on the team do you know how to do?
   All jobs
   Most jobs
   Some jobs
   A few jobs

5. Would you prefer to be rotating though more or fewer jobs in your team?
   More jobs
   Fewer jobs
   Like it as it is

6. How long did it take you to learn your job? (open-ended)

Chapter 6

1. How often do you feel the pace of your job is too fast?
   All the time
   Often
   Once in a while
   Never

2. How often does the line go too fast?
   All the time
   Often
   Once in a while
   Never

3. How long is your work cycle? (open-ended)

4. How often do you find that your job is physically tiring?
   All the time
   Often
   Once in a while
   Never

5. How often do you find your job stressful?
   All the time
   Often
   Once in a while
   Never

6. How often do you feel burned out when you get home from work?
   All the time
   Often
   Once in a while
   Never

7. How often does your job expose you to:
   A. Muscle fatigue and strains
   B. Repetitive strains (All the time, often, once in a while, never)

8. On your job do you have the chance to vary the pace at which you work? Yes or No

9. CAMI workers work harder than in an average auto plant. Agree or Disagree

10. Your team is doing too much work with too few people. Agree or Disagree

Chapter 7

1. What is the name of your team? (open-ended)

2. How many times did your team meet last week? (open-ended)

3. When does the team usually meet?
   Before shift
   After shift
   At lunch
   At breaks
   When the line is down

4. Are you required to attend team meetings? Yes or No

5. Do you always attend? Yes or No

6. Are team meetings usually "give and take" discussions or just brief information sessions?
   Discussions
   Information sessions
   A bit of both

7. Just off the top of your head, what does team concept mean to you? (open-ended)

8. What do you like about team concept at CAMI? (open-ended)

9. Is there anything you don't like about team concept at CAMI? (open-ended)

10. How much do you like the idea of working as part of a team?
    Very much
    Somewhat
    Not much
    Not at all

11. How much do you like being a member of your team?
    Very much
    Somewhat
    Not much
    Not at all

12. All things considered, working in a team (respondents were asked to agree or disagree with the following items):
    A. Helps me feel like I'm part of CAMI
    B. Gives me a say over how my job is done
    C. Is a waste of time
    D. Gives me a chance to get to know people
    E. Gives me a chance to raise my concerns
    F. Allows team members to act together to express complaints
    G. Is a way to get us to work harder
    H. Gets us all pressuring one another
    I. Helps CAMI but not me

13. In your experience, how often is team pressure put on members to do the following (all the time, often, once in a while, never):
    A. Work harder
    B. Improve quality
    C. Improve attendance
    D. Improve attitude
    E. Reduce waste
    F. Do housekeeping in work area
    G. Work slower
    H. File a grievance

14. How often has your team put special pressure on you?
    All the time
    Often
    Once in a while
    Never

15. Some people say that when team concept has been tried at other plants the teams work more for the good of the company than for the good of workers. Based on your experience at CAMI would you:
    Agree
    Agree somewhat
    Disagree

16. Would you like to become a team leader? Yes or No

17. Do you think there should be team leaders? Yes or No

18. Do you think team leaders should be elected? Yes or No

19. Do you think team leaders should be rotated? Yes or No

20. How often does your team leader cooperate with the team?
    All the time
    Often
    Once in a while
    Never

21. How often does your team leader think more like management than one of you?
    All the time
    Often
    Once in a while
    Never

22. How often does your team leader pressure you to submit suggestions?
    All the time
    Often
    Once in a while
    Never

23. How often do you get along with your team leader?
    All the time
    Often
    Once in a while
    Never

24. Have you ever done taiso? Yes or No

25. Do you do taiso now? Yes or No

Chapter 8

1. Do you think men and women workers are treated about equally at CAMI? Yes or No. If no, probe (open-ended).

2. In your experience, does team concept make it easier for men and women to participate equally in all aspects of work? Yes or No

3. Is your team leader a man or a woman?

4. In your experience, do women workers at CAMI tend to be assigned to certain departments because they are women? Yes or No

5. If yes [to the above question], which departments? (open-ended)

6. In your experience, do women workers tend to be assigned to certain jobs because they are women? Yes or No

7. If yes [to the above question], are these jobs:
   A. More skilled or Less skilled
   B. Easier or Harder
   C. More responsible or Less responsible
   D. With better working conditions or With worse working conditions

Chapter 10

1. Do you participate in the suggestion program? Yes or No

2. Do you think everyone should [participate]? Yes or No

3. Why do you or do you not think everyone should participate? (open-ended)

4. Do you belong to a quality circle? Yes or No

5. Do quality circles solve problems that are important to you as a worker? Yes or No (Yes and No answers were probed in an open-ended format.)

6. Is there any pressure to participate in quality circles? Yes or No

7. If yes [there is pressure], probe (open-ended).

8. If you participate in quality circles, do you participate because:
   You think they are a good idea
   Of pressure (Both responses were probed in an open-ended format.)

9. Which of the following questions best describes CAMI's efforts at reducing waste and increasing efficiency?
   A. Working smarter or Working harder
   B. Reducing jobs or Increasing jobs
   C. A more demanding work pace or A more comfortable work pace

10. How often do you have a say in the way you do your job?
    All the time
    Often
    Once in a while
    Never

11. In what way do you have a say over the way your job is done? (open-ended)

12. Are you actively involved in making decisions at work? Yes or No

13. If yes [to the above question], would you give me an example of what those decisions are? (open-ended)

14. If you find a way to do your job that is easier or faster than the specified way, what do you do?
    Keep it to yourself
    Share it with no one other than a few co-workers
    Tell the team leader
    Submit a suggestion
    I haven't found a better way

15. How often do you perform your job in conformity with the posted job standards?
    All the time
    Often
    Once in a while
    Never

16. Which of the following do you most agree with?
    Lunch break is a good time for us to get together as a team to go over things and solve problems.
    Lunch break is our personal time. It shouldn't be a time for team meetings or quality circles.

Chapter 11

1. Which of the following statements comes closest to your feelings about CAMI?
   A. CAMI is a special kind of experiment, designed to change the way people work in Canada. I am enthusiastic and excited about it.
   B. There is really nothing special about working at CAMI, and, in fact, all things considered CAMI really isn't any different than other corporations.

2. Many observers have commented that managers at CAMI and other team concept plants have gotten rid of many of the things that made them seem superior to workers. They point out that managers no longer have separate parking areas, cafeterias, and dress codes. Considering this issue, which of the following statements comes closest to your feelings about common cafeterias, dress codes, and parking areas?
   A. It's a good thing, it's starting to make managers and workers more equal.
   B. It is nothing but a smokescreen. The reality is that management still has all the power.

3. Which best characterizes the atmosphere at CAMI?
   A. Democratic or Undemocratic
   B. Cooperative and helpful or Competitive and stressful

4. Do you think managers at CAMI would "put one over" on workers if they had the chance? Yes or No

5. In your opinion, how interested is CAMI management in the welfare of workers?
   Very interested
   Mildly interested
   Not very interested
   Not at all interested

6. How would you best describe your job?
   Interesting and Challenging
   Boring and monotonous
   Somewhere in between

7. Overall, how satisfied are you with your job?
Very satisfied
Satisfied
Dissatisfied
Very dissatisfied

8. Do you think workers are empowered here? Yes or No

9. How satisfied are you with the amount of decision making power you have?
Very satisfied
Satisfied
Dissatisfied
Very dissatisfied

10. Have you ever been involved in kaizen/continuous improvement? Yes or No

Chapter 12

1. If you thought you or someone on your team was being subjected to some form of on-the-job harassment or unfair treatment, who would you most likely turn to in order to get something done?
Your team leader
Your union representative
Your area leader
The Personnel Department
Other

2. What do you think of the following statement?
We need a union at CAMI because no matter how cooperative the relationship, there will always be differences between workers and management.
Strongly agree
Agree
Disagree
Strongly disagree

References

Adler, Paul S. 1993a. "Time and Motion Regained." *Harvard Business Review,* January–February:97–108.

Adler, Paul S. 1993b. "'The Learning Bureaucracy': New United Motor Manufacturing Inc." *Organizational Behaviour,* 15:111–194.

Adler, Paul S. 1995. "'Democratic Taylorism': The Toyota Production System at NUMMI." Pp. 207–219 in Steve Babson (ed.), *Lean Work: Empowerment and Exploitation in the Global Auto Industry.* Detroit: Wayne State University Press.

Adler, Paul S., and Robert Cole. 1993. "Designed for Learning: A Tale of Two Auto Plants." *Sloan Management Review,* Spring:85–94.

Andersen, Robert C. A. 1994. "Worker Commitment under Lean Production: A Case Study of the Unionized CAMI Transplant in Ingersoll, Ontario." M.A. thesis, University of Western Ontario.

Andersen Consulting. 1993. *The Lean Enterprise Benchmarking Project.* London, England.

Automotive: Why People Count. Report of the Automotive Industry Human Resources Task Force. 1986. Ottawa: Employment and Immigration Canada.

Babson, Steve. 1993. "Lean or Mean: The MIT Model and Lean Production at Mazda." *Labor Studies Journal,* 18, Summer:3–24.

Babson, Steve. 1995. "Lean Production and Labor: Empowerment and Exploitation." Pp. 1–37 in Steve Babson (ed.), *Lean Work: Empowerment and Exploitation in the Global Auto Industry.* Detroit: Wayne State University Press.

Baritz, Lorne. 1965. *The Servants of Power.* New York: John Wiley and Sons.

Benedict, Daniel. 1985. "The 1984 GM Agreement in Canada: Significance and Consequences." *Relations Industrielles/Industrial Relations,* 40, 1:27–45.

Berggren, Christian. 1992. *Alternatives to Lean Production: Work in the Swedish Auto Industry.* Ithaca, New York: ILR Press.

Berggren, Christian. 1993. "Lean Production—The End of History?" *Work, Employment and Society,* 7, 2:163–188.

Berggren, Christian. 1994. "NUMMI Versus Uddevalla: Are Assembly Lines Just More Efficient?" *Sloan Management Review,* Winter:37–49.

Berggren, Christian, Torsten Bjorkman, and Ernst Hollander. 1991. "Are They Unbeatable?" Stockholm: Royal Institute of Technology.

Besser, Terry L. 1993. "The Commitment of Japanese and U.S. Workers: A Reassessment." *American Sociological Review,* 58, December:873–881.

Braid, Dean. 1994. "Strike Wins New Jobs from a Reluctant General Motors." *Labor Notes,* 188, November.

Bratton, John. 1992. *Japanization at Work.* London: Macmillan Press.

Braverman, Harry. 1974. *Labor and Monopoly Capital: The Degradation of Work in the Twentieth Century.* New York: Monthly Review Press.

Brown, Claire, and Michael Reich. 1989. "When Does Union-Management Cooperation Work?" *California Management Review,* Summer:26–44.

Burawoy, Michael. 1979. *Manufacturing Consent: Changes in the Labor Process Under Monopoly Capitalism.* Chicago: University of Chicago Press.

Burawoy, Michael. 1985. *The Politics of Production: Factory Regimes Under Capitalism and Socialism.* London: Verso.

Canadian Auto Workers. 1989. "CAW Statement on the Reorganization of Work." North York, Ontario.

Chappell, Lindsay. 1991. "CAMI Promises 13 Percent Rise in North American Content." *Automotive News,* May 20.

Chappell, Lindsay. 1992. "CAMI Strike Wilts Transplant Rose." *Automotive News,* September 4.

Chappell, Lindsay. 1996a. "Strike at Delphi Plants Fires a Shot Through the Industry." *Automotive News,* March 18.

Chappell, Lindsay. 1996b. "Mitsubishi Learns a Painful Public Relations Lesson." *Automotive News,* April 29:42.

Child, Charles, and David Sedgwick. 1996. "GM Makes a Point, but Pays Stiff Price." *Automotive News,* March 25.

Chinoy, Ely. 1955. *Automobile Workers and the American Dream.* Boston: Beacon Press.

Clarke, Simon. 1990. "The Crisis of Fordism or the Crisis of Social Democracy?" *Telos,* Spring:71–98.

Coch, Lester, and John R. P. French. 1948. "Overcoming Resistance to Change." *Human Relations,* 1:512–532.

Cockburn, Cynthia. 1981. "The Material of Male Power." *Feminist Review,* 9:41–59.

Cole, Robert E. 1979. *Work, Mobility and Participation: A Comparative Study of American and Japanese Industry.* Berkeley: University of California Press.

Cole, Robert E. 1989. *Strategies for Learning: Small Group Activities in American, Japanese and Swedish Industry.* Berkeley: University of California Press.

Confederation of Japanese Automobile Workers Union. 1992. "Japanese Automobile Industry in the Future." Tokyo.

Creese, Gillian. 1995. "Gender Equity or Masculine Privilege? Union Strategies and Economic Restructuring in a White Collar Union." *Canadian Journal of Sociology*, 20, Spring:143–166.

Crowther, Stuart, and Phillip Garrahan. 1988. "Corporate Power and the Local Economy." *Industrial Relations Journal*, 19, Spring:51–59.

Daley, Brian. 1995. "Canadian Auto Workers Beat Contracting Out: Wildcat Strike Convinces Management." *Labor Notes*, 194, May.

Dassbach, Carl H. A. 1995. "Lean Production, Labor Control, and Post-Fordism in the Japanese Automobile Industry." Pp. 19–40 in William G. Green and Ernest J. Yanarella (eds.), *North American Auto Unions in Crisis: Lean Production as Contested Terrain*. Albany, N.Y.: SUNY Press.

Dohse, Knuth, Ulrich Jürgens, and Thomas Malsch. 1985. "From 'Fordism' to 'Toyotism'? The Social Organization of the Labor Process in the Japanese Automobile Industry." *Politics and Society*, 14, 2:115–146.

Edwards, Richard. 1979. *Contested Terrain: The Transformation of Work in the Twentieth Century*. New York: Basic Books.

Edwards, Richard, and Michael Podgursky. 1986. "The Unraveling Accord: American Unions in Crisis." Pp. 14–60 in R. Edwards, P. Garonna, and F. Todtling (eds.), *Unions in Crisis and Beyond: Perspectives from Six Countries*. Dover, Mass.: Auburn House Publishing.

Elger, Tony, and Chris Smith. 1994. "Introduction." Pp. 1–24 in Tony Elger and Chris Smith (eds.), *Global Japanization? The Transnational Transformation of the Labour Process*. London: Routledge.

Faber, Seymour. 1976. "Working Class Organization." *Our Generation*, 11, Summer:13–26.

Feldman, Richard, and Michael Betzold. 1988. *End of the Line: Auto Workers and the American Dream*. New York: Weidenfeld and Nicolson.

Florida, Richard, and Martin Kenney. 1991. "Transplanted Organizations: The Transfer of Japanese Industrial Organization to the U.S." *American Sociological Review*, 56, June:381–398.

Forrest, Anne. 1993. "Women and Industrial Relations Theory: No Room in the Discourse." *Relations Industrielles*, 48, 3:409–40.

Friedman, Andrew. 1977. *Industry and Labour: Class Struggle at Work and Monopoly Capitalism*. London: Macmillan.

Fucini, Joseph, and Suzy Fucini. 1990. *Working for the Japanese: Inside Mazda's American Auto Plant*. New York: Free Press.

Gannagé, Charlene. 1986. *Double Day, Double Bind: Women Garment Workers*. Toronto: Women's Press.

Garrahan, Phillip, and Paul Stewart. 1992. *The Nissan Enigma: Flexibility at Work in a Local Economy*. London: Mansell Publishing.

Gartman, David. 1986. *Auto Slavery: The Labor Process in the American Automobile Industry, 1897–1950*. London: Rutgers University Press.

Gindin, Sam. 1989. "Breaking Away: The Formation of the Canadian Auto Workers." *Studies in Political Economy,* 29, Summer:63–89.

Gindin, Sam. 1995. *The Canadian Auto Workers: The Birth and Transformation of a Union.* Toronto: James Lorimer & Company.

Glaberman, Martin. 1983. "Building the Japanese Car." *Canadian Dimension,* 17, 1:17–19.

Gottfried, H., and L. Graham. 1993. "Constructing Difference: The Making of Gendered Subcultures in a Japanese Automobile Transplant," *Sociology,* 27, 4:611–628.

Graham, Laurie. 1993. "Inside a Japanese Transplant: A Critical Perspective." *Work and Occupations,* 20, 2:147–173.

Graham, Laurie. 1995. *On the Line at Subaru-Isuzu: The Japanese Model and the American Worker.* Ithaca, New York: ILR Press.

Green, William C. 1993. "The Tranformation of the NLRA Paradigm: The Future of Labor-Management Relations in Post-Fordist Auto Plants." Pp. 161–190 in William C. Green and Ernest J. Yanarella (eds), *North American Auto Unions in Crisis: Lean Production as Contested Terrain.* Albany, N.Y.: SUNY Press.

Halliday, Jon. 1975. *A Political History of Japanese Capitalism.* New York: Pantheon Books.

Hamper, Ben. 1991. *Rivethead: Tales from the Assembly Line.* New York: Warner Books.

Hargrove, Buzz. 1992. "Highlights of the Tentative Agreement Between CAW-Canada and CAMI." *CAW-Canada/CAMI Report.* October.

Herzenberg, Stephen. 1993. "Whither Social Unionism? Labor and Restructuring in the U.S. Auto Industry." Pp. 314–336 in Jane Jenson and Rianne Mahon (eds.), *The Challenge of Restructuring: North American Labor Movements Respond.* Philadelphia: Temple University Press.

Hodson, Randy, Gregory Hooks, and Sabine Rieble. 1992. "Customized Training in the Workplace." *Work and Occupations,* 19, 3:272–292.

Hodson, Randy, and Teresa A. Sullivan. 1995. *The Social Organization of Work.* Second Edition. Belmont, Calif.: Wadsworth.

Holmes, John. 1991. "The Globalization of Production and the Future of Canada's Mature Industries: The Case of the Automotive Industry." Pp. 153–180 in Daniel Drache and Meric S. Gertler (eds.), *The New Era of Global Competition: State Policy and Market Power.* Montreal: McGill-Queen's University Press.

Holmes, John, and A. Rusonik. 1991. "The Break-up of an International Labour Union: Uneven Development in the North American Auto Industry and the Schism in the UAW." *Environment and Planning,* 23:9–35.

Huxley, Christopher, David Kettler, and James Struthers. 1986. "Is Canada's Experience 'Especially Instructive'?" Pp. 113–132, 457–461 in S. M. Lipset (ed.),

Unions in Transition: Entering the Second Century. San Francisco: Institute for Contemporary Studies.

Huxley, Christopher, James Rinehart, and David Robertson. 1994. "Does Lean Production Have to be Mean? Worker and Union Responses to New Forms of Work Organization in the North American Auto Industry." Paper presented to Cars and Continentalism Conference II, Mexico City, December.

Huxley, C., D. Robertson, J. Rinehart, and H. Rosenfeld. 1995. "Le Travail en Equipe et le Kaizen. Une Application dans l'Industrie Automobile Canadienne: Le Cas CAMI." Pp. 139–165 in Diane-Gabrielle Tremblay (ed.), *Concertation et Performance Economique: Vers de Nouveaux Modeles?* Saint-Foy, Quebec: Presses de l'Universite du Quebec.

Jacobs, James. 1995. "Lean Production and Training: The Case of a Japanese Supplier Firm." Pp. 311–325 in Steve Babson (ed.), *Lean Work: Empowerment and Exploitation in the Global Auto Industry.* Detroit: Wayne State University Press.

Junkerman, John. 1982. "We Are Driven." *Mother Jones,* August:21–23, 38–40.

Junkerman, John. 1987. "Nissan, Tennessee." *The Progressive,* 51, 6:17–20.

Kamata, Satoshi. 1982. *Japan in the Passing Lane.* New York: Pantheon.

Kanawashi, Hirosuke. 1992. *Enterprise Unionism in Japan.* London: Kegan Paul.

Katz, Harry C. 1987. *Shifting Gears: Changing Labor Relations in the U.S. Automobile Industry.* Cambridge, Mass.: MIT Press.

Kendall, R.M. 1987. "Safety Management: Japanese Style." *Occupational Hazards,* 49, 2:48–51.

Kenney, Martin, and Richard Florida. 1988. "Beyond Mass Production: Production and the Labor Process in Japan." *Politics and Society,* 16, March:121–158.

Kenney, Martin, and Richard Florida. 1993. *Beyond Mass Production: The Japanese System and Its Transfer to the U.S.* New York: Oxford University Press.

Kettler, David, James Struthers, and Christopher Huxley. 1990. "Unionization and Labour Regimes in Canada and the United States: Considerations for Comparative Research," *Labour/Le Travail,* 25, Spring:161–187.

Klein, Janice. 1989. "The Human Costs of Manufacturing Reform." *Harvard Business Review,* 77, March–April:60–66.

Klein, Janice. 1991. "A Re-Examination of Autonomy in Light of New Manufacturing Practices." *Human Relations,* 44, 1:21–38.

Kochan, Thomas, Joel Cutcher-Gershenfeld, and John Paul MacDuffie. 1989. "Employee Participation, Work Redesign and New Technology." Draft paper for Commission on Workforce Quality and Labor Market Efficiency. MIT.

Krafcik, John F. 1988. "Complexity and Flexibility in Motor Vehicle Assembly: A Worldwide Perspective." MIT: International Motor Vehicle Program.

Krahn, Harvey J., and Graham S. Lowe. 1993. *Work, Industry, and Canadian Society.* Scarborough, Ontario: Nelson Canada.

Kumar, Pradeep, and John Holmes. 1996. "Continuity and Change: Evolving Human Resource Policies and Practices in the Canadian Automobile Industry." Unpublished paper. Kingston, Ontario: Queen's University.

Kusterer, Ken C. 1978. *Know-How on the Job: The Important Working Knowledge of "Unskilled" Workers.* Boulder, Colo.: Westview Press.

Lee, Bruce. 1988. "Worker Harmony Makes NUMMI Work." *New York Times,* December 25.

Lincoln, James, and Arne Kalleberg. 1990. *Culture, Control and Commitment: A Study of Work Organization and Work Activities in the United States and Japan.* New York: Cambridge University Press.

Lund, Caroline. 1994. "Union Beats 10-Hour Day at NUMMI." *Labor Notes,* 186, September.

MacDuffie, John Paul. 1988. "The Japanese Auto Transplants: Challenges to Conventional Wisdom." *ILR Report,* 26, 1:12–18.

MacDuffie, John Paul. 1995a. "International Trends in Work Organization in the Auto Industry: National-Level vs. Company-level Perspectives." Pp. 71–113 in K.S. Wever and L. Turner (eds.), *The Comparative Political Economy of Industrial Relations.* Madison: University of Wisconsin, Industrial Relations Research Association.

MacDuffie, John Paul. 1995b. "Workers' Roles in Lean Production: The Implications for Worker Representation." Pp. 54–69 in Steve Babson (ed.), *Lean Work: Empowerment and Exploitation in the Global Auto Industry.* Detroit: Wayne State University Press.

MacDuffie, John Paul, and John F. Krafcik. 1989. "The Team Concept: Models for Change." *The JAMA Forum,* 7, February:3–8.

MacDuffie, John Paul, and Fritz Pil. 1994. "The International Assembly Plant Study: Round Two Preliminary Findings." Paper presented to Conference on International Developments in Workplace Innovation: Implications for Canadian Competitiveness. Toronto.

MacDuffie, John Paul, and Fritz Pil. 1995. "The International Assembly Plant Study: Philosophical and Methodological Issues." Pp. 181–196 in Steve Babson (ed.), *Lean Work: Empowerment and Exploitation in the Global Auto Industry.* Detroit: Wayne State University Press.

Marsh, Robert M. 1992. "The Difference Between Participation and Power in Japanese Factories." *Industrial and Labor Relations Review,* 45, January:250–257.

Mayo, Elton. 1933. *The Human Problems of an Industrial Civilization.* Cambridge: Macmillan.

McCammon, Paula. 1989. "The Spinoffs: Tillsonburg Companies Have Risen to the Challenge of Supplying Parts and Services for CAMI's Rigid Guidelines." *London Business Monthly Magazine,* 3, May:112–115.

Messing, Karen, Julie Courville, Micheline Boucher, Lucie Dumais, and Ana Maria Seifert. 1994. "Can Safety Risks of Blue-Collar Jobs Be Compared by Gender?" *Safety Science*, 18:95–112.

Mills, C. Wright. 1949. "The Contribution of Sociology to Studies of Industrial Relations." *Proceedings of the First Annual Meeting of the Industrial Relations Research Association.* Madison: IRRA:199–222.

Mills, C. Wright. 1962. *The Marxists.* New York: Dell.

Monden, Yasuhiro. 1983. *Toyota Production System.* Norcross, Georgia: Industrial Engineering and Management Press.

Moody, Kim. 1996. "Sexual Harassment at Mitsubishi: Where Was the Union?" *Labor Notes,* 207, June:1,14.

Moore, Joe. 1983. *Japanese Workers and the Struggle for Power, 1945–1947.* Madison: University of Wisconsin Press.

National Film Board (Canada). 1984. *Final Offer.* Documentary film.

Nonaka, Ikujiro, and Keigo Sasaki. 1993. "Restructuring in the Japanese Automobile Industry." Paper presented at MIT IMVP Conference, Cape Cod, Mass., June.

Nemoto, M. 1992. *Shinshakaihatsu no saizensen.* Tokyo: Nikkagiren.

Neuman, W. Lawrence. 1994. *Social Research Methods: Qualitative and Quantitative Approaches.* Second Edition. Boston: Allyn and Bacon.

Office of Technology Assessment. 1990. *Worker Training: Competing in the New Economy.* Washington, D.C.: U.S. Government Printing Office.

Okayama, Reiko. 1987. "Industrial Relations in the Japanese Automobile Industry 1945–70: The Case of Toyota." Pp. 168–189 in Steven Tolliday and Jonathan Zeitlin (eds.), *The Automobile Industry and Its Workers.* New York: St. Martin's Press.

O'Reilly, Charles. 1989. "Corporations, Culture, and Commitment: Motivation and Social Control in Organizations." *California Management Review,* Summer:9–25.

Ouchi, W.G. 1981. *Theory Z—How American Business Can Meet the Japanese Challenge.* Reading: Addison-Wesley.

Parker, Mike. 1985. *Inside the Circle: A Union Guide to QWL.* Detroit: Labor Notes/ South End Press.

Parker, Mike. 1994. "Election of Dissident Reveals Discontent at Model 'Team Concept' Plant." *Labor Notes,* 184, July.

Parker, Mike, and Jane Slaughter. 1988. *Choosing Sides: Unions and the Team Concept.* Boston: South End Press.

Parker, Mike, and Jane Slaughter. 1988a. "Behind the Scenes at NUMMI Motors." *New York Times,* December 4.

Parker, Mike, and Jane Slaughter. 1994. *Working Smart: A Union Guide to Participation Programs and Reengineering.* Detroit: Labor Notes.

Perrucci, Robert. 1994. *Japanese Auto Transplants in the Heartland: Corporatism and Community*. Hawthorn, New York: Aldine.

Price, John. 1994. "Lean Production at Suzuki: A Historical Perspective." *Studies in Political Economy*, 45, Fall:66–99.

Price, John. 1995. "Lean Production at Suzuki and Toyota: A Historical Perspective." Pp. 81–107 in Steve Babson (ed.), *Lean Work: Empowerment and Exploitation in the Global Auto Industry*. Detroit: Wayne State University Press.

Rehder, Robert J. 1990. "Japanese Transplants: After the Honeymoon." *Business Horizons*, January-February:87–98.

Rinehart, James. 1984. "Appropriating Workers' Knowledge: Quality Control Circles at a General Motors Plant." *Studies in Political Economy*, 14, Summer:75–97.

Rinehart, James. 1986. "Improving the Quality of Working Life Through Job Redesign: Work Humanization or Work Rationalization?" *Canadian Review of Sociology and Anthropology*, 13, 4:507–530.

Rinehart, James. 1996. *The Tyranny of Work: Alienation and the Labour Process*. Third edition. Toronto: Harcourt Brace.

Rinehart, James, Christopher Huxley, and David Robertson. 1994. "Worker Commitment and Labour Management Relations under Lean Production at CAMI." *Relations Industrielles/Industrial Relations*, 49, 4:747–769.

Rinehart, James, Christopher Huxley, and David Robertson. 1995. "Team Concept at CAMI." Pp. 220–234 in Steve Babson (ed.), *Lean Work: Empowerment and Exploitation in the Global Auto Industry*. Detroit: Wayne State University Press.

Rinehart, James, David Robertson, Christopher Huxley, and Jeff Wareham. 1994. "Re-Unifying Conception and Execution of Work Under Japanese Production Management? A Canadian Case Study." Pp. 152–174 in Tony Elger and Chris Smith (eds.), *Global Japanization? The Transnational Transformation of the Labour Process*. London: Routledge.

Roberts, Glenda S. 1994. *Staying on the Line: Blue-Collar Women in Contemporary Japan*. Honolulu: University of Hawaii Press.

Robertson, David, James Rinehart, and Christopher Huxley. 1992. "Team Concept and Kaizen: Japanese Production Management in a Unionized Canadian Auto Plant." *Studies in Political Economy*, 39, Autumn:77–107.

Robertson, David, James Rinehart, and Christopher Huxley. 1993. "CAMI: Die kanadische Erfahrung." Pp. 81–85 in Boy Luthje and Christoph Scherrer (eds), *Jenseits des Sozialpakts: Neue Unternehmensstrategien, Gewerkschaften und Arbeitskampfe in den USA*. Munster: Westfalisches Dampfboot.

Robertson, David, James Rinehart, Christopher Huxley, Jeff Wareham, Herman Rosenfeld, Alan McGough, and Steve Benedict. 1992. *Japanese Production Management in a Unionized Auto Plant. Final Report to Labour Canada*. North York, Ontario: CAW Research Department.

Robertson D., J. Rinehart, C. Huxley, J. Wareham, H. Rosenfeld, A. McGough, and S. Benedict. 1993. *The CAMI Report: Lean Production in a Unionized Auto Plant.* North York, Ontario: CAW Research Department.

Robertson, David, and Jeff Wareham. 1987. *Technological Change in the Auto Industry.* CAW Technology Project. North York, Ontario: CAW Research Department.

Robertson, David, and Jeff Wareham. 1989. *Changing Technology and Work: Northern Telecom.* North York, Ontario: CAW Research Department.

Sandoval Godoy, Sergio A., and Pablo Wong Gonzales. 1994. "Labor Relations and Trade Union Action in Hermosillo's Ford Plant, 1986–1994: A Pending Agenda in the Face of the North American Integration." Paper presented to Cars and Continentalism I Conference, University of Toronto, May 20–22.

Schonberger, Richard J. 1983. "Japanese Manufacturing Techniques: Nine Hidden Lessons in Simplicity." *Operations Management Review,* Spring.

Shaiken, Harley. 1993. "The New International Division of Labor and Its Impact on Unions: A Case Study of High-Tech Mexican Export Production." Pp. 224–239 in J. Belanger, P.K. Edwards, and L. Haiven (eds.), *Workplace Industrial Relations and the Global Challenge.* Ithaca, N.Y.: ILR Press.

Sheppard, H.L. 1949. "Treatment of Unionism in 'Managerial Sociology.'" *American Sociological Review,* 14, April:310–313.

Shimada, Haruo. 1983. "Japanese Industrial Relations—A New General Model?" Pp. 3–27 in T. Shirai (ed.), *Contemporary Industrial Relations in Japan.* Madison: University of Wisconsin Press.

Shimada, Haruo, and John Paul MacDuffie. 1987. "Industrial Relations and 'Humanware.'" Boston: MIT International Motor Vehicle Program.

Shimokawa, Koichi. 1987. "Product and Labor Strategies in Japan." Pp. 224–243 in Steven Tolliday and Jonathan Zeitlin (eds.), *The Automobile Industry and Its Workers.* New York: St. Martin's Press.

Simon, Herbert. 1957. "Authority." Pp. 103–115 in Conrad M. Arensberg et al. (eds.), *Research in Industrial Human Relations: A Critical Appraisal.* New York: Harper and Brothers.

Slaughter, Jane. 1989. "Behind the UAW's Defeat at Nissan." *Labor Notes,* 126, September.

Sugiman, Pamela. 1992. "'That Wall's Comin' Down': Gendered Strategies of Worker Resistance in the UAW Canadian Region (1963–1970)." *Canadian Journal of Sociology,* 17, Winter:1–27.

Sugiman, Pamela. 1993. "Unionism and Feminism in the Canadian Auto Workers Union, 1961–1992." Pp. 172–188 in Linda Briskin and Patricia McDermott (eds.), *Women Challenging Unions: Feminism, Democracy, and Militancy.* Toronto: University of Toronto Press.

Sugiman, Pamela. 1994. *Labour's Dilemma: The Gender Politics of Auto Workers in Canada, 1937–1979.* Toronto: University of Toronto Press.

Taylor, Frederick W. 1947. *Scientific Management.* New York: Harper and Brothers.

Trist, Eric, and Kenneth Bamforth. 1951. "Some Social and Psychological Consequences of the Longwall Method of Coal Getting." *Human Relations,* 4:3–39.

Turnbull, Peter. 1988. "The Limits of 'Japanisation'—Just-in-Time, Labour Relations and the U.K. Automotive Industry." *New Technology, Work and Employment,* 3, Autumn:7–20.

Turner, Lowell. 1991. *Democracy at Work: Changing World Markets and the Future of Labor Unions.* Ithaca, N.Y.: Cornell University Press.

Van Helvoort, Ernest. 1979. *The Japanese Working Man. What Chance? What Reward?* Vancouver: University of British Columbia Press.

Vogel, Ezra. 1979. *Japan as Number One: Lessons for America.* Cambridge, Mass.: Harvard University Press.

Walker, C. R., and R. H. Guest. 1952. *Man on the Assembly Line.* Cambridge, Mass.: Harvard University Press.

Walmsley, Ann. 1992. "Trading Places." *Report on Business Magazine,* March:17–27.

Watanabe, Ben. 1993. "The Japanese Auto Industry: Is Lean Production on the Way Out?" Paper presented to The Lean Workplace Conference, Port Elgin, Ontario, October.

Wells, Donald. 1993. "Lean Production: The Challenges to Labour." Paper presented to The Lean Workplace Conference, Port Elgin, Ontario, October.

Wells, Donald. 1995. "New Dimensions for Labor in a Post-Fordist World." Pp. 191–207 in Willam C. Green and Ernest J. Yanarella (eds.), *North American Auto Unions in Crisis: Lean Production as Contested Terrain.* Albany, N.Y.: SUNY Press.

West, Jackie. 1990. "Gender and the Labour Process: A Reassessment." Pp. 244–73 in D. Knights and H. Willmott (eds.), *Labour Process Theory.* London: Macmillan.

Wickens, Peter D. 1993. "Lean Production and Beyond: The System, Its Critics and the Future." Inaugural Professorial Lecture, University of Sunderland, January.

Williams, Karel, C. Haslam, C. Williams, J. Cutler, A. Adcroft, and S. Johal. 1992. "Against Lean Production." *Economy and Society,* 21, 3:321–354.

Williams, Karel, C. Haslam, and C. Williams. 1993. "Ford Vs. 'Fordism': The Beginning of Mass Production." *Work, Employment and Society,* 6, 4:517–555.

Williams, Karel, C. Haslam, S. Johal, J. Williams, A. Adcroft, and R. Willis. 1995. "Management Practice or Structural Factors: The Case of America Versus Japan in the Car Industry." *Economic and Industrial Democracy,* 16:9–37.

Willis, Paul. 1990. "Masculinity and Factory Labor." Pp. 183–195 in Jeffrey C. Alexander and Steven Seidman (eds.), *Culture and Society: Contemporary Debates.* Cambridge: Cambridge University Press.

Womack, James. 1987. "The Japanification of the American Automobile Industry." Cambridge: MIT.

Womack, James, Daniel Jones, and Daniel Roos. 1990. *The Machine that Changed the World.* New York: Rawson and Associates.

Wood, Stephen. 1989. "The Japanese Management Model: Tacit Skills in Shop Floor Participation." *Work and Occupations,* 16, November:446–460.

Wood, Stephen. 1991. "Japanization and/or Toyotaism?" *Work, Employment and Society,* 5, 4:567–600.

Wood, Stephen. 1993. "The Lean Production Model." Paper presented to The Lean Workplace Conference, Port Elgin, Ontario, October.

Woodiwiss, Anthony. 1992. *Law, Labour and Society in Japan: From Repression to Reluctant Recognition.* London: Routledge.

Yanarella, Ernest J. 1995. "Worker Training at Toyota and Saturn: Hegemony Begins in the Training Center Classroom." Pp. 125–157 in William C. Green and Ernest J. Yanarella (eds.), *North American Auto Unions in Crisis: Lean Production as Contested Terrain.* Albany, N.Y.: SUNY Press.

Yanarella, Ernest J., and William C. Green. 1990. *The Politics of Industrial Recruitment: Japanese Automobile Investment and Economic Development in the American States.* New York: Greenwood Press.

Yates, Charlotte. 1993. *From Plant to Politics: The Autoworkers Union in Postwar Canada.* Philadelphia: Temple University Press.

Index

Technical control, 105–106
Time study, 29, 82, 151. *See also* Standardization
Total Productive Maintenance (TPM), 31,
  191
Toyota:
  and anti-unionism, 180–181
  and ease of manufacturability, 128
  and empowerment, 129
  and kaizen, 129
  production process at, 26, 27n
  and team autonomy, 86
  and team leaders, 90, 106
  and women, 110
Traditional auto plants. *See* Mass production
Training, 39–41, 60, 160, 167, 204
  on adherence to job standards, 150
  in Big Three auto plants, 36–39
  contrasted with shopfloor realities,
    166–170
  for kaizen, 130–131
  at NUMMI, 37–38
  for team leaders, 93–94
  in transplants, 36–39
  workers' views of, 41–43, 60
Transplants:
  in Canada, 11, 11n
  compared with CAMI, 195–199
  defined, 1–2
  and kaizen, 125–129
  and labor-management harmony, 8–10
  recruitment in, 33–34
  resistance in, 10, 196–199
  skill acquisition in, 45–46
  and teams, 85–89
  training in, 36–39
  women in, 108, 119–120
  and worker commitment, 159
  work intensity in, 65–66
  and unions, 180–183
Trist, Eric, 105
Turnbull, Peter, 9
Turner, Lowell, 182

Unions. *See* CAW; CAW Local 88; CTM;
  Enterprise unions; UAW
UAW (United Auto Workers union):
  and labor-management cooperation, 182,
    196
  and women, 110, 120

Visible management, 30
Volvo Uddevalla plant, 105

Wages and benefits, 4–5, 191–192
Wareham, Jeff, 208
Watanabe, Ben, 9
Welding Department, 18–19, 48
Wells, Donald, 170
Wickens, Peter D., 45
Wildcat strike, 191
Willis, Paul, 116
Womack, James, 37, 44, 85–86, 109, 125,
  158, 200
Women:
  in the auto industry, 109–110
  hiring of, 111–112
  in Japanese plants, 110
  and Local 88, 121–122
  and RSIs, 111, 115–116
  and seniority, 114, 122
  and team leader position, 96–97
  and teams, 115, 117–119, 122
  in transplants, 108
  and unions, 110
Women's Committee, 112
Wood, Stephen, 86, 124, 129
Workforce size and composition, 11, 16–18,
  24, 31, 35–36, 175, 214
Work intensification:
  and andon cords, 79
  in Big Three auto plants, 80
  and job enlargement, 62
  and kaizen, 78, 127–128
  and line speed increases, 79
  and overburdened jobs, 67, 81–84
  union response to, 81–83, 192
Work intensity (workloads, work pace),
  62, 202
  and age, 83–84
  and disputes mechanism, 82, 84
  and injuries, 80–81
  in Japan, 9
  at Lordstown, 66
  managers' views of, 78–80
  in transplants, 65–66
  workers' views of, 67–70
Work refusals, 72, 80n, 101, 153,
  189–190